Employment Relations and Human Resource Management

Readings, Cases, and Materials

By Raymond L. Hogler
Colorado State University

cognella
San Diego, CA

Bassim Hamadeh, Publisher
Michael Simpson, Vice President of Acquisitions
Christopher Foster, Vice President of Marketing
Jessica Knott, Managing Editor
Stephen Milano, Creative Director
Kevin Fahey, Cognella Marketing Program Manager
Al Grisanti, Acquisitions Editor
Jamie Giganti, Project Editor
Luiz Ferreira, Licensing Associate

First published in the United States of America in 2012 by University Readers, Inc.

16 15 14 13 12 1 2 3 4 5

Printed in the United States of America

ISBN: 978-1-60927-006-3

cognella

www.cognella.com 800.200.3908

Contents

Introduction

The photograph on the cover of this book shows two men making steel. At one time, the American steel industry was the largest and most important manufacturing activity in the world. Steelworkers played a dominant role in creating the modern labor movement when employees at the U.S. Steel Company agreed to unionize in 1937, under the leadership of John L. Lewis and the Committee for Industrial Organization, later called the Congress of Industrial Relations. Through World War II and into the 1970s, steelworkers helped to establish a middle class in this country through collective bargaining. Labor contracts offered good wages and benefits, job security, and secure retirement. Workers during those years expected to enjoy rising incomes for themselves and their families.

By 2011 private sector union membership had fallen to less than seven percent, and steel production had largely dispersed to other countries. Unions were a negligible factor in labor markets. Wages for American workers were stagnant or falling between the late 1970s and the first decade of the twenty-first century; unemployment rose above 10 percent in the worst recession since the Great Depression; most "baby boomers" lacked adequate retirement income; the federal deficit reached historic levels, and income inequality was at its highest point since 1929. Things had changed, and not necessarily for the better for most citizens.

The employment relations environment likewise underwent tremendous change. Along with collective bargaining laws, New Deal legislators enacted a number of protective laws for workers, such as fair labor standards, social security, and unemployment insurance. In 1964 Congress passed the Civil Rights Act, one part of which protected minorities against discrimination in employment. This was followed by additional laws regulating health and safety, disabilities in the workplace, family and medical leave, and most recently, health insurance. States have also been active in workplace regulation, and their laws supplement the basic federal statutes.

One result of the historical evolution of the employment system and overlapping federal and state authority is a complicated, sometimes contradictory, body of legal doctrine. In a thoughtful essay, law professor Orly Lobel analyzed "four pillars of work law."[1] She described employment law as the individual dealings between employees and employers, labor law as the study of unions and collective bargaining, employment antidiscrimination law as the legal protection of designated groups, and employee benefits law as dealing with pensions, health coverage, and workers' compensation. Because these four areas have different origins and concerns, they do not make up an integrated domain with coordinated rules. Instead, human resource managers and legal specialists must have a broad familiarity with a range of issues connected with work.

This book is designed as a supplement to courses in employment relations and human resource management. The book uses a historical perspective to study American employment. Chapter 1 focuses on the background prior to the New Deal revolution. An important part of that background was the idea of "employment-at-will," which permitted an employee without a fixed contract to quit work at any time, and permitted the employer to fire the employee at any time. This idea was so important that the U.S. Supreme Court created a constitutional rule prohibiting any legislative attempt to regulate work relations. The law now recognizes a number of exceptions to employment-at-will, and the Constitution has been reinterpreted to allow both state and federal laws regulating employment in many ways. Insurance to protect workers against on-the-job injuries came into existence in the 1920s, and its birth and development offer an interesting variation on modern regulation.

Chapter 1 takes up the expansion of federal power during Franklin D. Roosevelt's first term as president, which is generally known as the New Deal era. The economic collapse of the early 1930s transformed American ideas about the role of government in society, and Roosevelt undertook dramatic steps to regulate labor markets. The Great Recession, beginning in 2008, raised similar questions about the role of the state in managing the economy, and the discussion of the two events offers a framework to evaluate policies. In 1935 Roosevelt signed the Wagner Act to promote collective bargaining and unionism. Wage and hour laws limited hours of work and established a minimum wage, and social security created a pension system still in effect. Unemployment insurance remains an important part of the safety net for workers.

Chapter 3 describes the Occupational Safety and Health Act (OSHA) of 1970. The law is the basic protection for workers against unsafe working conditions. It has a simple and efficient design, but its implementation is sometimes problematic. Many employers agree with the proposition that workers deserve a safe and healthy workplace, but there is some disagreement about whether or not OSHA is the best way to achieve that goal. The conflict between rules and individual behaviors is endemic to our society, and OSHA is often attacked as a prime example of the "nanny state" interfering with personal liberties and industrial efficiency.

Chapter 4 explores the most controversial area of employment relations in our system. Take, for example, the recent case of a white firefighter in New Haven, Connecticut, who was denied a promotion because the city council refused to accept the results of

---

[1] Orly Lobel, "The Four Pillars of Work Law," *Michigan Law Review*, 104 (no. 6), 2006, pp. 1539–57.

a test. The council thought the test had an adverse impact on black applicants and was unfair. The white firefighter thought it was unfair to him because he suffered from a reading disability and hired a tutor to help him prepare for the test, on which he scored the high grade. Do you agree with him, or the minority test-takers? The materials in this chapter explore the scope and meaning of anti-discrimination laws.

Chapter 5 is devoted to the area of human resource management (HRM). This subject is often treated as a separate course of study, but it is included in this book for two reasons. First, the HRM function incorporates the legal principles set forth in the preceding chapters, and that learning informs the daily activities of an HR manager. Second, the field is practical and applied in nature. The treatment in this chapter gives an overview of the subject matter, and offers directions for further exploration.

Taken altogether, the materials are intended to engage students in critical analysis of key points. Many of the readings demand careful scrutiny and focus. The questions at various points in the text are designed to generate meaningful debate, and case problems invite research and opportunities for presentation. Used along with a more conventional text, this book could provide material for a two-semester course in employment relations. Standing alone, it is sufficient for a basic introductory class on the topic. One of my objectives was to control the cost of the text, and for that reason, all of the product is either my own or taken from the public domain.

A word of thanks goes to the staff at Cognella who helped put this project in print. Al Grisanti provided editorial guidance from the start and helped to shape the book. Amy Wiltbank located an ideal picture for the cover and designed the accompanying format. Jessica Knott, the Managing Editor, helped me to meet our agreed-upon deadlines. Jamie Giganti moved the manuscript through the editing phase of production, ensuring a consistent and accurate text. I'm grateful for all the help along the way.

1. The Origins of the American Employment System

I. American "Exceptionalism" Briefly Explained

In most industrialized countries, workers cannot be terminated from employment without a legitimate managerial justification. The United States follows the "employment-at-will" rule explained and illustrated below. Simply stated, employment-at-will means an employee can be fired at any time for a good reason, a bad reason, or no reason, provided the reason is not illegal. Since there were no legal protections for employees until the New Deal era in the 1930s, discharges were at the sole discretion of the employer. Workers who tried to form a union, for example, could be fired regardless of how well they performed their work.

Part of the reason there were no laws protecting workers generally was that the U.S. Supreme Court typically struck down legislation that interfered with the employment-at-will rule. The Court said that the Constitution safeguarded *liberty* and *property* rights in this country, and the government had no authority to deprive employers or employees of those rights. A worker who wanted to work in a unionized workplace, for example, had a right to seek out such employment; an employer who preferred to remain nonunion had a right to hire and retain nonunion workers. The Court did not deal with inequality of power between employees and employers, but assumed that the freedom to bargain for wages would sufficiently balance the various interests.

The constitutional doctrine had serious implications for the development of working-class movements, because employers could resist collective bargaining with trade unions, and workers consequently lacked a unified voice in economic matters. Another important factor was that our political system discouraged a national "labor party," which developed in other countries. Political influence was tied to two dominant parties that co-opted any splinter movements, and our state and federal system was largely decentralized in terms of labor relations until the New Deal. As a result, our politics tends to be more conservative, less egalitarian, and more congenial to business interests than those of many other national governments.[1]

In 1937 the Supreme Court issued a landmark decision in the *Jones & Laughlin Steel Corp. v. National Labor Relations Board*. It upheld federal legislation protecting the right of workers to join and form unions and engage in negotiations over wages, hours, and working conditions. Unions grew rapidly throughout the 1940s and 1950s, and labor contracts typically contained a clause stating that workers would not be discharged except for "just cause." The Civil Rights Act of 1964 prohibited employers from discriminating on the basis of race, religion, gender, and national origin, among other characteristics. Other legislation followed to prevent discrimination because of age, disability, or exercising rights of safety and health. Presently, there are numerous laws making it illegal to terminate employment for various protected groups, but the burden is on the employee to prove the discharge was for an unlawful reason, rather than on the employer to prove there was a justifiable reason.

In addition to the federal legislation, state courts began to create common law exceptions to the employment-at-will rule during the 1980s. They ruled that employees could not be terminated for reasons that were contrary to "public policy," or that employees could have contractual rights in employment, even if the hiring was for an indefinite period. Some state courts even recognized a "covenant of good faith and fair dealing" implicit in the employment relationship. These changes in judicial thinking added another layer of legal doctrine to employment relations and led to a surge of litigation. One state, Montana, reacted to the judicial activism by adopting a statute that accommodated the interests of employees and employers; since 1987, it has provided a model for a reasonable adjustment of the interests of the parties. Materials later in this chapter take up these points in more detail.

To begin the analysis, we first consider some early cases articulating the employment-at-will rule and how that rule fits into America's culture of free markets and individual economic dealings. The rule applied even under circumstances that we might now consider to be ethically unacceptable. An excerpt from a leading U.S. Supreme Court decision sets forth the constitutional dimension of employment-at-will and its connection with economic dimensions of our system. Turning to more recent developments, the California Supreme Court decided that a person using medically certified marijuana could be discharged from his job, despite the fact there was a law allowing its use, and that decision will be included later in the chapter. The discussion of employment-at-will concludes with an article summarizing the state of the common law at the beginning of this decade.

II. Major Judicial Developments

A. Origins

Legal historians trace the beginning of the employment-at-will rule to a treatise writer named Horace Gray Wood. Judges and lawyers in the early 19th century did not have easy access to the opinions issued by various state courts, and the treatise writers performed a valuable service by collecting and summarizing the doctrine on a given point of law. Wood, like others following his craft, reviewed judicial decisions and provided a summary and analysis of the cases. In 1877 Wood published a book titled *A Treatise on the Law of Master and Servant*. He stated the "American," as opposed to the British, rule of employment was as follows: "the rule is inflexible, that a general or indefinite hiring is prima facie a hiring at will, and if the servant seeks to make it out a yearly hiring, the burden is upon him to establish it by proof" (p. 272). By this, Wood meant that an employee who claimed to have a contractual right to employment had the burden of proving there was a contract. Otherwise, the law presumed there was not one.

One of the leading cases adopting the employment-at-will rule was *Payne v. Western & Atlantic R.R. Co.*, 81 Tenn. 507 (1884). The Tennessee Supreme Court said that "men must be left, without interference to buy and sell where they please, and to discharge or retain employees at will for good cause or for no cause, or even for bad cause without thereby being guilty of an unlawful act per se. It is a right which an employee may exercise in the same way, to the same extent, for the same cause or want of cause as the employer." The court explained that the policy underlying the rule rested on the idea that the law did not correct imbalances of power, but left the exercise of power to the negotiations of the parties. In the court's words, "The great and rich and powerful are guaranteed the same liberty and privilege as the poor and weak. All may buy and sell where they choose; they may refuse to employ or dismiss whom they choose, without being thereby guilty of a legal wrong, though it may seriously injure and even ruin others."

The legal principle remained in effect for more than a century, even though it resulted in grave injustices. In *Comerford v. International Harvester*, 178 So. 894 (1938), for example, a salesman was fired because he refused to allow his supervisor to have sex with his wife. The case reached the Alabama Supreme Court, where the justices ruled that Comerford had no right to be reinstated to his job, despite working for the company for more than 20 years, and even though levels of unemployment were still at Depression levels. According to the court, the company would not be liable for the action of its manager even if the act were malicious. Because the employment was at will, the company and its agent had a right to discharge Comerford, regardless of the reason. "If one does an act which is legal in itself and violates no right of another, the fact that this rightful act is done from bad motives or with bad intent toward the person so injured thereby does not give the latter a right of action against the former. Therefore, if the defendant's acts complained of in this case were legal in themselves, and violated no superior right of the plaintiff, they were not actionable."

More problematically for workers, the underlying theory of employment-at-will was used as a means to stop Congress from enacting any laws that might interfere with an employer's prerogatives. Labor leader Eugene Debs led a strike against the mighty Pullman Corporation in 1894, and one of the results of the strike was a massive disruption of the flow of commerce across the nation. Congress decided that a better policy would be to give railway workers a right to bargain with the owners, and they passed the Erdman Act in 1896 to accomplish that end. The United States Supreme Court struck down the law. Its opinion is a detailed articulation of how free markets work under capitalism. Relevant parts of the decision are printed below.

This case is lengthy and complicated, but the point is simple. The Court holds that Congress did not have authority under the Constitution to regulate employment on railroads. As a result of this case, and many others like it, the federal government could not pass laws protecting workers in their employment. The rule did not change until 1937. In the meantime, there were many destructive labor disputes as workers tried to force employers to negotiate terms of employment with union organizations. There are two dissenting opinions in this case that deserve attention. The opinion by Justice McKenna sets out a constitutional theory based on the federal power over interstate commerce; his point of view became the majority rule during the New Deal, and it now is the foundation for federal activism in work relations. Justice Holmes is one of the most famous people ever to serve on the Supreme Court, and this is one of his best-known dissents.

Here are some concepts you should take away from the case:

- Congress believed that the protection of unions would reduce labor conflict on the railroads.
- The Court said that liberty and property are the most important parts of the Constitution.
- Employment-at-will was protected as a constitutional right of employers and employees.
- "Due process" means that the Court has the power to strike down laws that it thinks are not reasonable.
- The federal power is limited by Article I of the Constitution to those matters which are specifically enumerated.

The dissenting opinions offer a different interpretation of many propositions adopted by the majority. You should be aware of what those differences are, and how they are explained.

B. Case Study

***Adair v. United States*, 208 U.S. 161 (1908)**

[This case involves the constitutionality of certain provisions of the Erdman Act of 1898, which covered railroad workers and provided that it would be illegal to discriminate against workers who joined a union. The Court describes the charge against the employer, which stated that its agent, William Adair, fired an employee named O. B. Coppage because Coppage belonged to the Order of Locomotive Firemen. After a trial, the district court found Adair guilty, and fined him $100. The Court's opinion continues:]

It thus appears that the criminal offense charged in the count of the indictment upon which the defendant was convicted was, in substance and effect, that being an agent of a railroad company engaged in interstate commerce and subject to the provisions of the above act of June 1, 1898, he discharged one Coppage from its service *because of his membership in a labor organization*—no other ground for such discharge being alleged.

May Congress make it a criminal offense against the United States—as by the tenth section of the act of 1898 it does—for an agent or officer of an interstate carrier, having full authority in the premises from the carrier, to discharge an employee from service simply because of his membership in a labor organization?

The first inquiry is whether the part of the tenth section of the act of 1898 upon which the first count of the indictment was based is repugnant to the Fifth Amendment of the Constitution declaring that no person shall be deprived of liberty or property without due process of law. In our opinion that section, in the particular mentioned, is an invasion of the personal liberty, as well as of the right of property, guaranteed by that Amendment. Such liberty and right embraces the right to make contracts for the purchase of the labor of others and equally the right to make contracts for the sale of one's own labor; each right, however, being subject to the fundamental condition that no contract, whatever its subject matter, can be sustained which the law, upon reasonable grounds, forbids as inconsistent the public interests or as hurtful to the public order or as detrimental to the common good. This court has said that "in every well-ordered society, charged with the duty of conserving the safety of its members, the rights of the individual in respect of his liberty may, at times, under the pressure of great dangers, be subjected to such restraint, to be enforced by reasonable regulations, as the safety of the general public may demand" ... Without stopping to consider what would have been the rights of the railroad company under the Fifth Amendment, had it been indicted under the act of Congress, it is sufficient in this case to say that as agent of the railroad company and as such responsible for the conduct of the business of one of its departments, it was the defendant Adair's right—and that right inhered in his personal liberty, and was also a right of property—to serve his employer as best he could, so long as he did nothing that was reasonably forbidden by law as injurious to the public interests. It was the right of the defendant to prescribe the terms upon which the services of Coppage would be accepted, and it was the right of Coppage to become or not, as he chose, an employee of the railroad company upon the terms offered to him. …

In *Lochner v. New York*, 198 U.S. 45, which involved the validity of a state enactment prescribing certain maximum hours for labor in bakeries, and which made it a misdemeanor for an employer to require or permit an employee in such an establishment to work in excess of a given number of hours each day, the court said: "The general right to make a contract in relation to his business is part of the liberty of the individual protected by the Fourteenth Amendment of the Federal Constitution" … Under that provision no State can deprive any person of life, liberty, or property without due process of law. The right to purchase or to sell labor is part of the liberty protected by this amendment, unless there are circumstances which exclude the right. There are, however, certain powers, existing in the sovereignty of each State in the Union, somewhat vaguely termed police powers, the exact description and limitation of which have not been attempted by the courts. Those powers, broadly stated and without, at present, any attempt at a more specific limitation, relate to the safety, health, morals and general welfare of the public. Both property and liberty are held on such reasonable conditions as may be imposed by the governing power of the State in the exercise of those powers, and with such conditions the Fourteenth Amendment was not designed to interfere. In every case that comes before this court, therefore, where legislation of this character is concerned and where the protection of the Federal Constitution is sought, the question necessarily arises: Is this a fair, reasonable and appropriate exercise of the police power of the State, or is it an unreasonable, unnecessary and arbitrary interference with the right of the individual to his personal liberty or to enter into those contracts in relation to labor which may seem to him appropriate or necessary for the support of himself and his family? Of course the liberty of contract relating to labor includes both parties to it. The one has as much right to purchase as the other to sell labor. Although there was a difference of opinion in [an earlier] case among the members of the court as to certain propositions, there was no disagreement as to the general proposition that there is a liberty of contract which cannot be unreasonably interfered with by legislation. The minority were of opinion that the business referred to in the New York statute was such as to require regulation, and that as the statute was not shown plainly and palpably to have imposed an unreasonable restraint upon freedom on contract, it should be regarded by the courts as a valid exercise of the State's power to care for the health and safety of its people.

While, as already suggested, the right of liberty and property guaranteed by the Constitution against deprivation without due process of law, is subject to such reasonable restraints as the common good or the general welfare may require, it is not within the functions of government—at least in the absence of contract between the parties—to compel any person in the course of his business and against his will to accept or retain the personal services of another, or to compel any person, against his will, to perform personal services for another. The right of a person to sell his labor upon such terms as he deems proper is, in its essence, the same as the right of the purchaser of labor to prescribe the conditions upon which he will accept such labor from the person offering to sell it. So the right of the employee to quit the service of the employer, for whatever reason, is the same as the right of the employer, for whatever reason, to dispense with the services of such employ. It was the legal right of the defendant Adair—however unwise such a course might have been—to discharge Coppage because of his being a member of a labor organization, as it was the legal right of Coppage, if he saw fit do so—however unwise such a course on his part might have been—to quit the service in which he was engaged, because the defendant employed some persons who were not members of a labor organization. In all such particulars the employer and the employee have equality of right, and any legislation that disturbs that equality is an arbitrary interference with the liberty of contract which no government can legally justify in a free land ...

Of course, if the parties by contract fix the period of service, and prescribe the conditions upon which the contract may be terminated, such contract would control the rights of the parties as between themselves, and for any violation of those provisions the party wronged would have his appropriate civil action. And it may be—but upon that point we express no opinion—that in the case of a labor contract between an employer engaged in interstate commerce and his employee, Congress could make it a crime for either party without sufficient or just excuse or notice to disregard the terms of such contract or to refuse to perform it. In the absence, however, of a valid contract between the parties controlling their conduct towards each other and fixing a period of service, it cannot be, we repeat, that an employer is under any legal obligation, against his will, to retain an employee in his personal service any more than an employee can be compelled, against his will, to remain in the personal service of another. ...

But it is suggested that the authority to make it a crime for an agent or officer of an interstate carrier, having authority in the premises from his principal, to discharge an employee from service to such carrier, simply because of his membership in a labor organization, can be referred to the power of Congress to regulate interstate commerce, without regard to any question of personal liberty or right of property arising under the Fifth Amendment. This suggestion can have no bearing in the present discussion unless the statute, in the particular just stated, is within the meaning of the Constitution a regulation of commerce among the States. If it be not, then clearly the Government cannot invoke the commerce clause of the Constitution as sustaining the indictment against Adair.

Let us inquire what is commerce, the power to regulate which is given to Congress?

This question has been frequently propounded in this court, and the answer has been—and no more specific answer could well have been given—that commerce among the several States comprehends traffic, intercourse, trade, navigation, communication, the transit of persons and the transmission of messages by telegraph—indeed, every species of commercial intercourse among the several States, but not to that commerce "completely internal, which is carried on between man and man, in a State, or between different parts of the same State, and which does not extend to or affect other States." The power to regulate interstate commerce is the power to prescribe rules by which such commerce must be governed. Of course, as has been often said, Congress has a large discretion in the selection or choice of the means to be employed in the regulation of interstate commerce, and such discretion is not to be interfered with except where that which is done is in plain violation of the Constitution. … Manifestly, any rule prescribed for the conduct of interstate commerce, in order to be within the competency of Congress under its power to regulate commerce among the States, must have some real or substantial relation to or connection with the commerce regulated. But what possible legal or logical connection is there between an employee's membership in a labor organization and the carrying on of interstate commerce? Such relation to a labor organization cannot have, in itself and in the eye of the law, any bearing upon the commerce with which the employee is connected by his labor and services. Labor associations, we assume, are organized for the general purpose of improving or bettering the conditions and conserving the interests of its members as wage-earners—an object entirely legitimate and to be commended rather than condemned. But surely those associations as labor organizations have nothing to do with interstate commerce as such … It is the employee as a man and not as a member of a labor organization who labors in the service of an interstate carrier. Will it be said that the provision in question had its origin in the apprehension, on the part of Congress, that if it did not show more consideration for members of labor organizations than for wage-earners who were not members of such organizations, or if it did not insert in the statute some such provision as the one here in question, members of labor organizations would, by illegal or violent measures, interrupt or impair the freedom of commerce among the States? We will not indulge in any such conjectures, nor make them, in whole or in part, the basis of our decision. We could not do so consistently with the respect due to a coordinate department of the Government. We could not do so without imputing to Congress the purpose to accord to one class of wage-earners engaged, it may be, in the same kind of labor and serving the same employer. Nor will we assume, in our consideration of this case, that members of labor organizations will, in any considerable numbers, resort to illegal methods for accomplishing any particular object they have in view.

Looking alone at the words of the statute for the purpose of ascertaining its scope and effect, and of determining its validity, we hold that there is no such connection between interstate commerce and membership in a labor organization as to authorize Congress to make it a crime against the United States for an agent of an interstate carrier to discharge an employee because of such membership on his part. If such a power exists in Congress it is difficult to perceive why it might not, by absolute regulation, require interstate carriers, under penalties, to employ in the conduct of its interstate business only members of labor organizations, or only those who are not members of such organizations—a power which could not be recognized as existing under the Constitution of the United States. No such rule of criminal liability as that to which we have referred can be regarded as, in any just sense, a regulation of interstate commerce. We need scarcely repeat what this court has more than once said, that the power to regulate interstate commerce, great and paramount as that power is, cannot be exerted in violation of any fundamental right secured by other provisions of the Constitution.

It results, on the whole case, that the provision of the statute under which the defendant was convicted must be held to be repugnant to the Fifth Amendment and as not embraced by nor within the power of Congress to regulate interstate commerce and as applied to this case it arbitrarily sanctions an illegal invasion of the personal liberty as well as the right of property of the defendant Adair.

Mr. JUSTICE MCKENNA, dissenting.

The opinion of the court proceeds upon somewhat narrow lines and either omits or does not give adequate prominence to the considerations which, I think, are determinative of the questions in the case. The principle upon which the opinion is grounded is, as I understand it, that a labor organization has no legal or logical connection with interstate commerce, and that the fitness of an employee has no dependence or relation with his membership in such organization. It is hence concluded that to restrain his discharge merely on account of such membership is an invasion of the liberty of the carrier guaranteed by the Fifth Amendment of the Constitution of the United States. The conclusion is irresistible if the propositions from which it is deduced may be viewed as abstractly as the opinion views them. May they be so viewed?

A summary of the act is necessary to understand Sec. 10. Detach that section from the other provisions of the act and it might be open to condemnation.

The first section of the act designates the carriers to whom it shall apply. The second section makes it the duty of the Chairman of the Interstate Commerce Commission and the Commissioner of Labor, in case of a dispute between carriers and their employees which threatens to interrupt the business of the carriers, to put themselves in communication with the parties to the controversy and use efforts to "mediation and conciliation." If the efforts fail, then Sec. 3 provides for the appointment of a board of arbitration—one to be named by the carrier, one by the labor organization to which the employees belong, and the two thus chosen shall select a third.

There is a provision that if the employees belong to different organizations they shall concur in the selection of the arbitrator. The board is to give hearings; power is invested in the board to summon witnesses, and provision is made for filing the award in the clerk's office of the Circuit Court of the United States for the district where the controversy arose. Other sections complete the scheme of arbitration thus outlined, and make, as far as possible, the proceedings of the arbitrators judicial, and pending them put restrictions on the parties and damages for violation of the restrictions.

Even from this meager outline may be perceived the justification and force of Sec. 10. It prohibits discrimination by a carrier engaged in interstate commerce, in the employment under the circumstances hereafter mentioned or the discharge from employment of members of labor organizations "because of such membership." This the opinion condemns. The actions prohibited, it is asserted, are part of the liberty of a carrier protected by the Constitution of the United States from limitation or regulation. I may observe that the declaration is clear and unembarrassed by any material benefit to the carrier from its exercise. It may be exercised with reason or without reason, though the business of the carrier is of public concern. This, then, is the contention, and I bring its elements into bold relief to submit against them what I deem to be stronger considerations, based on the statute and sustained by authority.

I take for granted that the expressions of the opinion of the court, which seem to indicate that the provisions of Sec. 10 are illegal because their violation is made criminal, are used only for description and incidental emphasis, and not as the essential ground of the objections to those provisions.

I may assume at the outset that the liberty guaranteed by the Fifth Amendment is not a liberty free from all restraints and limitations, and this must be so or government could not be beneficially exercised in many cases. Therefore in judging of any legislation which imposes restraints or limitations the inquiry must be, what is their purpose and is the purpose within one of the powers of government? Applying this principle immediately to the present case without beating about in the abstract, the inquiry must be whether Sec.

10 of the act of Congress has relation to the purpose which induced the act and which it was enacted to accomplish, and whether such purpose is in aid of interstate commerce and not a mere restriction upon the liberty of carriers to employ whom they please, or to have business relations with whom they please. In the inquiry there is necessarily involved a definition of interstate commerce and of what is a regulation of it. As to the first, I may concur with the opinion; as to the second, an immediate and guiding light is afforded by the *Employers' Liability Cases*. ... In those cases there was a searching scrutiny of the powers of Congress, and it was held to be competent to establish a new rule of liability of the carrier to his employees—in a word, competent to regulate the relation of master and servant, a relation apparently remote from commerce, and one which was earnestly urged by the railroad to be remote from commerce. To the contention the court said: "But we may not test the power of Congress to regulate commerce solely by abstractly considering the broad subject to which a regulation relates, irrespective of whether the regulation in question is one of interstate commerce. On the contrary, the test of power is not merely the matter regulated, but whether the regulation is directly one of interstate commerce or is embraced within the grant conferred on Congress to use all lawful means necessary and appropriate to the execution of that power to regulate commerce." In other words, that the power is not confined to a regulation of the mere movement of goods or persons.

And there are other examples in our decisions—examples, too, of liberty of contract and liberty of forming business relations (made conspicuous as ground of decision in the present case)—which were compelled to give way to the power of congress. [Justice McKenna here refers to earlier cases in which the court permitted regulation of business activities as an aspect of interstate commerce. He continues:] There as here an opposition was asserted between the liberty of the railroads to contract with one another and the power of Congress to regulate commerce. That power was pronounced paramount, and it was not perceived, as it seems to be perceived now, that it was subordinate and controlled by the provisions of the Fifth Amendment. Nor was the relation of the power of Congress to that amendment overlooked. It was commented upon and reconciled. ...

From these considerations we may pass to an inspection of the statute of which Sec. 10 is a part, and inquire as to its purpose, and if the means which it employs has relation to that purpose and to interstate commerce. The provisions of the act are explicit and present a well-coordinated plan for the settlement of disputes between carriers and their employees, by bringing the disputes to arbitration and accommodation, and thereby prevent strikes and the public disorder and derangement of business that may be consequent upon them. I submit no worthier purpose can engage legislative attention or be the object of legislative action. ...

We are told that labor associations are to be commended. May not then Congress recognize their existence; yes, and recognize their power as conditions to be counted with in framing its legislation? Of what use would it be to attempt to bring bodies of men to agreement and compromise of controversies if you put out of view the influences which move them or the fellowship which binds them—maybe controls and impels them—whether rightfully or wrongfully, to make the cause of one the cause of all? And this practical wisdom Congress observed—observed, I may say, not in speculation of uncertain provision of evils, but in experience of evils—an experience which approached to the dimensions of a National calamity. The facts of history should not be overlooked, nor the course of legislation. The act involved in the present case was preceded by one enacted in 1888 of similar purport. That act did not recognize labor associations, or distinguish between the members of such associations and the other employees of carriers. It failed in its purpose, whether from defect in its provisions or other cause we may only conjecture. At any rate, it did not avert the strike at Chicago in 1894. Investigation followed, and, as a result of it, the act of 1898 was finally passed. Presumably its provisions and remedy were addressed to the mischief which the act of 1888 failed to reach or avert. It was the judgment of Congress that the scheme of arbitration might be helped by engaging in it the labor associations. Those associations unified bodies of employees in every department of the carriers, and this unity could be an obstacle or an aid to arbitration. It was attempted to be made an aid, but how could it be made an aid if, pending the efforts of "mediation and conciliation" of the dispute, as provided in Sec. 2 of the act, other provisions of the act may be arbitrarily disregarded, which are of concern to the members in the dispute? How can it be an aid, how can controversies which may seriously interrupt or threaten to interrupt the business, of carriers (I paraphrase the words of the statute), be averted or composed if the carrier can bring on the conflict or prevent its amicable settlement by the exercise of mere whim and caprice? I say mere whim or caprice, for this is the liberty which is attempted to be vindicated as the Constitutional right of the carriers. And it may be exercised in mere whim and caprice. If ability, the qualities of efficient and faithful workmanship can be found outside of labor associations, surely they may be found inside of them. Liberty is an attractive theme, but the liberty which is exercised in sheer antipathy does not plead strongly for recognition. …

Mr. JUSTICE HOLMES, dissenting.

I also think that the statute is constitutional, and but for the decision of my brethren I should have felt pretty clear about it.

As we all know, there are special labor unions of men engaged in the service of carriers. These unions exercise a direct influence upon the employment of labor in that business, upon the terms of such employment and upon the business itself. Their very existence is directed specifically to the business, and their connection with it is at least as intimate and important as that of safety couplers, and, I should think, as the liability of master to servant, matters which, it is admitted, Congress might regulate, so far as they concern commerce among the States. I suppose that it hardly would be denied that some of the relations of railroads with unions of railroad employees are closely enough connected with commerce to justify legislation by Congress. If so, legislation to prevent the exclusion of such unions from employment is sufficiently near.

The ground on which this particular law is held bad is not so much that it deals with matters remote from commerce among the States, as that it interferes with the paramount individual rights, secured by the Fifth Amendment. The section is, in substance, a very limited interference with freedom of contract, no more. It does not require the carriers to employ any one. It does not forbid them to refuse to employ any one, for any reason they deem good, even where the notion of a choice of persons is a fiction and wholesale employment is necessary upon general principles that it might be proper to control. The section simply prohibits the more powerful party to exact certain undertakings, or to threaten dismissal or unjustly discriminate on certain grounds against those already employed. I hardly can suppose that the grounds on which a contract lawfully may be made to end are less open to regulation than other terms. So I turn to the general question whether the employment can be regulated at all. I confess that I think that the right to make contracts at will that has been derived from the word liberty in the amendments has been stretched to its extreme by the decisions; but they agree that sometimes the right may be restrained. Where there is, or generally is believed to be, an important ground of public policy for restraint the Constitution does not forbid it, whether this court agrees or disagrees with the policy pursued. It cannot be doubted that to prevent strikes, and, so far as possible, to foster its scheme of arbitration, might be deemed by Congress an important point of policy, and I think it impossible to say that Congress might not reasonably think that the provision in question would help a good deal to carry its policy along. But suppose the only effect really were to tend to bring about the complete unionizing of such railroad laborers as Congress can deal with, I think that object alone would justify the act. I quite agree that the question what and how much good labor unions do, is one on which intelligent people may differ,—I think that laboring men sometimes attribute to them advantages, as many attribute to combinations of capital disadvantages, that really are due to economic conditions of a far wider and deeper kind—but I could not pronounce it unwarranted if Congress should decide that to foster a strong union was for the best interest, not only of the men, but of the railroads and the country at large. …

Questions on the *Adair* Decision

1. What constitutional provisions are important to the result in this case? How does the majority interpret the meaning of "liberty" and "property?"
2. Does the majority concede that lawmakers may impose some limitations on rights of liberty and property? How does the Court know which limitations are constitutionally acceptable? As a philosophical proposition, could you argue that the notion of *liberty* is incompatible with the concept of property?
3. How does the practice of judicial review fit in with the idea of democracy? What is the basic idea of democracy in the United States?
4. How does the Court interpret the term "interstate commerce?" Where is that term found in the U.S. Constitution?
5. Compare the dissenting opinion of Justice McKenna with that of the majority. What are the major points of disagreement? Do you think McKenna's interpretation of the Commerce Clause is more convincing or less convincing than the majority's?
6. Justice Holmes is usually regarded as one of the most brilliant jurists to ever sit on the Supreme Court. What is his view of the constitutionality of the Erdman Act? How does his opinion differ from that of the majority? Does he agree with Justice McKenna on the matter of interstate commerce? What is Holmes's interpretation of the "due process" clause?

C. Modifications and Evolution of Employment-at-Will

The employment-at-will rule lasted nearly a century before judges began to reconsider whether it was good public policy to allow employers such power over employees. Beginning in the 1980s, courts began to modify the common law in certain situations and gave employees a right to challenge discharges. The judicial exceptions to the rule generally fall into three categories: the public policy exception, the contract exception, and the covenant of good faith exception. In each instance, the court permits an employee to file a lawsuit on the ground that some exception applies. In a famous case, the Arizona Supreme Court said a nurse could state a legal claim by alleging the employer fired her for her refusal to violate a public policy about indecent exposure (the nurse refused to participate with her fellow employees in a musical skit titled "Moon River").[2]

The article below discusses each exception and shows the law in each state. The essay appears in a government publication that covers employment issues and is prepared by the federal Department of Labor. The article has been edited for purposes of space.

Charles J. Muhl, "The employment-at-will doctrine: three major exceptions," *Monthly Labor Review*, January 2001 (pp. 3–11). Bureau of Labor Statistics: http://www.bls.gov/opub/mlr/2001/01/art1full.pdf.

In the United States, employees without a written employment contract generally can be fired for good cause, bad cause, or no cause at all; judicial exceptions to the rule seek to prevent wrongful terminations.

[M]any workers in the United States believe that satisfactory job performance should be rewarded with, among other benefits, job security. However, this expectation that employees will not be fired if they perform their jobs well has eroded in recent decades in the face of an increased incidence of mass layoffs, reductions in companies' workforces, and job turnover. In legal terms, though, since the last half of the 19th century, employment in each of the United States has been "at will," or terminable by either the employer or employee for any reason whatsoever. The employment-at-will doctrine avows that, when an employee does not have a written employment contract and the term of employment is of indefinite duration, the employer can terminate the employee for good cause, bad cause, or no cause at all.[1]

Traditionally and as recently as the early 1900s, courts viewed the relationship between employer and employee as being on equal footing in terms of bargaining power. Thus, the employment-at-will doctrine reflected the belief that people should be free to enter into employment contracts of a specified duration, but that no obligations attached to either employer or employee if a person was hired without such a contract. Because employees were able to resign from positions they no longer cared to occupy, employers also were permitted to discharge employees at their whim.

The Industrial Revolution planted the seeds for the erosion of the employment-at-will doctrine. When employees began forming unions, the collective bargaining agreements they subsequently negotiated with employers frequently had provisions in them that required just cause for adverse employment actions, as well as procedures for arbitrating employee grievances.[2] The 1960s marked the beginning of Federal legislative protections (including Title VII of the 1964 Civil Rights Act) from wrongful discharge based on race, religion, sex, age, and national origin.[3] These protections reflected the changing view of the relationship between employer and employee. Rather than seeing the relationship as being on equal footing, courts and legislatures slowly began to recognize that employers frequently have structural and economic advantages when negotiating with potential or current employees. The recognition of employment as being central to a person's livelihood and well-being, coupled with the fear of being unable to protect a person's livelihood from unjust termination, led to the development of common-law, or judicial, exceptions to the employment-at-will doctrine beginning in the late 1950s. The bulk of the development of these exceptions did not take place until the 1980s, but as we enter the new millennium, the employment-at-will doctrine has been significantly eroded by statutory and common-law protections against wrongful discharge.

This article focuses on the three major exceptions to the employment-at-will doctrine, as developed in common law, including recognition of these exceptions in the 50 States. The exceptions principally address terminations that, although they technically comply with the employment-at-will requirements, do not seem just. The most widespread exception prevents terminations for reasons that violate a State's public policy. Another widely recognized exception prohibits terminations after an implied contract for employment has been established; such a contract can be created through employer representations of continued employment, in the form of either oral assurances or expectations created by employer handbooks, policies, or other written assurances. Finally, a minority of States has read an implied covenant of good faith and fair dealing into the employment relationship. The good-faith covenant has been interpreted in different ways, from meaning that terminations must be for cause to meaning that terminations cannot be made in bad faith or with malice intended. Only six western States—Alaska, California, Idaho, Nevada, Utah, and Wyoming—recognize all three of the major exceptions.[4] Three southern States—Florida, Georgia, and Louisiana—and Rhode Island do not recognize any of the three major exceptions to employment-at-will. (See Exhibit 1.)

Exhibit 1.

Recognition of employment-at-will exceptions, by state, as of Oct. 1, 2000

State	Public-policy exception	Implied-contract exception	Covenant of good faith and fair dealing
Total	43	38	11
Alabama	no	yes	yes
Alaska	yes	yes	yes
Arizona	yes	yes	yes
Arkansas	yes	yes	no
California	yes	yes	yes
Colorado	yes	yes	no
Connecticut	yes	yes	no
Delaware	yes	no	yes
D.C.	yes	yes	no
Florida	no	no	no
Georgia	no	no	no
Hawaii	yes	yes	no
Idaho	yes	yes	yes
Illinois	yes	yes	no

Indiana	yes	no	no
Iowa	yes	yes	no
Kansas	yes	yes	no
Kentucky	yes	yes	no
Louisiana	no	no	no
Maine	no	yes	no
Maryland	yes	yes	no
Massachusetts	yes	no	yes
Michigan	yes	yes	no
Minnesota	yes	yes	no
Mississippi	yes	yes	no
Missouri	yes	no	no
Montana	yes	no	yes
Nebraska	no	yes	no
Nevada	yes	yes	yes
New Hampshire	yes	yes	no
New Jersey	yes	yes	no
New Mexico	yes	yes	no
New York	no	yes	no
North Carolina	yes	no	no
North Dakota	yes	yes	no
Ohio	yes[1]	yes	no
Oklahoma	yes	yes	no
Oregon	yes	yes	no
Pennsylvania	yes	no	no
Rhode Island	no	no	no
South Carolina	yes	yes	no
South Dakota	yes	yes	no
Tennessee	yes	yes	no
Texas	yes	no	no
Utah	yes	yes	yes
Vermont	yes	yes	no
Virginia	yes	no	no
Washington	yes	yes	no
West Virginia	yes	yes	no
Wisconsin	yes	yes	no
Wyoming	yes	yes	yes

[1]Overturned previous decision that was contrary to current doctrine.

SOURCE: Data are from David J. Walsh and Joshua L. Schwarz, "State Common Law Wrongful Discharge Doctrines: Up-date, Refinement, and Rationales," *33 Am. Bus. L.J. 645* (summer 1996). Case law was [verified] to update the recognition of exceptions through Oct. 1, 2000.

Public-Policy Exception

Under the public-policy exception to employment-at-will, an employee is wrongfully discharged when the termination is against an explicit, well-established public policy of the State. For example, in most States, an employer cannot terminate an employee for filing a workers' compensation claim after being injured on the job, or for refusing to break the law at the request of the employer. The majority view among States is that public policy may be found in either a State constitution, statute, or administrative rule, but some States have either restricted or expanded the doctrine beyond this bound. The public-policy exception is the most widely accepted exception, recognized in 43 of the 50 States (see map on next page).

Although the significant development of exceptions to employment-at-will occurred in the 1980s, the first case to recognize a public-policy exception occurred in California in 1959. In *Petermann v. International Brotherhood of Teamsters*,[5] Peter Petermann was hired by the Teamsters Union as a business agent and was told by its secretary-treasurer that he would be employed for as long as his work was satisfactory. During his employment, Petermann was subpoenaed by the California legislature to appear before, and testify to, the Assembly Interim Committee on Governmental Efficiency and Economy, which was investigating corruption inside the Teamsters Union. The union directed Petermann to make false statements to the committee during his testimony, but he instead truthfully answered all questions posed to him. He was fired the day after his testimony.

In recognizing that an employer's right to discharge an employee could be limited by considerations of public policy, the California appellate court found that the definition of public policy, while imprecise, covered acts that had a "tendency to be injurious to the public or against the public good."[6] The court noted that, in California as elsewhere, perjury and the solicitation of perjury were criminal offenses and that false testimony in any official proceeding hindered the proper administration of both public affairs and justice. Even though employer and employee could otherwise be prosecuted under the criminal law for perjury or solicitation of perjury, the court found that applying the public policy exception in this context would more fully effectuate California's declared policy against perjury. Holding otherwise would encourage criminal conduct by both employer and employee, the court reasoned.

Courts in other States were slow to follow California's lead. No other State considered adopting such an exception until after 1967, and only 22 States had considered the exception by the early 1980s.[7] Courts clearly struggled with the meaning of the phrase "public policy," with some finding that a policy was public only if it was clearly enunciated in a State's constitution or statutes and others finding that a public policy could be inferred from a statute even where the statute neither required nor permitted an employee to act in a manner that

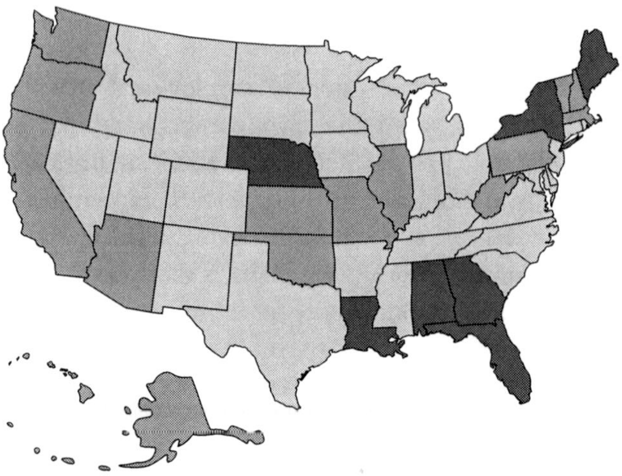

Yes, based on public policy from State constitution and statutes, as well as broader notions of public good and civic duty

Yes, based strictly on public policy from State constitution and statutes

No

SOURCE: Data are from David J. Walsh and Joshua L. Schwarz, "State Common Law Wrongful Discharge Doctrines: Up-date, Refinement, and Rationales," *33 Am. Bus. L.J. 645* (summer 1996). Reprinted from the Bureau of Labor Statistics: http://www.bls.gov/opub/mlr/2001/01/art1full.pdf.

subsequently resulted in the employee's termination. The courts that refused to recognize the exception generally found that, given the vagueness of the term "public policy," such exceptions to employment-at-will should be created by legislative, not judicial, act.[8]

In 1981, one of the broadest definitions of "public policy" was adopted by the Illinois Supreme Court in *Palmateer v. International Harvester Company.*[9] In this case, Ray Palmateer alleged that he was fired from his job with International Harvester after he provided information to local law enforcement authorities about potential criminal acts by a co-worker and indicated that he would assist in any criminal investigation and subsequent trial. The court noted that the traditional employment-at-will rule was grounded in the notion that the employment relationship was based on reciprocal rights, and because an employee was free to end employment at any time for any condition merely by resigning, the employer was entitled to the same right in return. Rejecting this "mutuality theory," the court pointed to the rising number of large corporations that conduct increasingly specialized operations, leading their employees' skills to become more specialized in turn and, hence, less marketable. These changes made it apparent to the court that employer and employee are not on equal footing in terms of bargaining power. Thus, the public-policy exception to the employment-at-will doctrine was necessary to create a "proper balance … between the employer's interest in operating a business efficiently and profitably, the employee's interest in earning a livelihood, and society's interest in seeing its public policies carried out."[10]

The Illinois court found that matters of public policy "strike at the heart of a citizen's social rights, duties, and responsibilities" and could be defined in the State constitution or statutes.[11] Beyond that, when the constitution and statutes were silent, judicial decisions could also create such policy, the court said in creating a broad scope for its exception. In this case, nothing in the Illinois Constitution or statutes required or permitted an employee to report potential criminal activity by a co-worker. However, the court found that public policy favored citizen crime fighters and the exposure of criminal activity. Thus, Palmateer brought an actionable claim for retaliatory discharge.

Two years after *Palmateer*, the Wisconsin Supreme Court rejected such an expansive definition of public policy and limited the application of this employment-at-will exception in its State to cases in which the public policy was evidenced by a constitutional or statutory provision. In *Brockmeyer v. Dun & Bradstreet*,[12] the court found that the public-policy exception should apply neither to situations in which actions are merely "consistent with a legislative policy" nor to "judicially conceived and defined notions of public policy."[13]

In *Brockmeyer*, the plaintiff worked for Dun & Bradstreet from August 1969 to May 1980, the last 3 years as district manager of the Credit Services Division in Wisconsin. Brockmeyer had an above-average performance record, but in February 1980, his immediate supervisors learned that he was vacationing with his secretary when it was understood by others that he was performing his normal duties as district manager. The supervisors also learned that Brockmeyer had smoked marijuana in the presence of other employees. The supervisors confronted him with the allegations and stated unequivocally that he would be terminated or reassigned if his performance did not improve. They also suggested that either he or his secretary would have to find a reassignment within Dun & Bradstreet so that they would not continue to work together. When Brockmeyer tried unsuccessfully to find another position for his secretary, the supervisors sought and obtained her resignation. After leaving, the former secretary filed a sex discrimination claim against Dun & Bradstreet; Brockmeyer indicated to his supervisors that he would tell the truth if called to testify at a trial regarding this complaint. Dun & Bradstreet settled the sex discrimination suit, and Brockmeyer was fired 3 days later.

Brockmeyer contended that his termination violated Wisconsin statutes that prohibited (1) perjury, (2) willful and malicious injuring of another in his or her reputation, trade, business, or profession, and (3) the use of threats, intimidation, force, or coercion to keep a person from working. Rejecting these claims, the Wisconsin Supreme Court found that Dun & Bradstreet did not engage in any behavior that violated these statutes. Dun & Bradstreet had legitimate reasons for terminating Brockmeyer, and no evidence demonstrated that Dun & Bradstreet had asked him to lie in the event that the sex discrimination action by his secretary went to trial. The court held that it was not the State's public policy to prevent discharge of an employee because the employee may testify in a manner contrary to his employer's interests.

The court in *Brockmeyer* decided to limit the application of the public-policy exception to "fundamental and well-defined public policy as evidenced by existing law" and held that a wrongful-discharge claim should not be actionable merely because an "employee's conduct was praiseworthy or because the public may have derived some benefit from it."[14] The court justified its limitation by saying that it would safeguard employee job security interests against employer actions that undermine fundamental policy preferences, while still providing employers with flexibility to make personnel decisions in line with changing economic conditions. Later, the court issued a clarification to the effect that public policy could support a wrongful-termination suit in cases where an explicit constitutional or legislative statement did not evidence that policy, as long as the policy was evident from "the spirit as well as the letter" of the constitutional and legislative provisions.[15] The court also now permits public policy to be evidenced by administrative rules and regulations.[16]

Seven states have rejected the public-policy exception in its entirety: Alabama, Florida, Georgia, Louisiana, Nebraska, New York, and Rhode Island.[17] In *Murphy v. American Home Products Corporation*,[18] the Court of Appeals of New York (the state's highest court) forcefully argued that such exceptions to the employment-at-will doctrine were the province of legislators, not judges. While recognizing that many other jurisdictions had created a public-policy exception, the court found that legitimacy of the principal justification for such adoption—namely, inadequate bargaining power on the part of employees—was better left to the New York legislature to evaluate. The court found that legislators have "greater resources and procedural means to discern the public will" and "elicit the view of the various segments of the community that would be directly affected."[19] Because the recognition of such an exception requires some sort of principal scheme for its application, the configuration of that scheme must be determined by the legislature after the public has had its opportunity to communicate its views, according to the court. Finally, the court found that any such change in the employment at-will doctrine would fundamentally alter rights and obligations under the employment relationship and thus should be applied prospectively by the legislature, rather than retrospectively by the court.[20]

To summarize, the vast majority of States do recognize some form of a public-policy exception to the employment-at-will doctrine. Such a regulation prevents employees from being terminated for an action that supports a State's public policy. The definition of public policy varies from State to State, but most States either narrowly limit the definition to clear statements in their constitution or statutes, or permit a broader definition that enables judges to infer or declare a State's public policy beyond the State's constitution or statutes.

Implied-Contract Exception

The second major exception to the employment-at-will doctrine is applied when an implied contract is formed between an employer and employee, even though no express, written instrument regarding the employment relationship exists. Although employment is typically not governed by a contract, an employer may make oral or written representations to employees regarding job security or procedures that will be followed when adverse employment actions are taken. If so, these representations may create a contract for employment. This exception is recognized in 38 of the 50 states (see map below).

A common occurrence in the recent past was courts finding that the contents and representations made in employee handbooks could create an implied contract, absent a clear and express waiver that the guidelines and policies in such handbooks did not create contract rights. The typical situation involves handbook provisions which state that employees will be disciplined or terminated only for "just cause" or under other specified circumstances, or provisions which indicate that an employer will follow specific procedures before disciplining or terminating an employee.[21] A hiring official's oral

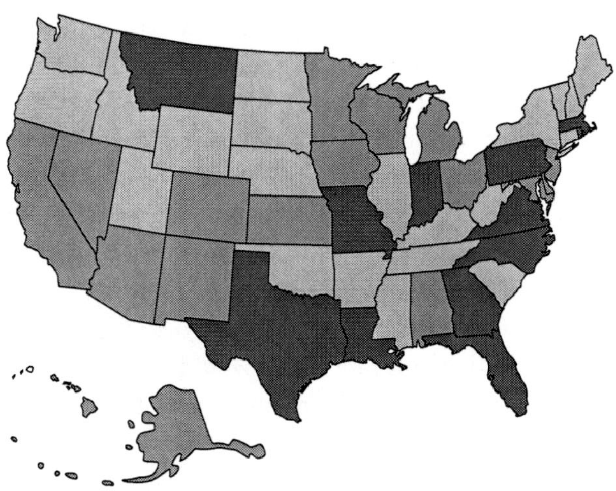

Yes, including oral and written assurances by employers; disclaimers not per se defense

Yes, limited to written assurances; disclaimers nullity employer representation if unambiguous and prominent

No

SOURCE: Data are from David J. Walsh and Joshua L. Schwarz, "State Common Law Wrongful Discharge Doctrines: Up-date, Refinement, and Rationales," *33 Am. Bus. L.J. 645* (summer 1996). Reprinted from the Bureau of Labor Statistics: http://www.bls.gov/opub/mlr/2001/01/art1full.pdf.

representations to employees, such as saying that employment will continue as long as the employee's performance is adequate, also may create an implied contract that would prevent termination except for cause.

The leading case having to do with the implied-contract exception is *Toussaint v. Blue Cross & Blue Shield of Michigan*,[22] decided by the Supreme Court of that State in 1980. Charles Toussaint had been employed in a middle management position with Blue Cross for 5 years before his employment was terminated. When he was hired, he asked his hiring official about his job security and was told that his employment would continue "as long as [he] did [his] job." Toussaint also was provided with a manual of Blue Cross personnel policies some 260 pages long; within the manual were statements that disciplinary procedures would be applied to all Blue Cross employees who completed their probationary period and that it was Blue Cross' policy to terminate employees only for "just cause."

The court ruled that, even if employment is not for a definite term, a provision indicating that an employee would be fired only for just cause was enforceable and that such a provision could create an implied contract if it engendered legitimate expectations of job security in the employee. If the employee is arbitrarily fired thereafter, then a claim for wrongful discharge is actionable. The court noted that Blue Cross could have established a policy giving it the right to terminate employees for no cause at all, but chose instead to follow a "just cause" termination policy. The court argued that employer policies and practices create a "spirit of cooperation and friendliness" in the workforce, making employees "orderly, cooperative, and loyal" by giving them peace of mind regarding job security and the belief that they will be treated fairly when termination decisions are made.[23] If an employer's actions lead an employee to believe that the policies and guidelines of the employer are "established and official at any given time, purport to be fair, and are applied consistently and uniformly to each employee," then the employer has created an obligation.[24] That obligation is created even though the parties may not have mutually agreed that contract rights would be established by the policies.

An implied contract for employment cannot be disregarded at the employer's whim, but the employer can prevent the contract from being created by including in its policies and provisions a clear and unambiguous disclaimer stating that its policies and guidelines do not create contractual rights.[25] If a company does this, no employee could reasonably expect that the policies and guidelines provided a contractual right to job security or any other benefit described therein.

In *Pine River State Bank v. Mettilee*,[26] the Minnesota Supreme Court agreed with the rationale behind *Toussaint*. In *Pine River*, an employee handbook was given to an employee after he had been working for the bank for several months. The handbook contained two sections that the employee claimed created contract rights. The first was a section titled "Job Security" that described employment in the banking industry (though not the specific bank) as secure. The second involved the bank's "Disciplinary Policy," which outlined specific procedures, including reprimands and opportunities to correct one's behavior, that would be followed if an employee was alleged to have violated a company policy. The court found that the "Job Security" section was insufficient to create contract rights, but that the "Disciplinary Policy" section was sufficient. The court analyzed that provision according to traditional requirements for the creation of a contract: offer, acceptance, and consideration for the contract. The court found that the employer offered employment subject to the terms in the employee handbook; the employee accepted the employment offer by showing up for work. The employee's labor was the consideration in support of the contract. Thus, argued the court, the employer breached the employment contract by terminating the employee without following the specific procedures outlined in the handbook that created the implied contract. The court reasoned that, when an employer chooses to prepare and distribute a handbook, the employer is choosing to "implement or modify its existing contracts with all employees covered by the handbook."[27]

Among the states rejecting the application of an implied-contract exception to employment-at-will are Florida, Pennsylvania, and Texas. In *Muller v. Stromberg Carlson Corporation*,[28] a Florida appellate court rejected the exception because of fear that it would lead to uncertainty in the application of the law. Walter H. Muller sued Stromberg Carlson following his termination and alleged that, pursuant to the company's merit pay plan that required an annual review of an employee's performance and a recommendation as to pay increases based on that performance, he had an annual implied-employment contract. The Florida court rejected Muller's claim, finding no justification to depart from the "long established principles that an employment contract requires definiteness and certainty in its terms."[29] The court reasoned that, if indefinite terms or assurances were used to imply an employment contract, the courts in Florida would be "flooded with claims that judicial discretion be substituted for employer discretion."[30] Addressing the arguments made by the Michigan Supreme Court in *Toussaint*, the court said that the longstanding view in Florida, contrary to that in Michigan, was that beneficial social or economic policy should not be advanced by judicial decisions. The Florida court believed the judicial function to be advancing certainty in business relationships by providing meaningful criteria that lead to predictable consequences. The court had "serious reservations as to the advisability of relaxing the requirements of definiteness in employment contracts considering the concomitant uncertainty which would result in the employer–employee relationships."[31] The court added that the inequality of bargaining power between employers and their employees was not a sufficient basis to create implied contracts of employment based on oral or written assurances.

Texas refused to recognize the implied-contract exception in the 1986 case *Webber v. M. W. Kellogg Company.*[32] In that case, the court found that a letter offering a position of employment, the classification of an employee as "permanent" rather than "temporary," and the identification in company documents of a scheduled retirement date for the employee some 22 years after employment was initiated were insufficient in sum to create an implied contract of employment for a specific duration. Likewise, in *Richardson v. Charles Cole Memorial Hospital*,[33] the Supreme Court of Pennsylvania rejected the implied-contract exception, finding that policies published in an employee handbook did not create a "meeting of the minds," one of the traditional standards for evaluating whether a contract has been created between two parties. Because the terms of the handbook were not bargained for in the traditional sense, the court reasoned, the benefits conferred upon the parties by the handbook were mere gratuities and not rights that were contracted for.

To summarize, then, employers' oral or written assurances regarding job tenure or disciplinary procedures can create an implied contract for employment under which the employer cannot terminate an employee without just cause and cannot take any other adverse employment action without following such procedures. Employers can prevent written assurances from creating an implied contract by including a clear and unambiguous disclaimer characterizing those assurances as company policies that do not create contractual obligations. Oral assurances must create a reasonable expectation in the employee in order for an implied contract to be created.

Covenant-of-Good-Faith Exception

Recognized by only eleven states (see map on next page), the exception for a covenant of good faith and fair dealing represents the most significant departure from the traditional employment-at-will doctrine.[34] Rather than narrowly prohibiting terminations based on public policy or an implied contract, this exception—at its broadest—reads a covenant of good faith and fair dealing into *every* employment relationship. It has been interpreted to mean either that employer personnel decisions are subject to a "just cause" standard or that terminations made in bad faith or motivated by malice are prohibited.[35]

As with the public-policy exception, California courts were the first to recognize an implied covenant of good faith and fair dealing in the employment relationship. In *Lawrence M. Cleary v. American Airlines, Inc.*,[36] an American Airlines employee who had worked satisfactorily for the company for 18 years was terminated without any reason given. A California appellate court held that, in virtue of the airline's express policy of adjudicating personnel disputes *and the longevity of the employee's service*, the employer could not fire the

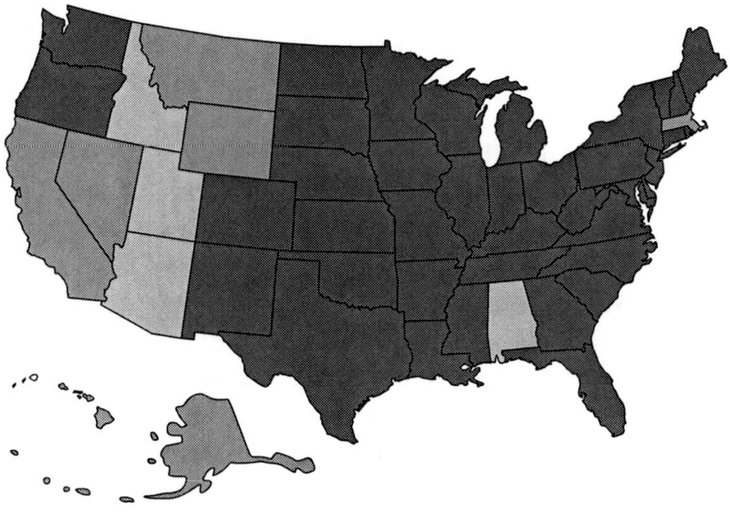

Yes, plaintiff can sue in tort or contract, or otherwise broader application

Yes, limited to contractual remedies or narrower application

No

SOURCE: Data are from David J. Walsh and Joshua L. Schwarz, "State Common Law Wrongful Discharge Doctrines: Up-date, Refinement, and Rationales," *33 Am. Bus. L.J. 645* (summer 1996). Reprinted from the Bureau of Labor Statistics: http://www.bls.gov/opub/mlr/2001/01/art1full.pdf.

employee without good cause. The court stated that "Termination of employment without legal cause after such a period of time offends the implied-in-law covenant of good faith and fair dealing" and that, from the covenant, "a duty arose on the part of … American Airlines … to do nothing which would deprive … the employee … of the benefits of the employment … having accrued during [the employee's] 18 years of employment."[37] This California appellate case was decided in 1980, and the factual situation included an implied employment contract. However, the court did not hold that a covenant of good faith and fair dealing was actionable only if an employee had an express or implied employment contract from which the covenant could arise. Rather, the appellate court found that a tort action could be maintained for breach of the covenant of good faith and fair dealing in every employment relationship, not just those covered by an express or implied contract. The California Supreme Court subsequently rejected this formulation and eliminated the tort action.[38]

Later, however, in *Kmart Corporation v. Ponsock*, the Supreme Court of Nevada permitted a cause of action in tort for breach of an implied covenant of good faith and fair dealing in every employment relationship.[39] Ponsock was a tenured employee at Kmart, hired until retirement or as long as economically possible. At trial, the jury found that Kmart terminated Ponsock to avoid having to pay him retirement benefits. As part of his case, he claimed that Kmart's discharge was in "bad faith" and that, even without a contract,[40] such a termination gave rise to tort liability. The court agreed, citing the employer–employee relationship as one of the "rare and exceptional cases that the duty [of law] is of such a nature as to give rise to tort liability."[41]

In its opinion, the court recognized the changes that many feel have occurred in the employment relationship:

> We have become a nation of employees. We are dependent upon others for our means of livelihood, and most of our people have become completely dependent upon wages. If they lose their jobs they lose every resource except for the relief supplied by the various forms of social security. Such dependence of the mass of the people upon others for all of their income is something new in the world. For our generation, the substance of life is in another man's hands.[42]

The court found that Ponsock was dependent on Kmart's commitment to extended employment and to retirement benefits based on that employment and that the "special relationships of trust" required a tort remedy in addition to any available contractual remedy if the employer conducts an "abusive and arbitrary" dismissal. Providing such a remedy, the court reasoned, would deter employers from engaging in such malicious behavior. Because the termination in *Ponsock* was motivated by the company's desire to serve its own financial ends, the employee was entitled to recover for a bad-faith agreement.

The vast majority of courts have rejected reading such an implied covenant into the employment relationship. The reasoning used by a Florida appellate court in *Catania v. Eastern Airlines, Inc.*,[43] is representative. Four employees alleged that Eastern had wrongfully discharged them and claimed, among other things, that they were entitled to a good-faith review of the discharge. The court summarized the plaintiffs' argument as follows:

> To require employers to demonstrate valid grounds and methods for an employee's discharge does not unduly restrict employers; it merely provides some balance of power. It is apparent that there is not truly freedom of contract between an employer and employee; the individual employee has no power or ability at all to negotiate an employment contract more favorable to himself. And the traditional common law [the employment-at-will doctrine] totally subordinates an interest of the employee to the employer's freedom.

Rejecting the "plaintiff's invitation to be a 'law giver'" and applying reasoning that had been accepted by the Nevada Supreme Court, the Florida court found that the burden on courts of having to determine an employer's motive for terminating an employee was too great an undertaking.

The employment relationship is forever evolving. Additional statutory and common-law exceptions to the employment-at-will doctrine may be developed in the future, but the traditional doctrine has already been significantly eroded by the public-policy and implied-contract exceptions. In addition to the three exceptions detailed in this article, other common-law limitations on employment-at-will have been developed, including actions based on the intentional infliction of emotional distress, intentional interference with a contract, and promissory estoppel or detrimental reliance on employer representations. Suits seeking damages for "constructive discharge," in which an employee alleges that he or she was forced to resign, and for "wrongful transfer" or "wrongful demotion" have increased in recent years. Accordingly, nowadays employers must be wary when they seek to end an employment relationship for good cause, bad cause, or, most importantly, no cause at all.

Notes to Muhl's "Employment-at-Will Doctrine"

[1] Shane and Rosenthal, *Employment Law Deskbook*, § 16.02 (1999).

[2] Jeanne Duquette Gorr, *The Model Employment Termination Act: Fruitful Seed or Noxious Weed?* 31 DUQLR 111 (fall 1992); see also Robert W. Fisher, "When workers are discharged—an overview," *Monthly Labor Review*, June 1973, pp. 4–17.

[3] 42 U.S.C. § 2000e *et seq.* This article does not address statutory exceptions to employment-at-will. Many such exceptions have been enacted at both the Federal and State level. For example, Federal law prevents employment discrimination, including termination for engaging in lawful union activities (see National Labor Relations Act, 29).

U.S.C. § 201–219, (1978) and for safety and health violations at the workplace (see Occupational Safety and Health Act, 29 U.S.C. § 651–678, 1985), among others. Certain States have laws preventing employers from terminating employees for whistle-blowing (reporting potential violations of law committed by the employer); other State laws prohibit employers from terminating employees who file a workers' compensation claim or serve on a jury. (See, generally, Shane and Rosenthal, *Employment Law Deskbook.*) However, only two States—Arizona and Montana—have enacted comprehensive wrongful termination legislation. Montana passed the Wrongful Discharge from Employment Act in 1987, and Arizona enacted its Employment Protection Act in 1996. Of the two, the Montana statute is broader in the scope of its protections for employees.

[4] Courts in Arizona had recognized all three exceptions until passage of the Employment Protection Act.

[5] 174 Cal.App.2d 184 (1959).

[6] 174 Cal.App.2d at 188.

[7] Deborah A. Ballum, "Employment-at-will: The Impending Death of a Doctrine," 37 *Am. Bus. L.J.* 653, 660 (summer 2000).

[8] See, for example, *Pacheco v. Raytheon*, 623 A.2d 464 (R.I. 1993); and *Murphy v. American Home Products Corp.*, 58 N.Y.2d 293, 448 N.E.2d (1983).

[9] 85 Ill.2d 124, 421 N.E.2d 876 (1981).

[10] *Id.* at 878.

[11] *Id.*

[12] 113 Wis.2d 561, 335 N.W.2d 834 (1983).

[13] *Id.* at 839–40.

[14] *Id.* at 840, citing *Palmateer v. International Harvester Co.*, 421 N.E.2d at 883.

[15] See *Wandry v. Eye Credit Union*, 129 Wis.2d 37, 384 N.W.2d 325 (1986).

[16] See *Winkelman v. Beloit Memorial Hosp.*, 168 Wis.2d 12, 483 N.W.2d 211 (1992).

[17] At this time, it is unclear how Maine views the public-policy exception, as no decision has addressed it directly.

[18] 58 N.Y.2d 293, 448 N.E.2d 86 (1983).

[19] *Id.* at 302.

[20] One year after the decision was rendered, the New York legislature enacted the Retaliatory Action by Employers Act, amending the State's labor law so that it would protect whistle-blowers from wrongful termination. See N.Y. LAB. LAW § 740 (*Gould's New York Consolidated Laws Unannotated*, 1988).

[21] Shane and Rosenthal, *Employment Law Deskbook*, § 16.03[5].

[22] 408 Mich. 579, 292 N.W.2d 880 (1980).

[23] *Id.* at 644.

[24] *Id.*

[25] The following is a sample disclaimer, which must be clear and unambiguous in the handbook or policy in order to be effective: "This policy is not intended as a contractual obligation of the company. The company reserves the right to amend this policy from time to time at its discretion and in accordance with applicable law."

[26] 333 N.W.2d 622 (1983).

[27] *Id.* at 626–27.

[28] 427 So.2d 266 (1983).

[29] *Id.* at 268.

[30] *Id.* at 269.

[31] *Id.* at 270.

[32] 720 S.W.2d 124 (1986).

[33] 320 Pa.Super. 106, 466 A.2d 1084 (1983).

[34] Shane and Rosenthal, *Employment Law Deskbook*, § 16.03[8].

[35] *Id.*

[36] 111 Cal.App.3d 443 (1980).

[37] *Id.* at 455.

[38] See *Foley v. Interactive Data Corp.*, 47 Cal.3d 654, 765 P.2d 373.
(Cal. 1988).

[39] 103 Nev. 39, 732 P.2d 1364 (1987).
[40] In the trial, the court did find that an employment contract existed that Kmart had breached.
[41] *Id.* at 49.
[42] *Id.* at 51, quoting F. Tannenbaum, *A Philosophy of Labor* (1951).
[43] 381 So.2d 265 (1980).

D. Medical Marijuana and the Public Policy Exception to Employment-at-Will

In the case below, an employee was discharged after testing positive for drug use. He said that he had a right to use marijuana under California statutes, and for that reason, he should not be discriminated against by prospective employers as a matter of public policy. Is this an argument that courts should accept? Since employment is so important in our society, it could be said that an approved use of marijuana is no different than using a prescribed medication. Note how the California Supreme Court disposes of the claim. The plaintiff also said that he could not be discriminated against because of his disability—that is, the condition for which he used marijuana. Again, the court rejects this proposition. The case thus illustrates how judges may be reluctant to involve themselves in a case that is more appropriate for legislators to deal with.

***Ross v. RagingWire Telecommunications, Inc.*, 174 P.3d 200 (S.Ct.CA, 2008)**
[Ross was fired by the defendant company for testing positive for THC, the active ingredient in marijuana. He claimed that his certification as a user of medical marijuana prevented the company from discharging him as a result of drug use. The California Supreme Court ruled that Ross did not have a disability that was protected under the state law against disability discrimination. This particular area of the law is treated more fully in Chapter 4. More relevant at this point is the court's treatment of employment-at-will and its exception for "public policy" violations. Portions of the opinion are quoted below. Some citations have been omitted.]

Wrongful Termination in Violation of Public Policy

Plaintiff also attempts, based on defendant's refusal to accommodate his use of marijuana, to state a cause of action for wrongful termination in violation of public policy. The legal principles that underlie such a claim are well established: Either party to a contract of employment without a specified term may terminate the contract at will, but this ordinary rule is subject to the exception that an employer may not discharge an employee for a reason that violates a fundamental public policy of the state. *Tameny v. Atlantic Richfield Co.*, 610 P.2d 1330. To support such a cause of action, the policy in question must satisfy four requirements: "First, the policy must be supported by either constitutional or statutory provisions. Second, the policy must be 'public' in the sense that it 'inures to the benefit of the public' rather than serving merely the interests of the individual. Third, the policy must have been articulated at the time of the discharge. Fourth, the policy must be 'fundamental' and 'substantial.' Defendant contends his discharge violated fundamental public policies supported by the Compassionate Use Act, and the privacy clause of the California Constitution. We disagree.

The Compassionate Use Act, as we have explained, simply does not speak to employment law. Nothing in the act's text or history indicates the voters intended to articulate any policy concerning marijuana in the employment context, let alone a fundamental public policy requiring employers to accommodate marijuana use by employees. Because the act articulates no such policy, to read the FEHA in light of the Compassionate Use Act leads to no different result. Plaintiff argues that the statutory provision on which a wrongful termination claim is based "does not have to ... prohibit the employer's precise act. ..." Even so, the provision in question still "must sufficiently describe the type of prohibited conduct to enable an employer to know the fundamental public policies that are expressed in that law" and to "have adequate notice of the conduct that will subject [the employer] to tort liability to the employees [it] discharge[s]." (The Compassionate Use Act did not put defendant on notice that employers would thereafter be required under the FEHA to accommodate the use of marijuana.)

Plaintiff also argues that his discharge violated the public policy that underlies an adult patient's right "to determine whether or not to submit to lawful medical treatment"—a right we have located both in the privacy clause of the state Constitution and in the common law. The body of law to which plaintiff refers protects the right of competent adult patients to refuse medical treatment and imposes, inferentially, an obligation on health care providers to seek patients' informed consent before undertaking medical procedures. Defendant's decision not to accommodate plaintiff's marijuana use does not implicate plaintiff's right to refuse medical treatment.

In the course of this argument, plaintiff attempts to describe a right of medical self-determination broader than the right to refuse treatment we recognized in [various cases]. Plaintiff relies on *Abigail Alliance v. von Eschenbach* (D.C.Cir.2006) 445 F.3d 470, 486, in which a federal court held that a terminally ill patient with no other government-approved treatment options had a due process right under the United States Constitution to have access to an investigational new drug that the Food and Drug Administration had not approved for commercial sale but had determined to be sufficiently safe for testing on human beings. Analogizing to *Abigail Alliance,* plaintiff argues that "[i]n California, medical marijuana use is legal, so under the state [Constitution] RagingWire was not permitted to prohibit [plaintiff] from using it." Assuming for the sake of argument *Abigail Alliance* has any relevance to the case before us, the decision does not compel a different result because defendant has not prevented plaintiff from having access to marijuana. Defendant has only refused to employ plaintiff. To assert that defendant's refusal to employ plaintiff affects his access to marijuana is merely to restate the argument that the Compassionate Use Act gives plaintiff a right to use marijuana free of hindrance or inconvenience, enforceable against third parties. That argument we have already rejected.

We thus conclude plaintiff cannot state a cause of action for wrongful termination in violation of public policy.

Questions

1. How does the court define a "public policy?" If the policy of the marijuana law is not to protect users, what is it?
2. Is marijuana use always inconsistent with an employment relationship? Consider someone suffering from alcoholism who has a sales job and is told to take a client to a club and "have a good time." Can the worker refuse, based on his disability, to go to a place where alcohol is served?
3. Assume a female marketing employee is told to take a client to an "adult entertainment" venue. She refuses, and is subsequently discharged. Is this a case where public policy is violated, or is it a violation of some other employment law?

E. Montana's Wrongful Discharge Act: A Legislative Exception to the Rule

In 1985 the state of Montana passed a statute that protected employees from discharge without cause and protected employers from tort damages in termination cases. Commentators generally agree that the statute fulfills its basic objectives and has not discouraged businesses from locating in the state. The policy underlying the statute, in fact, aims to reasonably accommodate the interests of employers and employees. Relevant provisions of the law are set forth below.

39-2-902. Purpose. This part sets forth certain rights and remedies with respect to wrongful discharge. Except as provided in 39-2-912, this part provides the exclusive remedy for a wrongful discharge from employment.

39-2-903. Definitions. In this part, the following definitions apply:

(1) "Constructive discharge" means the voluntary termination of employment by an employee because of a situation created by an act or omission of the employer which an objective, reasonable person would find so intolerable that voluntary termination is the only

reasonable alternative. Constructive discharge does not mean voluntary termination because of an employer's refusal to promote the employee or improve wages, responsibilities, or other terms and conditions of employment.

(2) "Discharge" includes a constructive discharge as defined in subsection (1) and any other termination of employment, including resignation, elimination of the job, layoff for lack of work, failure to recall or rehire, and any other cutback in the number of employees for a legitimate business reason.

(3) "Employee" means a person who works for another for hire. The term does not include a person who is an independent contractor.

(4) "Fringe benefits" means the value of any employer-paid vacation leave, sick leave, medical insurance plan, disability insurance plan, life insurance plan, and pension benefit plan in force on the date of the termination.

(5) "Good cause" means reasonable job-related grounds for dismissal based on a failure to satisfactorily perform job duties, disruption of the employer's operation, or other legitimate business reason. The legal use of a lawful product by an individual off the employer's premises during nonworking hours is not a legitimate business reason, unless the employer acts within the provisions of 39-2-313(3) or (4).

(6) "Lost wages" means the gross amount of wages that would have been reported to the internal revenue service as gross income on Form W-2 and includes additional compensation deferred at the option of the employee.

(7) "Public policy" means a policy in effect at the time of the discharge concerning the public health, safety, or welfare established by constitutional provision, statute, or administrative rule.

39-2-904. Elements of wrongful discharge—presumptive probationary period.

(1) A discharge is wrongful only if:

(a) it was in retaliation for the employee's refusal to violate public policy or for reporting a violation of public policy;

(b) the discharge was not for good cause and the employee had completed the employer's probationary period of employment; or

(c) the employer violated the express provisions of its own written personnel policy.

(2) (a) During a probationary period of employment, the employment may be terminated at the will of either the employer or the employee on notice to the other for any reason or for no reason.

(b) If an employer does not establish a specific probationary period or provide that there is no probationary period prior to or at the time of hire, there is a probationary period of 6 months from the date of hire.

39-2-905. Remedies. (1) If an employer has committed a wrongful discharge, the employee may be awarded lost wages and fringe benefits for a period not to exceed 4 years from the date of discharge, together with interest on the lost wages and fringe benefits. Interim earnings, including amounts the employee could have earned with reasonable diligence, must be deducted from the amount awarded for lost wages. Before interim earnings are deducted from lost wages, there must be deducted from the interim earnings any reasonable amounts expended by the employee in searching for, obtaining, or relocating to new employment.

(2) The employee may recover punitive damages otherwise allowed by law if it is established by clear and convincing evidence that the employer engaged in actual fraud or actual malice in the discharge of the employee in violation of 39-2-904(1)(a).

(3) There is no right under any legal theory to damages for wrongful discharge under this part for pain and suffering, emotional distress, compensatory damages, punitive damages, or any other form of damages, except as provided for in subsections (1) and (2).

39-2-911. Limitation of actions. (1) An action under this part must be filed within 1 year after the date of discharge.

(2) If an employer maintains written internal procedures, other than those specified in 39-2-912, under which an employee may appeal a discharge within the organizational structure of the employer, the employee shall first exhaust those procedures prior to filing an action under this part. The employee's failure to initiate or exhaust available internal procedures is a defense to an action brought under this part. If the employer's internal procedures are not completed within 90 days from the date the employee initiates the internal procedures, the employee may file an action under this part and for purposes of this subsection the employer's internal procedures are considered exhausted. The limitation period in subsection (1) is tolled until the procedures are exhausted. In no case may the provisions of the employer's internal procedures extend the limitation period in subsection (1) more than 120 days.

(3) If the employer maintains written internal procedures under which an employee may appeal a discharge within the organizational structure of the employer, the employer shall within 7 days of the date of the discharge notify the discharged employee of the existence of such procedures and shall supply the discharged employee with a copy of them. If the employer fails to comply with this subsection, the discharged employee need not comply with subsection (2).

39-2-912. Exemptions. This part does not apply to a discharge:

(1) that is subject to any other state or federal statute that provides a procedure or remedy for contesting the dispute. The statutes include those that prohibit discharge for filing complaints, charges, or claims with administrative bodies or that prohibit unlawful discrimination based on race, national origin, sex, age, disability, creed, religion, political belief, color, marital status, and other similar grounds.

(2) of an employee covered by a written collective bargaining agreement or a written contract of employment for a specific term.

39-2-913. Preemption of common-law remedies. Except as provided in this part, no claim for discharge may arise from tort or express or implied contract.

39-2-914. Arbitration. (1) A party may make a written offer to arbitrate a dispute that otherwise could be adjudicated under this part.

(2) An offer to arbitrate must be in writing and contain the following provisions:

(a) A neutral arbitrator must be selected by mutual agreement or, in the absence of agreement, as provided in 27-5-211.

(b) The arbitration must be governed by the Uniform Arbitration Act, Title 27, Ch. 5. If there is a conflict between the Uniform Arbitration Act and this part, this part applies.

(c) The arbitrator is bound by this part.

(3) If a complaint is filed under this part, the offer to arbitrate must be made within 60 days after service of the complaint and must be accepted in writing within 30 days after the date the offer is made.

(4) A discharged employee who makes a valid offer to arbitrate that is accepted by the employer and who prevails in such arbitration is entitled to have the arbitrator's fee and all costs of arbitration paid by the employer.

(5) If a valid offer to arbitrate is made and accepted, arbitration is the exclusive remedy for the wrongful discharge dispute and there is no right to bring or continue a lawsuit under this part. The arbitrator's award is final and binding, subject to review of the arbitrator's decision under the provisions of the Uniform Arbitration Act.

39-2-915. Effect of rejection of offer to arbitrate. A party who makes a valid offer to arbitrate that is not accepted by the other party and who prevails in an action under this part is entitled as an element of costs to reasonable attorney fees incurred subsequent to the date of the offer.

Questions

1. If the Montana law is sound legal policy, why haven't other states followed Montana's lead?
2. Assume you are a state legislator and a version of the bill is introduced. Would you vote in favor or against its passage?
3. What arguments can be made in favor of arbitrating employment disputes? If you were an employee in a firm that required you to arbitrate a termination rather than bring a lawsuit, do you think that would be to your advantage or disadvantage?
4. Should the federal government pass a law giving all workers covered under civil rights laws the choice of arbitrating an employment dispute or proceeding under the civil rights laws?
5. Why does the law exempt from its coverage claims based on a labor contract or federal civil rights law?

III. Workers' Compensation Laws

Protection against work-related injuries makes up a major component of our employment relations system. The laws developed in the 1910s and quickly spread across the United States. Workers' compensation schemes are unique in several respects. First, the legislation consists of state, rather than federal, law, and the conditions for recovery of benefits and the amounts of compensation are determined strictly by the respective states. Second, employers supported the enactment of compensation laws, even though they represented an important deviation from the principle that contractual agreement governed employment relations. Third, the statutes displaced an existing system of common law, which in many cases favored employers and precluded workers from any remedy for workplace injuries.[3]

Given the seeming contradictions that workers' compensation posed for the contractual regime of employment, why would employers ever consent to the system? The figure below shows the evolution of workers' compensation laws and their administration. Certain key elements make up the compromise that enables employers to buy into the system while allowing workers to be protected against hazards of work. Under a workers' compensation scheme, the injured worker receives regular and fixed amounts of money for job-related illnesses and injuries. In exchange, the worker surrenders the right to sue the employer in court for damages arising out of the worker's loss of earning capacity. The arrangement protects the employer against the costs of litigation and jury awards, which eventually would be passed onto the consumer in the form of higher prices for the product. It protects employees from the uncertainty of a judicial proceeding, and it protects the public from the economic burdens associated with incapacitated workers.

Figure 1. How Workers' Compensation Works

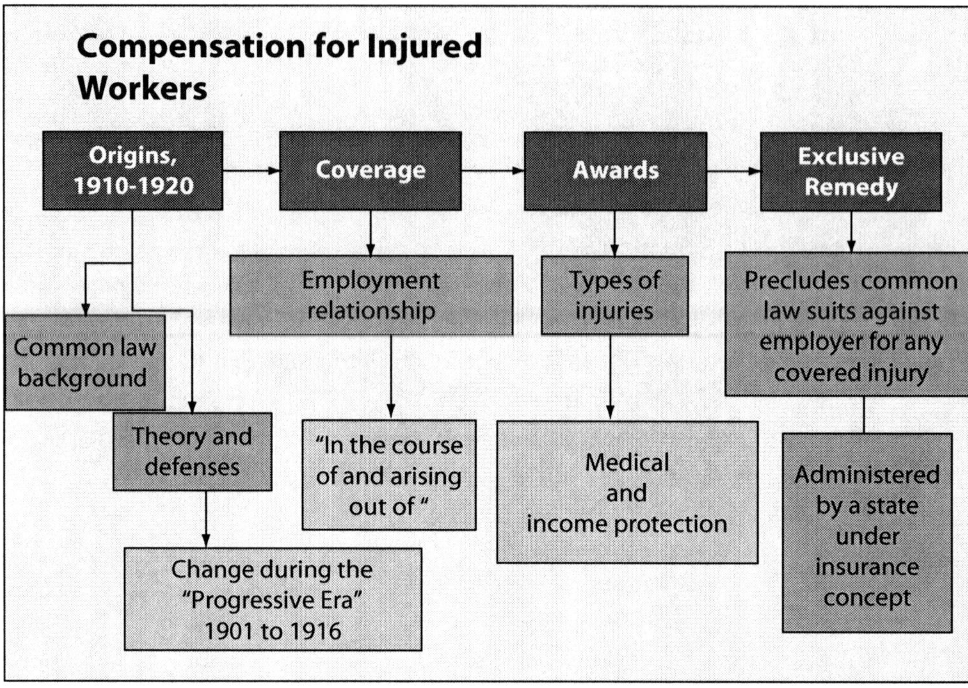

The growth of the factory system as a model for industrial production was accompanied by sharp increases in the number of industrial accidents, and the common law doctrines governing employment were inadequate to deal with the problem of injured workers. The result was a surge of state legislative activity in the first two decades of the century; that activity eventually resulted in the particular system of industrial insurance which now exists. Prior to the 1830s, the issue of an employer's duty to compensate an employer for injuries received little legal attention. As cases arose, American judges looked to English common law precedent to determine standards of liability. Under the English rule, an employee was required to prove as a condition of recovery that the employer's negligence had caused the injury. American courts followed that precedent in decisions such as *Farwell v. Boston and Worcester R.R. Corp.*, 4 Metcalf 49 (1842), decided in Massachusetts in 1842. Chief Justice Lemuel Shaw ruled in favor of the railroad, stating that the relationship between an employee and his employer was governed by express or implied contract, and said that wages would factor in the possibility of injury. In his words (p. 57):

> The general rule, resulting from considerations of justice as of policy, is, that he who engages in the employment of another for their performance of specified duties and services, for compensation, takes upon himself the natural and ordinary risks and perils incident to the performance of such services, and in legal presumption, the compensation is adjusted accordingly.

Labor markets, in Shaw's view, reflected a premium for hazardous work, and in theory, the negligence system promoted an efficient method of allocating the costs of industrial injury. By emphasizing the contractual nature of employment, losses due to injury could be regarded as a cost of work.

The common law system of compensation for workers' injuries was inadequate in a number of respects. The injured worker had no recourse for injury other than litigating against the employer. Such litigation was both expensive and time consuming, and the worker and his family required immediate aid. Even assuming the worker prevailed in the suit, the remedies were often not sufficient to defray the costs of litigation and to provide maintenance for the worker and his family, which resulted in a burden to the community. Finally, the common law system became progressively disadvantageous to the employer during the first decade of this century. Although it was difficult for a worker to obtain a remedy through the system, there were an increasing number of suits where the employer was found to be at fault, and the damages awarded to the injured worker were sometimes quite large.

One study concluded that "the rising value of the injured worker's right of action against the employer was at the center of capital's interest in a new system" of compensation for injury. As industrial injuries became more widespread, public attention focused on the problem, and judges and juries grew more sympathetic to claims. Premiums for insurance against such claims rose from $203,132 in 1887 to $35 million in 1911, and insurance companies were unable to develop sound actuarial standards for industrial injuries. There was also an obvious political dimension at stake; workers as a class reacted against the perceived callousness of employers and the hardships inflicted on workers' families. Several other aspects of labor unrest contributed to a "crisis of confidence" in business during the period; the compensation issue, however, was particularly symbolic, and it "became the focal point for a debate as to whether the American state could be modified to provide even a minimum floor to cushion the physical and financial risks of the employment relationship." Eventually, then, "The compensation crisis of the first decade reached the point where a solution imported from Europe, Workers' Compensation, presented itself as a form of social insurance that could be adopted to conditions in the United States."[4]

A. The Components of Workers' Compensation

1. *There must be an employment relationship.* Workers' compensation claims are appropriate only where an actual employer–employee relationship exists, and only the employee is covered. Generally, an employee is an individual who routinely and regularly performs remunerative work for another, and is subject to the control and direction of the other. An independent contractor, in contrast, is paid an agreed amount for completion of a task, and the accomplishment of the task is typically within the discretion of the contractor, who is in a position to make a profit or suffer a loss from the venture. Some other major exemptions usually found in statutory

provisions include those for agricultural employment, casual employment not in the employer's course of business, and for employers with less than a specified number of employees.

2. *Coverage is automatic for compensable injuries.* A compensable injury is defined as any injury "arising out of and in the course of employment." The standard ensures that the injury has some close and substantial connection to the employment relationship. Courts and administrative bodies interpret the phrase very broadly because the legislation is protective in nature. Thus, if a claimant proves that his or her injury resulted from a risk related to employment, as opposed to risks incurred by the general public, compensation will be awarded. Certain issues are particularly problematic, such as the case of employees who are injured away from the workplace or by a natural phenomenon such as a tornado. The cases in the next section help to define the meaning of the formula. In the case of a preexisting condition causing the injury, such as a propensity for heart attacks, the burden of proof rests on the employee to prove that the injury suffered was aggravated by his or her working conditions. Every state now provides coverage for occupational diseases connected with the employment, either through a broad definition of the term "injury," or by specific provisions within the statute.
3. *Negligence is not a necessary element of recovery.* Under workers' compensation, fault is usually irrelevant. In contrast to the common law, the worker need not prove that the employer's negligence caused the injury in order to recover, nor, typically, will the employee's own negligence defeat recovery. One exception to that rule is the situation in which the employee's acts constitute misconduct that has been expressly prohibited by the employer and that is consequently outside the course of the employment. Examples might include an injury incurred while using the employer's tools to make an item for personal use. A second exception to the no-fault principle is based on specific statutory provisions. For example, defenses to a compensation claim may include a showing of the employee's "willful misconduct," the violation of safety rules or positive law, self-induced intoxication, and an intentional self-injury or suicide, unless the suicide is the result of mental derangement produced by the work related injury. In most cases, nevertheless, the focus is on the source and nature of the harm, rather than on an evaluation of the parties' conduct.
4. *The right to compensation is an exclusive remedy.* In return for a prompt and certain remedy, the worker typically surrenders his or her right to sue the employer for any injury arising out of the employment relationship. Accordingly, the workers' compensation remedy is deemed to be "exclusive," and the amount recoverable is the only award to which the employee is entitled. The limitation of the exclusivity concept is offset by the relative ease and efficiency of recovery. Moreover, under some statutes, employer misconduct may affect the principle of exclusive remedy and permit recovery of additional damages. Such misconduct includes intentional injury to the employee, a failure to provide safety equipment, or the employer's willful misconduct that harms the employee. Courts may reach a similar conclusion in the absence of

specific provisions when the employer personally inflicts an intentional injury on the employee, under the theory that the injury is no longer "accidental." In addition, exclusivity may not apply when the injury arises from the negligence of a third party outside the employment relationship, and the worker may proceed against the third party. It should also be observed that employers may be criminally liable for intentional harm to an employee, regardless of the employee's right to workers' compensation or to a civil remedy. Indeed, criminal prosecutions against employers are viewed by some scholars as a more effective means of protecting employees than the workers' compensations systems or the occupational safety and health laws.

5. *The statutory system is administered by a governmental body.* Workers' compensation is the responsibility in the first instance of a designated agency created by the state. The function of the agency is to provide prompt and efficient handling of claims for compensation by avoiding the expense and delays associated with litigation. The agency is not bound by the formalities of a judicial proceeding and can thus avoid legal technicalities about evidence and procedure. Hearing officers have substantial expertise and familiarity with the statutory provisions. Typically, once a compensable claim is filed, the claimant will become eligible for benefits in two to seven days.
6. *The employer bears the cost of providing the compensation insurance.* The employer is not permitted to deduct the cost of his workers' compensation premiums from the employee's paycheck, but must assume the initial cost of the insurance. The employer will theoretically pass the costs of the insurance along to his customers in the form of higher prices for goods and services. Likewise, employers also pass some costs on to employees in the form of lower wages, but, in contrast to Social Security, the worker does not directly participate in underwriting the scheme. The arrangement gives employers an incentive to provide a safe workplace.

B. The Benefit System

Once a compensable injury has occurred and the claimant has initiated a valid claim for compensation, the claimant may be eligible for several types of cash benefits. It should be emphasized that the primary concern of workers' compensation is the loss of earning capacity or "disability." This concept has several dimensions that figure in the policy considerations underlying workers' compensation. The broad categories of benefits available to a worker and his or her family are discussed below.

- Medical. In every state an injured worker is entitled to recover for medical expenses incurred as a result of the injury. These expenses broadly include the costs of hospitalization, physician's care, and other necessary expenses, such as transportation and supplies. In addition, the employee may be entitled to rehabilitation services that will enable him or her to return to gainful employment. The medical benefits in most states are not limited either in duration or length of time, and if limited, the period can be extended by administrative decisions.

- Disability resulting in loss of earnings. To deal adequately with the matter of lost wages, compensation systems typically utilize a four-part scheme of classification. Benefits may be paid for disabilities within any of the following categories:
    a. temporary partial—a disability that incapacitates a worker only in part and only for a limited time;
    b. temporary total—a disability that prevents the worker from performing any suitable work for a definite period of time;
    c. permanent partial—a disability that impairs the worker's earning capacity and that will continue to do so in the foreseeable future;
    d. permanent total—a disability that prevents the worker from performing any suitable work and will continue to do so in the foreseeable future.

The amounts paid in each case will depend on the workers' earnings, the extent of disability, and the state's formula for awarding benefits. Those points are discussed more fully below. Keep in mind that the law is subject to legislative modification, so benefits can vary.

- Scheduled benefits. A second type of compensable claim, which is distinct from loss due to impaired earning capacity, is loss or loss of use of a member of the body. In all but seven states, there is a scheduled award of benefits for a specified injury of this kind. The award is usually computed by an award of a fixed number of weeks of payment. Note that the awards have no necessary relationship to a given worker's capacity to perform work or to whether the worker has suffered a wage loss. For example, if a computer operator suffered the loss of a foot in a compensable injury, but returned to work shortly thereafter at the same salary, the operator nevertheless would be entitled to the scheduled award of compensation. The inconsistency is compounded when the amount of the award is based on past earnings; in this case, a high wage earner and a low wage earner receive different amounts for the identical injury.
- Death and dependency benefits. In addition to payments to an injured worker, the compensation system pays benefits to the worker's dependents in the event of his or her death from a work-related injury. The amounts may vary from state to state, both in terms of the maximum benefit and the duration; but most states pay benefits to a widow for life or until remarriage, and to children until they reach a specified age. In Pennsylvania, for example, the spouse and family who survive the worker are entitled to the same maximum as the deceased worker, and they receive the award throughout widow- or widowerhood and until age 18, unless disabled or a student under age 23. Most states presume the dependency of surviving spouses and children. Other persons may be entitled to benefits if they prove dependency, but in some relationships, proof of dependency does not

result in entitlement. The death benefit in all states includes some payment for the expenses of funeral and burial.

- Calculating the award. Generally, workers' compensation statutes use a workers' "average weekly wage" (AWW) as a basis for calculating awards of benefits. This figure is derived from the actual earnings of the worker or from a wage that fairly approximates the worker's earning capacity, including such items as tips, bonuses, or other related income. Once the AWW is determined, it may be reduced to a percentage fixed by statute, such as 66 2/3%. The award may be further subject to a statutory minimum and maximum based on a statewide average weekly wage (SAWW) or some other figure. Thus, for example, a worker in Colorado who is temporarily totally disabled as a result of compensable injury will be eligible for payments amounting to 66 2/3% of the worker's average weekly wage. However, if the worker has high earnings, the award will be limited by the state maximum. That maximum is set at 91% of the state average weekly wage (SAWW), which was $1,216 in 2010. The highest award under the statute is therefore $801 per week. For temporary partial and permanent partial disabilities, benefits will be determined by the extent of the disability, or, if applicable, a scheduled award of benefits.
- How workers' compensation is funded. Workers' compensation systems are highly politicized, and states have substantial flexibility to alter benefits according to the political climate. In determining levels of benefits, the state must consider the interest of the employee in receiving adequate financial assistance, the interest of the employer in not being unduly burdened by insurance premiums, and the state's own interest in attracting and retaining business activities to provide employment for state citizens. These interests are frequently a topic of legislative and public debate, and they are especially significant in a period of intense competition among states and among the industrialized nations of the world.

C. A Case Study of "In the Course of and Arising out of Employment"

Tolbert v. Martin Marietta Corp., 759 P.2d 17 (Colo.1988)

[The plaintiff in this case worked for Martin Marietta. On her way to lunch, she was assaulted and raped by a custodian also employed by the company. She brought suit in federal court, claiming that the assault was not covered under the exclusive remedy provisions of Colorado workers' compensation law and that she had a right to sue under a tort theory for injuries suffered in the incident. The Tenth Circuit Court of Appeals sent the case to the Colorado Supreme Court for an interpretation of Colorado law. The state Supreme Court held that the tort claim was barred by the exclusive remedy provision of the Colorado statute. Selections from the court's opinion follow.]

The United States Court of Appeals for the Tenth Circuit has certified to the Supreme Court of Colorado a two-part question of law pertaining to a pending federal case: Does the Workmen's Compensation Act of Colorado provide an exclusive remedy for an employee against her employer: (1) for injuries resulting from a sexual assault by a co-worker which was motivated by considerations neither personal to the injured employee nor distinctly associated with the employment; and (2) when the employee has fixed hours and place of employment in a secure facility and the injury occurred while the employee was in her building of employment, but away from her work station, on her way to lunch in the employer's cafeteria? This court has agreed to answer the interrogatory, and now responds to both parts of the question in the affirmative.

In March 1983 Deborah Tolbert was employed by Martin Marietta as an entry level professional. Arthur Martinez was a janitor, a co-employee at Martin Marietta. Tolbert was on her way to lunch in the company cafeteria on the Martin Marietta premises when she was attacked and raped by Martinez. Tolbert also filed a tort action in federal district court, alleging that Martin Marietta had negligently hired Martinez and negligently failed to keep the premises reasonably safe.

Martin Marietta filed a motion for summary judgment in federal district court raising the Colorado Workmen's Compensation Act (Act) as a complete defense. In its motion, Martin Marietta asserted that workers' compensation is Tolbert's exclusive remedy and as a result, her tort action is barred.

The Workmen's Compensation Act provides:

8-52-102. Conditions of recovery. (1) The right to the compensation provided for in articles 40 to 54 of this title, in lieu of any other liability to any person for any personal injury or death resulting therefrom, shall obtain in all cases where the following conditions occur:

a) Where, at the time of the injury, both employer and employee are subject to the provisions of said articles and where the employer has complied with the provisions thereof regarding insurance;
b) Where, at the time of the injury, the employee is performing service arising out of and in the course of his employment;
c) Where the injury or death is proximately caused by an injury or occupational disease arising out of and in the course of his employment and is not intentionally self-inflicted.

In ruling on Martin Marietta's motion for summary judgment, the federal district court held that it was "undisputed that condition (a) is met, and condition (b) does not appear to be seriously disputed." Thus, the narrow issue of law presented here is whether the injury suffered by Tolbert "arose out of and in the course of" her employment, thus meeting the third requirement.

Our response to the two-part question will determine whether recovery under the Workmen's Compensation Act is Tolbert's exclusive remedy, thereby barring her tort action in negligence. "Recovery under the Act is meant to be exclusive and to preclude employee tort actions against an employer." If we conclude that Tolbert's injury is not compensable under the Act, then her tort action against Martin Marietta is not barred.

The phrases "arising out of" and "in the course of" found in section 8-52-102(1)(c) are not synonymous, and a claimant must prove both requirements. The parties do not dispute that this incident occurred "in the course of" Tolbert's employment with Martin Marietta, so "arising out of" is the phrase at issue here.

An accident "arises out of" employment when there is a causal connection between the work conditions and the injury. For an injury to be compensable under the Act there must be a sufficient nexus between the employment and the injury. The determination of whether an employee's injuries arose out of an employment relationship depends largely on the facts presented in a particular case. "The totality of the circumstances must be examined in each case to see whether there is a sufficient nexus between the employment and the injury."

This nexus or causality requirement is subject to more than one definition. As the federal district court stated, the phrase "arising out of" has been interpreted "in a number of different ways" in various jurisdictions which "have developed different tests of causality." The court also rested its analysis on the observation that "Colorado courts have not consistently applied any single test to determine whether an assault by a co-employee arises out of the employment relationship." The issue becomes what test or standard to apply to this "arising out of" language of the Act.

This court has most frequently used the positional-risk or "but for" standard to define the "arising out of" language. An important and growing number of courts are accepting the full implications of the positional-risk test: An injury arises out of the employment if it would not have occurred but for the fact that the conditions and obligations of the employment placed claimant in the position where he was injured. ...

This theory supports compensation, for example, in cases of stray bullets, roving lunatics, and other situations in which the only connection of the employment with the injury is that its obligations placed the employee in the particular place at the particular time when he was injured by some neutral force, meaning by "neutral" neither personal to the claimant nor distinctly associated with the employment.

The positional-risk test is formulated to assess whether there is a sufficient relationship between the employment and the injury to justify compensation under the Act. "Whether worker's compensation coverage is invoked as a defense by an employer, or as the basis of a claim by an employee, the test of applicability is the same. Compensation is to be awarded, and the tort remedy is abolished, if the statute's conditions are all met." By reviewing the totality of the circumstances using this test, the act's intentional or non-intentional character alone is not dispositive. Rather, the "neutral force" provides the necessary distinction between conflicts imported into the workplace from outside work, as opposed to a neutral force which would have happened to the employee who happened to be in that particular place at that particular time.

Determination of the Act's coverage of assaults by co-workers requires the positional-risk analysis. This interpretation of the Act is supported by the rationale that "instead of being so placed by his duties as to receive the impact of a random bullet or a falling cornice, the claimant is so placed as to receive the impact of his co-worker's personality." Applying the positional-risk doctrine, the test is whether the employee, in the course of her employment, was reasonably required to be at a particular place at a particular time and there met with a "neutral force," meaning that any other person then and there present would have met with attack. The "only connection" required between the employment and the injury is that the job "placed the employee in the particular place at the particular time when she was injured by some neutral force, meaning by 'neutral' neither personal to the claimant nor distinctly associated with the employment."

Does the Workmen's Compensation Act of Colorado provide an exclusive remedy for an employee against her employer: (1) for injuries resulting from a sexual assault by a co-worker which was motivated by considerations neither personal to the injured employee nor distinctly associated with the employment?

As to the time element, it is evident that Tolbert's work obligations caused her to be present on the grounds of Martin Marietta. The mere fact that an employee is on lunch hour does not prohibit workers' compensation coverage, as long as the incident occurred within a time during which the worker is employed. "Courts generally have been liberal in protecting workers during the noon hour," as long as the worker was at a place where the worker may reasonably be, at a time during which the worker is employed, doing what he or she may reasonably do. The employee need not necessarily be engaged in the actual performance of work at the moment of injury in order to receive compensation. Tolbert was also at a place where she "may reasonably be," on the premises of Martin Marietta during her lunch hour. Finally, she was doing what she "may reasonably do": walking to the company cafeteria.

It arises out of the employment if it is connected with the nature, conditions, operations or incidents of the employment. … "No break in the employment is caused by the mere fact that the workman is ministering to his personal comforts or necessities, as by warming himself, or seeking shelter, or by leaving his work to relieve nature, or to procure drink, refreshments, food, or fresh air, or to rest in the shade." An employee need not necessarily be engaged in the actual performance of work at the moment of the injury. Clearly, this case meets the time requirement. This court has quoted with approval the following passage regarding preparatory acts:

"The course of employment, for employees having a fixed time and place of work, embraces a reasonable interval before and after official working hours while the employee is on the premises engaged in preparatory or incidental acts, such as washing or changing his clothes. The rule is not limited to activities that are absolutely necessary; it is sufficient if they can be said to be reasonably incidental to the work.

The "place" element requires that the injury have occurred at a place where the worker may reasonably be. "Under even the broadest rule, the but-for test, it must be emphasized that the test is not 'but for the bare existence of the employment,' but rather 'but for the conditions and obligations of the employment.'" Tolbert's presence in the Martin Marietta building where the attack took place was a direct result of her employment. "But for" the conditions and obligations of her employment with Martin Marietta—being at work on the day in question and using the cafeteria provided by her employer—Tolbert would not have been present at this particular location, traveling to the company cafeteria, which caused her to be vulnerable to her attacker. An employee walking from a work station to the employer cafeteria is certainly in a place where a worker "may reasonably be at the time." The place requirement, therefore, is met.

The third requirement is that the injury must have been caused by a neutral force. Willful assaults upon the claimant, like injuries generally, can be divided into three categories: those that have some inherent connection with the employment, those that are inherently private, and those that are neither, and may therefore be called "neutral."

The first category, assaults which have an inherent connection with employment, are those in which a dispute arises out of "enforced contacts" which result from the duties of the job. The second category, assaults which are inherently private, are those in which "the animosity or dispute that culminates in an assault is imported into the employment from claimant's domestic or private life, and is not exacerbated by the employment." Such assaults do "not arise out of the employment under any test." It is "universally agreed" that an assault is compensable if it grew out of an argument over performance of work, possession of work tools or equipment, delivery of a paycheck, quitting or being terminated, or mediating between quarreling co-employees. Further, even if the "subject of the dispute is unrelated to the work," injuries are compensable if work brought the employees together and "created the relations and conditions" resulting in the dispute. Inherently private assaults typically involve disputes over spouses. Compensation is usually denied "when the fight was caused by a quarrel between the employee's wives, when the argument was concerned with the assailant's misconduct with another employee's wife, or the employee's misconduct with the assailant's wife, and when the assault was occasioned by a remark to the co-employee's wife."

The third category of neutral assaults includes "assaults which are in essence equivalent to blind or irrational forces, such as attacks by lunatics, drunks, small children, and other irresponsibles; completely unexplained assaults; and assaults by mistake." The characteristic of a neutral or unexplained assault is that "nothing connects it with the victim privately; neither can it be shown to have had a specific employment origin." If an employee is exposed to the unexplained assault "because he is discharging his duties at that time and place," then the injuries are generally compensable. "A minority of jurisdictions are inclined to regard the neutral category as noncompensable, for want of affirmative proof of distinctive employment risk as the cause of the harm; but a growing majority, sometimes expressly applying the positional or but-for test, make awards for such injuries when sustained in the course of employment." Under the 'but-for test,' assaults by co-workers are compensable as long as they are not motivated by personal vengeance stemming from contact with the employee outside of the employment. There is a marked distinction between the holdup in which the robber says to himself, "I am going to track down Henry Davis wherever he may be and steal the gold watch which I know he has," and the holdup in which the robber says, "I am going to rob whoever happens to be on duty as night watchman at the Consolidated Lumber Company or whoever happens to come down the dark, hidden path from the factory to the rear gate."

The parties agree that there was no personal or private motivation for Martinez' attack and rape of Tolbert. The rape was not directly associated with Tolbert's employment and there was no indication that Martinez had specifically selected Tolbert as a victim. Prior to the assault, Tolbert and Martinez "had only the slightest contacts, and those were only at Martin Marietta." The federal district court held: "There is nothing to indicate that any other woman—whether or not a Martin employee—who happened to be in the same area at the time of the attack would not have become the victim." The parties agree that Tolbert was not on duty when attacked; she was on her lunch hour. She was not at her assigned work place, nor was she at a place where her job expressly required her to be at that moment. Tolbert was on Martin Marietta premises walking from her work station to the employee cafeteria at the time of her assault. The parties agree that there are no facts or circumstances "tending to show that the attack was directed against [Tolbert] as opposed to any other woman who might have been present at the place and time." The undisputed facts and circumstances surrounding this attack meet the definition of a "neutral" attack.

Does the Workmen's Compensation Act of Colorado provide an exclusive remedy for an employee against her employer: (2) when the employee has fixed hours and place of employment in a secure facility and the injury occurred while the employee was in her building of employment, but away from her work station, on her way to lunch in the employer's cafeteria?

The same three-part positional-risk test must be applied. The "fixed hours" aspect of Tolbert's employment establishes that Tolbert would not have been present at this time but for the conditions and obligations of her work. Tolbert was free to leave her work area during the lunch hour, but was expected to return after lunch. In this case Tolbert stayed on her employer's premises during lunch hour, thus meeting the time requirement.

The fact that she remained on Martin Marietta premises creates another link between the employment and the injury. Tolbert was on Martin Marietta premises walking to the employee cafeteria, which is a fringe benefit provided by Martin Marietta to its employees. These facts establish that the conditions and obligations of Tolbert's employment caused her to be at this particular place at this time.

We recognize that [our] ruling may seem to produce an unfair result, in the respect that Tolbert is now barred from bringing a civil action against Martin Marietta. While not unmindful of the dilemma, it must be noted that "the Workmen's Compensation Act should be given a liberal construction because its purpose is highly remedial and beneficent." We agree with New Jersey's response to this issue: "Even though in this case the injured employee is resisting compensability, presumably in order to obtain a larger recovery in a civil action, we are bound by the principle requiring liberal interpretation of the Workmen's Compensation Act in order to afford a certain remedy. 'Consistency requires us to use the same legal yardstick. …' In keeping with the broad underlying policies and the remedial nature of the Act, we answer both parts of the interrogatory in the affirmative.

Questions

1. Why does the plaintiff try to avoid coverage under the workers' compensation statute?
2. What would she have to prove in order to prevail on a tort claim against the employer? What defenses would the employer raise?
3. Does the plaintiff have a claim against her attacker? Why might that not be an adequate remedy?
4. Do you think employers would agree to a workers' compensation insurance scheme without the exclusive remedy provision?
5. If you were a state legislator, would you vote to do away with workers' compensation and permit workers to sue their employers?
6. Should the cap on recovery under workers' compensation be removed?

D. A Note on Independent Contracting

There is an important distinction between an employment relationship and an independent contractor who stands in a much different legal position. If an individual is an employee, then the primary incidents of employment automatically attach to the job, including workers' compensation and other protections discussed later. The key element in determining independent contractor status is whether the individual is under direct and detailed control while performing work. If the seller of labor exercises discretion over the methods, execution, and manner of completing the task, he or she has a contractual relationship with the buyer. Some common examples include doctors, dentists, builders, painters, and hairdressers. Conversely, an employee performs under instructions issued by the employer and can be separated from employment if the work is not satisfactory. Independent contractors are not "fired," but can be sued for failure to satisfy the contract.

Whether an individual is an independent contractor or an employee matters to the person and to the state. The person may lose important protections if he or she is an independent contractor, and the state may lose revenues necessary to sustain vital programs such as workers' compensation, Social Security, and unemployment insurance. The respective interests are illustrated by ongoing litigation involving FedEx, the freight carrier.

One aspect of the FedEx case has to do with a suit brought by the state of Massachusetts, alleging the company's failure to pay appropriate employment taxes. The company argued that the affected drivers were independent contractors rather than employees, but the state asserted that by accepted legal guidelines, the drivers were actually employees. Without admitting any liability, FedEx offered a settlement of $3 million, and the state accepted the offer in July 2010. The settlement resolves governmental claims against the company, but legal claims by the drivers are continuing.

Drivers for FedEx in Massachusetts brought a class action suit against the company in August 2010. According to an article in Reuters news service, "The suit, which was filed in U.S. District Court in Boston and seeks class-action status, contends the degree of control FedEx exerts over its drivers—including setting rules on uniforms and equipment—amounts to an employer-employee relationship, not a customer-contractor relationship." If drivers are designated as employees, they will have a right to unionize and engage in collective bargaining as do employees at United Parcel Service. One explanation for FedEx's designation of drivers as independent contractors is that FedEx gains a competitive advantage in labor costs over the unionized workers at rival UPS.

The standard test for employee status is one of control. Over the years, the Internal Revenue Service has formulated a series of factors that indicate control. The following material is taken from the IRS Web site at http://www.irs.gov/businesses/small/article/0,,id=99921,00.html.

Independent Contractor (Self-Employed) or Employee?

It is critical that you, the business owner, correctly determine whether the individuals providing services are employees or independent contractors. Generally, you must withhold income taxes, withhold and pay Social Security and Medicare taxes, and pay unemployment tax on wages paid to an employee. You do not generally have to withhold or pay any taxes on payments to independent contractors. If you are an independent contractor and hire or subcontract work to others, you will want to review the information in this section to determine whether individuals you hire are independent contractors (subcontractors) or employees.

Facts that provide evidence of the degree of control and independence fall into three categories:

1. ***Behavioral: Does the company control or have the right to control what the worker does and how the worker does his or her job?***

Behavioral Control

Behavioral control refers to facts that show whether there is a right to direct or control how the worker does the work. A worker is an employee when the business has the right to direct and control the worker. The business does not have to actually direct or control the way the work is done—as long as the employer has the right to direct and control the work.

The behavioral control factors fall into the categories of:

- Type of instructions given
- Degree of instruction
- Evaluation systems
- Training

Types of Instructions Given

An employee is generally subject to the business's instructions about when, where, and how to work. All of the following are examples of types of instructions about how to do work.

- When and where to do the work.
- What tools or equipment to use.
- What workers to hire or to assist with the work.
- Where to purchase supplies and services.
- What work must be performed by a specified individual.
- What order or sequence to follow when performing the work.

Degree of Instruction

Degree of Instruction means that the more detailed the instructions, the more control the business exercises over the worker. More detailed instructions indicate that the worker is an employee. Less detailed instructions reflects less control, indicating that the worker is more likely an independent contractor. **Note:** The amount of instruction needed varies among different jobs. Even if no instructions are given, sufficient behavioral control may exist if the employer has the right to control how the work results are achieved. A business may lack the knowledge to instruct some highly specialized professionals; in other cases, the task may require little or no instruction. The key consideration is whether the business has retained the right to control the details of a worker's performance or instead has given up that right.

2. ***Financial: Are the business aspects of the worker's job controlled by the payer? (These include things like how worker is paid, whether expenses are reimbursed, who provides tools/supplies, etc.)***

Financial Control

Financial control refers to facts that show whether or not the business has the right to control the economic aspects of the worker's job.

The financial control factors fall into the categories of:

- Significant investment
- Unreimbursed expenses
- Opportunity for profit or loss
- Services available to the market
- Method of payment

Significant Investment

An independent contractor often has a significant investment in the equipment he or she uses in working for someone else. However, in many occupations, such as construction, workers spend thousands of dollars on the tools and equipment they use and are still considered to be employees. There are no precise dollar limits that must be met in order to have a significant investment. Furthermore, a significant investment is not necessary for independent contractor status as some types of work simply do not require large expenditures.

Unreimbursed Expenses

Independent contractors are more likely to have unreimbursed expenses than are employees. Fixed ongoing costs that are incurred regardless of whether work is currently being performed are especially important. However, employees may also incur unreimbursed expenses in connection with the services that they perform for their business.

Opportunity for Profit or Loss

The opportunity to make a profit or loss is another important factor. If a worker has a significant investment in the tools and equipment used and if the worker has unreimbursed expenses, the worker has a greater opportunity to lose money (i.e., their expenses will exceed their income from the work). Having the possibility of incurring a loss indicates that the worker is an independent contractor.

Services Available to the Market

An independent contractor is generally free to seek out business opportunities. Independent contractors often advertise, maintain a visible business location, and are available to work in the relevant market.

Method of Payment

An employee is generally guaranteed a regular wage amount for an hourly, weekly, or other period of time. This usually indicates that a worker is an employee, even when the wage or salary is supplemented by a commission. An independent contractor is usually paid by a flat fee for the job. However, it is common in some professions, such as law, to pay independent contractors hourly.

3. ***Type of Relationship: Are there written contracts or employee type benefits (i.e. pension plan, insurance, vacation pay, etc.)? Will the relationship continue and is the work performed a key aspect of the business?***

Type of Relationship

Type of relationship refers to facts that show how the worker and business perceive their relationship to each other.

The factors, for the type of relationship between two parties, generally fall into the categories of:

- Written contracts
- Employee benefits
- Permanency of the relationship
- Services provided as key activity of the business

Written Contracts

Although a contract may state that the worker is an employee or an independent contractor, this is not sufficient to determine the worker's status. The IRS is not required to follow a contract stating that the worker is an independent contractor, responsible for paying his or her own self-employment tax. How the parties work together determines whether the worker is an employee or an independent contractor.

Employee Benefits

Employee benefits include things like insurance, pension plans, paid vacation, sick days, and disability insurance. Businesses generally do not grant these benefits to independent contractors. However, the lack of these types of benefits does not necessarily mean the worker is an independent contractor.

Permanency of the Relationship

If you hire a worker with the expectation that the relationship will continue indefinitely, rather than for a specific project or period, this is generally considered evidence that the intent was to create an employer–employee relationship.

Services Provided As Key Activity of the Business

If a worker provides services that are a key aspect of the business, it is more likely that the business will have the right to direct and control his or her activities. For example, if a law firm hires an attorney, it is likely that it will present the attorney's work as its own and would have the right to control or direct that work. This would indicate an employer–employee relationship.

> Businesses must weigh all these factors when determining whether a worker is an employee or independent contractor. Some factors may indicate that the worker is an employee, while other factors indicate that the worker is an independent contractor. There is no "magic" or set number of factors that "makes" the worker an employee or an independent contractor, and no one factor stands alone in making this determination. Also, factors which are relevant in one situation may not be relevant in another.

In September 2010 Senator John Kerry of Massachusetts and Representative Jim McDermott of Washington State introduced legislation to address problems associated with the definition of independent contractor. The bill, titled "The Fair Playing Field Act of 2010 (S. 3786, H. 6128)," corrected perceived weaknesses of the Internal Revenue Code, which allowed companies to avoid tax obligations. In addition to strengthening the tax code, the proposal also requires buyers of labor to disclose that an individual is classified as an independent contractor and the reasons for the classification. The bill includes the following statement of findings in Section 1(b)(4):

> Many workers are properly classified as independent contractors. In other instances, workers who are employees are being treated as independent contractors. Such misclassification for tax purposes contributes to inequities in the competitive positions of businesses and to the Federal and State tax gap, and may also result in misclassification for other purposes, such as denial of unemployment benefits, workplace health and safety protections, and retirement or other benefits or protections available to employees.

To conclude, the distinction between an independent contractor and an employee is important in several respects. Employees have rights attaching to their status, and independent contractors have rights according to their agreement. The state has an interest in the classification, because employment contributes to such programs as Social Security, unemployment insurance, and protections against injuries on the job.

Suggested Exercises

1. In an assigned group, develop a strategy to adopt the Montana wrongful discharge act in your state. Anticipate and address arguments against the legislation, and formulate arguments in favor of it.
2. Engage in a debate on the majority and dissenting opinions in *Adair*. Focus particularly on the values articulated in each position.
3. Review the article on employment-at-will. Discuss the patterns, if any, in the states adopting exceptions to the rule.

4. How did the workers' compensation system originate in the United States? Write an essay describing the beginnings and principle elements of the system.
5. Do a group presentation of the *Tolbert* case. Explain the case to an audience, including the facts, the holding, and the reasoning in the case.
6. Assume you are the director of human resources for a large electronics manufacturing company. You want to provide several intern positions in the marketing and distribution departments. Draw up a description of the position that will avoid any legal issues with the Internal Revenue Service.

Notes

1. For a good recent analysis, see David Soskice, "American Exceptionalism and Comparative Political Economy," in *Labor in the Age of Globalization*, ed. Clair Brown, Barry Eichengreen, & Michael Reich (New York: Cambridge University Press, 2010), pp. 51–93.
2. *Wagenseller v. Scottsdale Memorial Hospital*, 147 Ariz. 370, 710 P.2d 1025 (1985).
3. An excellent book on the subject is Price V. Fishback and Shawn Everett Kantor, *A Prelude to the Welfare State: The Origins of Workers' Compensation* (Chicago: University of Chicago Press, 2000).
4. Anthony Balle, "America's First Compensation Crisis: Conflict Over the Value and Meaning of Workplace Injuries Under the Employer's Liability System," in *Dying for Work: Workers Safety and Health in Twentieth Century America*, ed. David Rosner and Gerald Markowitz (Bloomington.: University of Indiana Press, 1987), pp. 34; 47–49.

2. The Foundations of Modern Employment Regulation

I. Overview of the Chapter

Prior to the 1930s, American employment law was governed by Supreme Court decisions that limited state and federal regulation in important ways. Attempted federal legislation, such as the Erdman Act discussed in Chapter 1, exceeded the constitutional powers granted to the federal government. State laws were subject to review on due process grounds; any exercise of state police powers, as in the *Lochner* case, could be overturned on the theory that the law deprived employers of their property rights. As a result, workers had little recourse against the abusive powers of corporations, and they were subject to legal persecution for engaging in organized action against employers. The onset of the Great Depression led to a transformation in our political and economic system.

The New Deal era initiated by President Franklin D. Roosevelt revolutionized employment in the United States. First, the Roosevelt administration enacted sweeping changes in the legal environment, beginning with the National Labor Relations Act and culminating with the Social Security program. The Supreme Court changed the constitutional theory articulated in its previous decisions, and settled on a rule that authorized regulation under the interstate commerce clause found in Article I of the Constitution. Following that breakthrough, the federal government could legitimately regulate all matters that affected commerce. This clause is the basis for all subsequent employment laws, such as the Civil Rights Act of 1964, and more recently, the Affordable Health Care Act passed in 2010. One of the important debates during the New Deal addressed the reasons for the Depression and the policies that were necessary to correct the economic collapse. The debate continued in the first years of the Obama administration. We begin with an overview of the subject.

II. From the Great Depression to the Great Recession: Causes and Consequences

In late 2007 the American economy began to unravel. Financial problems sparked a global crisis in banking and credit, and the international system of exchange faced paralysis. Swift action by the Federal Reserve and the U.S. Treasury avoided a worldwide bank collapse by massive injections of liquidity and guarantees of solvency that enabled firms to continue business. In the 2010 midterm elections, the effectiveness of the stimulus and "bailout" activities became a central point of campaign debate. Critics of President Obama's administration described the efforts as a failure that led to unsustainable expansion of the federal deficit. Other economists argued that the federal government's intervention did not go far enough in dealing with unemployment. Nobel laureate Paul Krugman, for example, wrote in October 2010 that President Obama failed to act decisively enough in delivering economic stimulus. He said, "When Mr. Obama took office, he inherited an economy in dire straits—more dire, it seems, than he or his top economic advisers realized. They knew that America was in the midst of a severe financial crisis. But they don't seem to have taken on board the lesson of history, which is that major financial crises are normally followed by a protracted period of very high unemployment."[1]

The severity of the 2007 collapse did not lead to the same levels of unemployment or to massive deflation as in the 1930s. Many commentators, though, viewed the event as potentially devastating as the earlier crash. Two highly regarded economists wrote in 2010, "Eighteen months ago, the global financial system was on the brink of collapse and the U.S. was suffering its worst economic downturn since the 1930s. Real GDP was falling at about a 6% annual rate, and monthly job losses averaged close to 750,000."[2] They argued that the federal stimulus bills and the intervention of the Federal Reserve prevented a much more serious deterioration.

The chairman of the Federal Reserve in 2007, Ben Bernanke, received his doctoral degree in economics from Princeton University. He wrote his dissertation on the fiscal conditions underlying the Great Depression of the 1930s. Because Bernanke had a deep understanding of how the country fell into the most severe domestic crisis since the Civil War, he was able to avert another financial panic during his term in office. His decisions followed closely from the main conclusions he drew from his research on the Depression. Some three years before the onset of the Great Recession of 2008, as it has come to be called, Bernanke delivered an address at the College of William and Mary. His speech discusses the major policy elements from the Depression that appeared again in the 2008 banking crisis. Bernanke began with a survey of the nature and depth of the 1930s crisis.[3] His description explains why the federal government acted in the 1930s to reverse the effects of the economic downturn.

> The impact that the experience of the Depression has had on views about the role of the government in the economy is easily understood when we

> recall the sheer magnitude of that economic downturn. During the major contraction phase of the Depression, between 1929 and 1933, real output in the United States fell nearly 30 percent. During the same period, according to retrospective studies, the unemployment rate rose from about 3 percent to nearly 25 percent, and many of those lucky enough to have a job were able to work only part-time. For comparison, between 1973 and 1975, in what was perhaps the most severe U.S. recession of the World War II era, real output fell 3.4 percent and the unemployment rate rose from about 4 percent to about 9 percent. Other features of the 1929–33 decline included a sharp deflation—prices fell at a rate of nearly 10 percent per year during the early 1930s—as well as a plummeting stock market, widespread bank failures, and a rash of defaults and bankruptcies by businesses and households. The economy improved after Franklin D. Roosevelt's inauguration in March 1933, but unemployment remained in the double digits for the rest of the decade, full recovery arriving only with the advent of World War II. Moreover ... the Depression was international in scope, affecting most countries around the world not only the United States.

Bernanke went on in his speech to describe the monetary dimensions of the crash. He summarized the views of economists prior to the 1980s, who tended to focus mainly on the experience of the United States. Bernanke argued that the best way to understand what took place was to examine the problem in a global framework. He said:

> To explain the current consensus on the causes of the Depression, I will first describe the debate as it existed before 1980, and then discuss how the recent focus on international aspects of the Depression and the comparative analysis of the experiences of different countries have helped to resolve that debate. I have already mentioned the sharp deflation of the price level that occurred during the contraction phase of the Depression, by far the most severe episode of deflation experienced in the United States before or since. Deflation, like inflation, tends to be closely linked to changes in the national money supply, defined as the sum of currency and bank deposits outstanding, and such was the case in the Depression. Like real output and prices, the U.S. money supply fell about one-third between 1929 and 1933, rising in subsequent years as output and prices rose.
>
> While the fact that money, prices, and output all declined rapidly in the early years of the Depression is undeniable, the interpretation of that fact has been the subject of much controversy. Indeed, historically, much of the debate on the causes of the Great Depression has centered on the role of monetary factors, including both monetary policy and other influences on the national money supply, such as the condition of the banking system. Views have changed over time. During the Depression itself, and in several

decades following, most economists argued that monetary factors were not an important cause of the Depression. For example, many observers pointed to the fact that nominal interest rates were close to zero during much of the Depression, concluding that monetary policy had been about as easy as possible yet had produced no tangible benefits to the economy. The attempt to use monetary policy to extricate an economy from a deep depression was often compared to "pushing on a string."

During the first decades after the Depression, most economists looked to developments on the real side of the economy for explanations, rather than to monetary factors. Some argued, for example, that overinvestment and overbuilding had taken place during the ebullient 1920s, leading to a crash when the returns on those investments proved to be less than expected. Another once-popular theory was that a chronic problem of "under-consumption"—the inability of households to purchase enough goods and services to utilize the economy's productive capacity—had precipitated the slump.

However, in 1963, Milton Friedman and Anna J. Schwartz transformed the debate about the Great Depression. That year saw the publication of their now-classic book, *A Monetary History of the United States, 1867–1960.* The *Monetary History*, the name by which the book is instantly recognized by any macroeconomist, examined in great detail the relationship between changes in the national money stock—whether determined by conscious policy or by more impersonal forces such as changes in the banking system—and changes in national income and prices. The broader objective of the book was to understand how monetary forces had influenced the U.S. economy over a nearly a century. In the process of pursuing this general objective, however, Friedman and Schwartz offered important new evidence and arguments about the role of monetary factors in the Great Depression. In contradiction to the prevalent view of the time, that money and monetary policy played at most a purely passive role in the Depression, Friedman and Schwartz argued that "the [economic] contraction is in fact a tragic testimonial to the importance of monetary forces."

According to Bernanke, the Federal Reserve sparked the financial downturn early in 1928 by raising interest rates and tightening the money supply. When the stock market crashed in October 1929, the proximate cause was a policy of "tight money." What followed was a period of falling prices, rising unemployment, and political inactivity by the Hoover administration. Prominent economists, including Hoover's treasury secretary, Andrew Mellon, thought that the Depression was a self-correcting business cycle and that the economy would stabilize when the "excess" credit was liquidated from the system. In theory, lower prices would lead to more consumption, lower wages would enable employers to hire more labor, and production would rise. In actual fact, however, consumers hoarded cash, banks were unable to lend, and as unemployment rose, fewer people were able to purchase goods and services. Richard Posner, a federal appeals court judge and a prolific writer on economic matters, titled his recent book *A Failure of Capitalism* (2009). He showed how the experience of 1929 paralleled the crisis of 2007, except for the fact that Bernanke and others responded with the right strategies to prevent a repeat of the Great Depression. Conditions worsened through Hoover's remaining years in office.

Franklin D. Roosevelt's election in 1932 led to a series of measures generally known as the New Deal. Roosevelt initiated far-reaching economic legislation that transformed the economy. Many of the New Deal programs continue today, and will be dealt with later in this chapter; they include Social Security, unemployment insurance, and minimum wage and overtime laws. For the moment, we focus on laws that deal with unionization and collective bargaining. Labor law provided the basis for a new line of constitutional interpretation, the creation of administrative bureaucracies, and the foundation for three decades of middle-class prosperity and economic growth. That prosperity began to fade in the mid-1970s, when average real incomes became stagnant or declining until the late 1990s. They rose briefly, and then continued a downward trend through the next decade. A large body of economic research concludes that declining union membership was a significant factor in the downward wage spiral, for reasons explained below.

III. The National Labor Relations Act and Collective Bargaining Practices

A. Background

In 1936 the famous economist John Maynard Keynes published his best-known work on how economies function.[4] Keynes argued that business conditions were not dynamic, and the system could not extricate itself from depression, either through low interest rates or falling prices, as was predicted by classical economic theory. Keynes said that only some form of stimulus, such as government spending or improved consumer demand, would lead to recovery. Keynes's ideas fit closely with Roosevelt's programs. The centerpiece of Roosevelt's plan was an ambitious attempt to impose government oversight on wages and prices; the statute was known as the National Industrial Recovery Act (NIRA), and it passed in early 1933.

Prior to the New Deal, Supreme Court rulings like the *Adair* case in Chapter 1 discouraged legislators from enacting broad worker protections, which were likely to be found unconstitutional. Roosevelt believed that the federal government should have the power to act in periods of extreme crisis, and he proceeded with his comprehensive legislative scheme to restore the economy. To gain organized labor's support for the NIRA, Roosevelt invited William Green of the American Federation of Labor to participate in creating the legislation. Green wanted protections for the right to unionize, the right to negotiate, and a ban on company unions. Conceding to those demands, the

Roosevelt administration inserted Section 7(a) into the NIRA. Roosevelt chose Senator Robert Wagner (D-NY) to oversee the new National Labor Board and develop a body of law implementing Section 7(a).

The Supreme Court ruled the NIRA unconstitutional in the *Schechter Poultry Company* case of 1935. The Court held that the regulation of poultry farming within the borders of New York State had no direct connection with interstate commerce. Wagner, despite the Court's ruling, continued to draft a comprehensive bill protecting the rights of workers and unions to engage in collective bargaining. He introduced the bill into the Senate in June 1935, just months after the *Schechter Poultry* decision. Wagner's theory was that the federal power to regulate interstate commerce was sufficient to allow federal oversight in the employment regime, and he proved to be correct on that point two years later. Wagner also viewed the legislation as a key element of economic recovery. Consistent with the ideas of John Maynard Keynes, Wagner thought that consumer demand was essential to economic activity, and collective bargaining would provide enough income to workers that they would be able to begin purchasing goods and services. When he introduced his legislation into the Senate in February 1935, Wagner explained how unions would contribute to the recovery. His comments are reprinted below. This speech is a central document in the New Deal legislative effort, and a cogent policy justification for the policy of collective bargaining.

Senator Robert F. Wagner, Speech on the National Labor Relations Act (February 21, 1935). *Congressional Record*, 74th Cong., 1st sess., Vol. 79, 2371–72, reprinted in *Legislative History of the National Labor Relations Act*, vol. 1 (Govt. Printing Office, 1985), pp. 1311–15.

> The recovery program has sought to bestow upon the business man and the worker a new freedom to grapple with the great economic challenges of our times. We have released the business man from the undiscriminating enforcement of the antitrust laws, which had been subjecting him to the attacks of the price cutters and wage reducers—the pirates of industry. In order to deal out the equal treatment upon which a just democratic society must rest, we at the same time guaranteed the freedom of action of the worker. In fact, the now famous section 7(a), by stating that employees should be allowed to cooperate among themselves if they desired to do so, merely restated principles that Congress has avowed for half a century.
>
> Congress is familiar with the events of the past 2 years. While industry's freedom of action has been encouraged until the trade association movement has blanketed the entire country, employees attempting in good faith to exercise their liberties under section 7(a) have met with repeated rebuffs. It was to check this evil that the President in his wisdom created the National Labor Board in August 1933, out of which has emerged the present National Labor Relations Board.

The Board has performed a marvelous service in composing disputes and sending millions of workers back to their jobs upon terms beneficial to every interest. But it was handicapped from the beginning, and it is gradually but surely losing its effectiveness, because of the practical inability to enforce its decisions. At present it may refer its findings to the National Recovery Administration and await some action by that agency, such as the removal of the Blue Eagle. We all know that the entire enforcement procedure of the N.R.A. is closely interlinked with the voluntary spirit of the codes. Business in the large is allowed to police itself through the code authorities. This voluntarism is without question admirable in respect to provisions for fair competition that have been written by industry and with which business is in complete accord. But it is wholly unadapted to the enforcement of a specific law of Congress which becomes a crucial issue only in those very cases where it is opposed by the guiding spirits of the code authorities. Secondly, the Board may refer a case to the Department of Justice. But since the Board has no power to subpoena records or witnesses, its hearings are largely ex parte and its records so infirm that the Department of Justice is usually unable to act. Finally, the existence of numerous industrial boards whose interpretations of section 7(a) are not subject to the coordinating influence of a supreme National Labor Relations Board, is creating a maze of confusion and contradictions. While there is a different code for each trade, there is only one section 7(a), and no definite law written by Congress can mean something different in each industry. These difficulties are reducing section 7(a) to a sham and a delusion.

The break-down of section 7(a) brings results equally disastrous to industry and to labor. Last summer it led to a procession of bloody and costly strikes, which in some cases swelled almost to the magnitude of national emergencies. It is not material at this time to inquire where the balance of right and wrong rested in respect to these various controversies. If it is true that employees find it difficult to remain acquiescent when they lose the main privilege promised them by the Recovery Act, it is equally true that employers are tremendously handicapped when it is impossible to determine exactly what their rights are. Everybody needs a law that is precise and certain.

There has been a second and even more serious consequence of the break-down of section 7(a). When employees are denied the freedom to act in concert even when they desire to do so, they cannot exercise a restraining influence upon the wayward members of their own groups, and they cannot participate in our national endeavor to coordinate production and purchasing power. The consequences are already visible in the widening gap between wages and profits. If these consequences are allowed to produce their full harvest, the whole country will suffer from a new economic decline.

The national labor relations bill which I now propose is novel neither in philosophy nor in content. It creates no new substantive rights. It merely provides that employees, if they desire to do so, shall be free to organize for their mutual protection or benefit. Quite aside from section 7(a), this principle has been embodied in the Norris-LaGuardia Act, in amendments to the Railway Labor Act passed last year, and in a long train of other enactments of Congress.

There is not a scintilla of truth in the wide-spread propaganda to the effect that this bill would tend to create a so-called "labor dictatorship." It does not encourage national unionism. It does not favor any particular union. It does not display any preference toward craft or industrial organizations. Most important of all, it does not force or even counsel any employee to join any union if he prefers to deal directly or individually with his employers. It seeks merely to make the worker a free man in the economic as well as the political field. Certainly the preservation of long-recognized fundamental rights is the only basis for frank and friendly relations in industry.

The erroneous impression that the bill expresses a bias for some particular form of union organization probably arises because it outlaws the company-dominated union. Let me emphasize that nothing in the measure discourages employees from uniting on an independent- or company-union basis, if by these terms we mean simply an organization confined to the limits of one plant or one employer. Nothing in the bill prevents employers from maintaining free and direct relations with their workers or from participating in group insurance, mutual welfare, pension systems, and other such activities. The only prohibition is against the sham or dummy union which is dominated by the employer, which is supported by the employers, which cannot change its rules or regulations without his consent, and which cannot live except by the grace of the employer's whims. To say that that kind of a union must be preserved in order to give employees freedom of selection is a contradiction in terms. There can be no freedom in an atmosphere of bondage. No organization can be free to represent the workers when it is the mere creature of the employer.

Equally erroneous is the belief that the bill creates a closed shop for all industry. It does not force any employer to make a closed-shop agreement. It does not even state that Congress favors the policy of the closed shop. It merely provides that employers and employees may voluntarily make closed-shop agreements in any State where they are now legal. Far from suggesting a change, it merely preserves the status quo.

A great deal of interest centers around the question of majority rule. The national labor relations bill provides that representatives selected by the majority of employees in an appropriate unit shall represent all the employees within that unit for the purposes of collective bargaining. This does not imply that an employee who is not a member of the majority group can be forced to enter the union which the majority favors. It means simply that the majority may decide who are to be the spokesmen for all in making agreements concerning wages, hours, and other conditions of employment. Once such agreements are made the bill provides that their terms must be applied without favor or discrimination to all employees. These provisions conform to the democratic procedure that is followed in every business and in our governmental life, and that was embodied by Congress in the Railway Labor Act last year. Without them the phrase "collective bargaining" is devoid of meaning, and the very few unfair employers are encouraged to divide their workers against themselves.

Finally, the National Labor Relations Board is established permanently, with jurisdiction over other boards dealing with cases under section 7(a) or under its equivalent as written into this bill. Nothing could be more unfounded than the charges that the Board would be invested with arbitrary or dictatorial or even unusual powers. Its powers are modeled upon those of the Federal Trade Commission and numerous other governmental agencies. Its orders would be enforceable not by the Board, but by recourse to the courts of the United States, with every affected party entitled to all the safeguards of appeal.

The enactment of this measure will clarify the industrial atmosphere and reduce the likelihood of another conflagration of strife such as we witnessed last summer. It will stabilize and improve business by laying the foundations for the amity and fair dealing upon which permanent progress must rest. It will give notice to all that the solemn pledge made by Congress when it enacted section 7(a) cannot be ignored with impunity, and that a cardinal principle of the new deal for all and not some of our people is going to be supported and preserved by the government.

Some Questions about Wagner's Speech

1. How does Wagner describe the effect of the NIRA on business? What did the bill do for labor?
2. Why does Wagner believe that new legislation is needed?
3. What was the result of employers' refusal to deal with workers' organizations? How does his bill address the problem?
4. Does Wagner's speech set out an economic theory? What is that theory?
5. Why does Wagner discuss the idea of a "labor dictatorship?" Is it dictatorial to require workers in a bargaining unit to provide financial support to the union? Should an individual have a right to decide whether to pay taxes?

6. What does Wagner say about majority rule? Why is it important to eliminate the "company unions"?
7. Do you think that workers now have more, or less, bargaining power than they did in the 1950s and 1960s? For one answer, see the following Web site (it's "less"): http://www.epi.org/economic_snapshots/entry/what_workers_gave_and_what_they_got/.
8. Two economists devised a way a measuring income distribution in the United States, and they found that inequality presently is at its highest level since 1929. The Center for Budget Policy and Priorities has a graph of the data at http://www.cbpp.org/cms/index.cfm?fa=view&id=2908.

B. The Structure of the Wagner Act

Wagner's vision for workers began with the fundamental proposition that employers should have no control over the preferences of employees as to unionization. The so-called "company unions" of the time were not strong enough to bargain effectively for employees in place of independent trade unions. If a union representative was selected according to NLRA procedures, that representative had a right to bargain for all employees covered in the unit, regardless of whether the employee had favored representation. Finally, unions had a right to compel all employees covered under an agreement to provide financial support in the form of union dues. Those three elements are the crucial features of the law, and they continue to be central in understanding the statute.[5] Along with a broad statement of principles, Wagner enumerated five unfair labor practices, which employers were prohibited from engaging in. To enforce the law, the Wagner Act created the National Labor Relations Board, which still serves today as the administrative body responsible for protecting workers' rights. We begin by examining the policy and findings of the Act, reprinted below.

1. Findings and Policies of the National Labor Relations Act

NATIONAL LABOR RELATIONS ACT
Also cited NLRA or the Act; 29 U.S.C. §§ 151–169
FINDINGS AND POLICIES

Section 1§151.] The denial by some employers of the right of employees to organize and the refusal by some employers to accept the procedure of collective bargaining lead to strikes and other forms of industrial strife or unrest, which have the intent or the necessary effect of burdening or obstructing commerce by (a) impairing the efficiency, safety, or operation of the instrumentalities of commerce; (b) occurring in the current of commerce; (c) materially affecting, restraining, or controlling the flow of raw materials or manufactured or processed goods from or into the channels of commerce, or the prices of such materials or goods in commerce; or (d) causing diminution of employment and wages in such volume as substantially to impair or disrupt the market for goods flowing from or into the channels of commerce.

The inequality of bargaining power between employees who do not possess full freedom of association or actual liberty of contract and employers who are organized in the corporate or other forms of ownership association substantially burdens and affects the flow of commerce, and tends to aggravate recurrent business depressions, by depressing wage rates and the purchasing power of wage earners in industry and by preventing the stabilization of competitive wage rates and working conditions within and between industries.

Experience has proved that protection by law of the right of employees to organize and bargain collectively safeguards commerce from injury, impairment, or interruption, and promotes the flow of commerce by removing certain recognized sources of industrial strife and unrest, by encouraging practices fundamental to the friendly adjustment of industrial disputes arising out of differences as to wages, hours, or other working conditions, and by restoring equality of bargaining power between employers and employees.

Experience has further demonstrated that certain practices by some labor organizations, their officers, and members have the intent or the necessary effect of burdening or obstructing commerce by preventing the free flow of goods in such commerce through strikes and other forms of industrial unrest or through concerted activities which impair the interest of the public in the free flow of such commerce. The elimination of such practices is a necessary condition to the assurance of the rights herein guaranteed.

It is declared to be the policy of the United States to eliminate the causes of certain substantial obstructions to the free flow of commerce and to mitigate and eliminate these obstructions when they have occurred by encouraging the practice and procedure of collective bargaining and by protecting the exercise by workers of full freedom of association, self-organization, and designation of representatives of their own choosing, for the purpose of negotiating the terms and conditions of their employment or other mutual aid or protection.

2. Unfair Labor Practices

The original Wagner Act prohibited only certain activities by employers. Wagner said that his bill was intended to aid unions and workers; consequently, he was not concerned about ways in which unions should be regulated. When the NLRA was modified in 1947 by a Republican Congress in the Taft-Hartley Act, a series of union unfair labor practices was inserted into the law. As a result, the law now consists of sections 8(a)1–5, and 8(b)1–7. Each of the unfair practices is summarized in the table below.

Employer ULPs	Prohibited Acts	Union ULPS	Prohibited Acts
Section 8(a)(1)	Unlawful to interfere with or coerce employees in the exercise of their rights	Section 8(b)(1)	Unlawful to coerce or restrain employees in the exercise of their rights
Section 8(a)(2)	Unlawful to control or dominate an entity which represents employees ("company union")	Section 8(b)(2)	Unlawful to cause employer to discriminate against an employee, except for required union dues
Section 8(a)(3)	Unlawful to discriminate against an employee to encourage or discourage union activity—except to pay union dues under the labor contract	Section 8(b)(3)	Unlawful to refuse to bargain with an employer
Section 8(a)(4)	Unlawful to retaliate against an employee who participates in NLRB proceedings	Section 8(b)(4)	Unlawful to engage in specified "secondary" activities involving a neutral party
Section 8(a)(5)	Unlawful to refuse to bargain with a certified representative	Section 8(b)(5)	Unlawful to charge excessive dues or fees
		Section 8(b)(6)	Unlawful to require employer to pay for services not performed or not to be performed
		Section 8(b)(7)	Unlawful to engage in certain types of picketing

The National Labor Relations Board has established procedures for adjudicating unfair labor practice charges. Charges may be filed against the union or the employer. The NLRB has field investigators who will take up the charge and determine whether it is supported by some evidence. If it is, then the Board will commence a proceeding before an Administrative Law Judge (ALJ). The ALJ is an independent judge who serves outside the direct control of the Board. The judge convenes a hearing, takes evidence, and applies the appropriate law. If the charged party is found to be in violation, the judge will order a remedy. Neither the Board nor the ALJ has the power to compel enforcement of an order; instead, the Board will take the case to a federal court and request enforcement. At that point, the charged party can argue the entire case again before the court and try to get the Board's decision reversed. Occasionally, the federal judge will set aside the Board's order because the Board was incorrect about the law, or the evidence clearly does not support the order.

These rules can be illustrated with a simple fact pattern that shows how the law can be strategically used to a party's (usually the employer's) advantage. Assume a union tries to organize a company's employees. During that process, described more fully below, the employer singles out the pro-union employees and fires them. The remaining employees decide they want nothing more to do with the union. The union can file charges against the employer, and the Board will investigate, conduct a hearing, and issue a decision ordering reinstatement of the employees. The employer then appeals to the full five-member NLRB in Washington, D.C. Most likely the NLRB will uphold the ALJ decision and confirm the order of reinstatement. The employer refuses to comply, and the Board files in federal court for enforcement. The judge upholds the Board's order. At this point, the employer may be liable for reinstatement and back pay to the fired employees. In the meantime, between three and four years have passed. The discharged employees probably have new jobs, so back pay is not significant. They most likely are not interested in going back to their old place of employment. Employees at the company have lost their desire to unionize. In short, the employer's unlawful act had a number of beneficial outcomes for the employer. Most labor law experts acknowledge the weaknesses of the NLRA, but it is difficult to make substantive changes in the law. The most recent attempt is discussed later.

3. Union Organizing: Election Procedures and Certification of a Representative

The second major function of the NLRB is to conduct elections to determine if a group of employees wants union representation. Sketched briefly, a union decides that a workplace is suitable for an organizing attempt. The union first recruits sympathetic employees for an in-plant committee. The employees have certain rights inside the workplace and cannot be discriminated against for their union support. These employees try to collect "authorization cards" from their fellow workers. The cards indicate that the signer wants the union to represent him or her for purposes of bargaining. Once the union has enough cards to make a "showing of interest," the union files a petition, asking the Board to hold an election. The Board decides on a time, day, and place—usually the place of employment—and the parties then begin to campaign. There are a number of rules regulating the campaign process, but the overall objective is to maintain "laboratory conditions," under which employees can vote free from coercion and undue influence. After the balloting closes, the Board counts the vote and declares a winner. If the union wins, it has the legal right to demand negotiations for a labor agreement. The union's goal is to gain a contract setting forth wages, hours, and working conditions. The contract typically has an arbitration clause to enforce the terms of the document. The union collects dues from the employees to pay the costs of representation and maintain the bargaining unit. The figure summarizes the various steps in the process.

Figure 1. Aspects of the Union Organizing Process

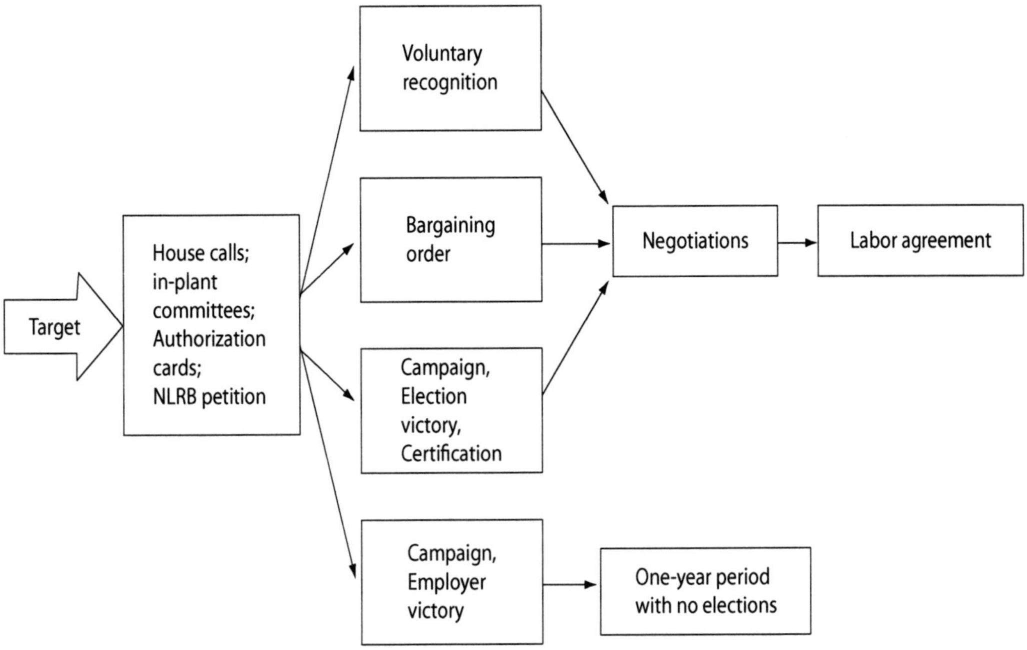

4. Unions from the Wagner Act to the Employee Free Choice Act

As Robert Wagner insisted, his bill was designed to protect workers and promote the interests of unions. Most employers in 1935 thought the law would be declared unconstitutional, and they decided not to vigorously oppose the bill in Congress. As a result, the Wagner Act passed fairly quickly and was signed into law. Unions made massive gains in organizing, despite the uncertain legal environment and employer resistance. The foundation was laid in October 1936, when John L. Lewis and several other union leaders formed the Congress of Industrial Organizations (CIO). The organization's objective was to organize the mass production workers that the American Federation of Labor tended to ignore. Lewis's first success came at General Motors, where the CIO led a sit-down strike that paralyzed the company and forced it to recognize and deal with the union. Shortly thereafter, Lewis convinced the United States Steel Corporation to sign a labor agreement. Within two years of the Wagner Act, major sectors of the economy had been organized, and collective bargaining established basic workplace standards going into the future. The Supreme Court in 1937 upheld the NLRA as a constitutional exercise of the federal power to regulate interstate commerce.

America entered World War II in 1941 when the Japanese attacked Pearl Harbor in Hawaii. President Roosevelt created the National War Labor Board to administer industrial relations during the conflict, and the NWLB helped to sustain union membership by means of "maintenance of membership" clauses, which required anyone belonging to the union at the beginning of a contract to remain a member until the contract expired. In exchange, the major national unions agreed not to strike and disrupt the production of war materials. Unions emerged from the war period in a strong position to demand improved wages and benefits; their major achievement came with the "Treaty of Detroit" in 1951, when the United Autoworkers negotiated an agreement that formed the institutional basis of American employment relations. It also, as two well-known economists explained, made up the "Golden Age" of economic development between 1947 and 1973. They said, "A central feature of that Golden Age was mass upward mobility: individuals saw sharply rising incomes through much of their career and each successive generation was living better than the last."[6] What happened next was a trajectory of stagnant real wages for most workers and an increased accretion of wealth for the top one percent of income holders. In their recent book on American politics, Jacob S. Hacker and Paul Pierson attribute much of the rise in wealth for the already rich to a decline in the institutional role played by labor unions.[7] The chart below illustrates the loss in membership density over the period. Particularly important is the deterioration of collective bargaining in the private sector, where unions played a major role in determining wage and compensation patterns.

Why did unions sharply decline from the mid-1970s forward? One explanation is that employers in the United States never accepted unions as a legitimate institution in this country. After the Supreme Court upheld the Wagner Act in 1937, employers waged intense political battles against labor on both the state and federal levels. Several states passed laws during the war that were aggressively directed to undermine unions. Colorado's Labor Peace Act of 1943 illustrated the depth and intensity of antiunion sentiment, and that law provided a model for the 1947 Taft-Hartley amendments to the Wagner Act.[8] The new modifications to the NLRA included Section 14(b), which permitted states to prohibit union security agreements that forced anyone covered by the contract to pay union dues. The legislation is known as "right to work," and such laws are now in effect in 22 states, primarily in the south and west. According to some research, the presence of right-to-work laws is the most significant factor in union decline.[9] Other labor relations experts argue that weak and ineffective labor laws are the primary culprit in falling union density. On this view, employers engage in unlawful tactics to discourage union organizing, and the law lacks effective remedies to protect workers. The result is a downward trend, in which weakened unions confront more powerful employers and employees are discouraged from collective action.

Organized labor attempted during President Carter's administration (1976–1980) to change the legal environment to its advantage. The Labor Reform Act of 1977 proposed to increase the membership of the National Labor Relations Board from five to seven members to expedite elections and decision making. It also substantially increased the monetary consequences of employer unfair acts, and it provided for a means of arbitration to resolve impasses in bargaining. The legislation passed in the House of

Representatives, and Carter indicated he would sign the bill. Opponents in the Senate mounted a filibuster. Despite numerous attempts to bring the bill for a vote, it died as a consequence of Senate rules. Labor leaders declared that they had been betrayed by business.

When Barack Obama was elected president in 2008, he had the unanimous approval of labor organizations. Obama had expressed support for new labor legislation in 2007 known as the Employee Free Choice Act (EFCA). The bill proposed unionization through "card check certification," or approval of a union based on signed cards from employees. Like the Labor Reform Act, EFCA also increased penalties for illegal activities by employers and included a means of impasse resolution through binding arbitration. EFCA never came forward in the next legislative session, because the Obama administration faced daunting economic problems along with the reform of the health care system. Ongoing criticism of EFCA indicated that there would be little chance of successful enactment, and after the 2010 midterm election cycle in which Republicans took control of the House, EFCA appeared to have no chance of passage in the foreseeable future.

Most likely, organized labor will continue to lose power and influence in the American economy. That outcome may be disadvantageous for many Americans. Unions were the main source of bargaining strength for workers generally, and to the extent they stabilized or increased wages and fringe benefits for their members, they helped to sustain the institutional basis of American employment relations. With little effective resistance to corporate power, workers have scant means of maintaining incomes and other forms of economic security. The environment is not likely to change for years into the future.

5. Public Sector Unionism

Section 2(2) of the Wagner Act excludes governments from the definition of an "employer" covered by the law. This section provides that the term employer "shall not include the United States or any wholly owned Government corporation, or any Federal Reserve Bank, or any State or political subdivision thereof, or any person subject to the Railway Labor Act. ..." The reasons for not giving public employees the same rights as private sector employees are both practical and constitutional. In practical terms, public employees worked for a sovereign authority and were paid by the citizens of the governmental unit; consequently, they were historically regarded as a special type of employee. At the constitutional level, Wagner believed that the federal government could not dictate to state and local governments how they should organize their employment relations. As a result, government workers were not and still are not subject to federal collective bargaining laws. Those employees may have rights under federal, state, and local laws, and many of them are covered by union contracts. In fact, union density in the public sector is now substantially higher than in the private sector. The figure below shows total, private, and public union density levels from 1950 to 2010.[10]

Figure 2. Trends in Union Membership

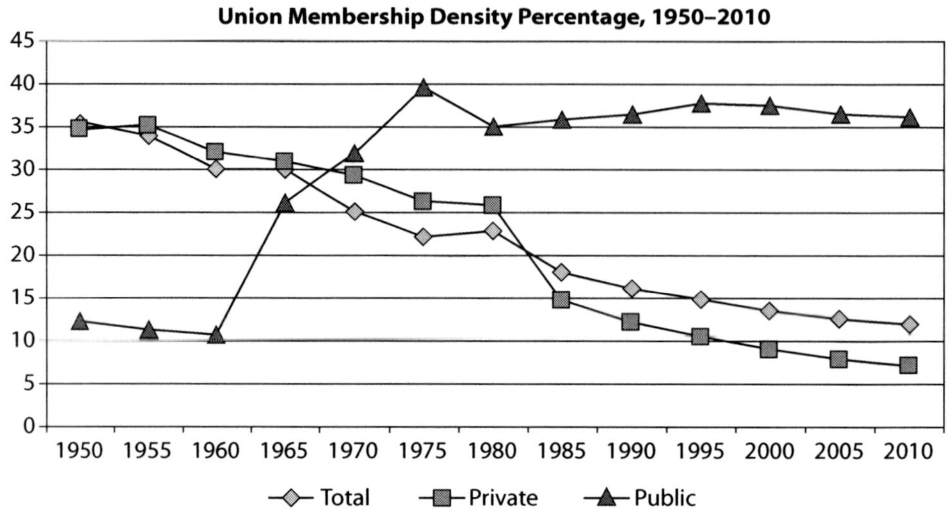

Federal employees bargain under the Civil Service Reform Act (CSRA), which was enacted in 1978 during the Carter Administration. It protects rights to organize, to bargain over a limited scope of subjects, and to enter into contracts. The Federal Labor Relations Authority (FLRA) enforces the provisions of the CSRA, and functions similarly to the National Labor Relations Board. It has authority to adjudicate unfair labor practices, to certify bargaining units, and to resolve disputes in negotiations between the parties. Federal employees generally have no right to bargain over wages and compensation, and they cannot legally strike. When members of the Professional Air Traffic Controllers Organization (PATCO) attempted a work stoppage in 1981, President Ronald Reagan fired them and kept air traffic in operation using supervisors, military personnel, and nonstrikers. Members of the American Postal Workers Union bargain under the National Labor Relations Act, except they are forbidden to strike and can use interest arbitration to resolve bargaining impasses.[11]

State and local governments can enact their own laws dealing with union organization, and a majority of states have done so. A number of states permit strikes by nonessential workers, usually those not involved in public safety. Where strikes are banned, binding interest arbitration or some nonbinding alternative, such as mediation, may be used to settle bargaining disputes. Each option has weaknesses, and there is no consensus among lawmakers about the best method for allowing employees to unionize while protecting the public interest in levels of service and taxation. The legal environment for public unions became increasingly favorable during the 1960s, when union membership surged dramatically. Following the inflationary spike in the late 1970s and President Reagan's confrontation with PATCO, public sector unionism stabilized at levels significantly above private sector density.

The economic concerns that dominated the 2010 Congressional elections provoked sharp attacks on the "excessive" wages and benefits conferred on public workers. This line of argument focused on the budget problems confronting state and local governments and proposed that employee compensation, particularly for unionized workers, was a major factor in the fiscal shortfalls. To address the issue, legislatures debated ways to restrict the power of unions. According to an article in the *New York Times* in January 2011, "Faced with growing budget deficits and restive taxpayers, elected officials from Maine to Alabama, Ohio to Arizona, are pushing new legislation to limit the power of labor unions, particularly those representing government workers, in collective bargaining and politics."[12] *The Economist* magazine featured a cover story on public sector unions, and documented the fact that public workers' compensation gains exceeded those of private sector workers over the past three decades.[13] Much of the increase in labor costs is associated with defined benefit pension plans, which public employers continue to provide even though most private employers offer only defined contribution retirement plans. Most importantly, the article points out, public workers exercise substantial political power over the officials who oversee their work. The impending confrontation between unions and political forces will undoubtedly affect the labor relations climate for years to come.

Questions About the NLRA

1. What policies are explicitly set forth in the text of the National Labor Relations Act? What is the relationship between those policy objectives and the legal rules adopted in the Act?
2. What are the legal rules governing employer conduct when a union tries to organize the employer's workplace?
3. What is the process by which a union gains recognition? Do unions need stronger protections, or should they be less protected?
4. Why do some states have laws protecting public sector workers and others do not? In 2011 the state of Ohio repealed a law in effect for three decades that allowed government workers to bargain collectively and to strike. Why would voters support such a law?

IV. Wage and Hour Laws

The Fair Labor Standards Act of 1938 placed a floor under wages and a ceiling on hours of work. Current law establishes a minimum wage for covered employment and requires the payment of a wage premium for hours of work over forty in a work week. There are a number of issues associated with the FLSA, including the proper level of minimum wage, the definition of exempt and nonexempt employees, and categories of employees excluded from coverage. The FLSA was amended in 1963 to include the Equal Pay Act

(EPA). This law requires that women receive equal pay for performing work equal to that of men. Congress recently overturned a Supreme Court decision interpreting the EPA, and pending legislation proposes to broaden the protections under the EPA. This section deals first with minimum wage and overtime issues and then turns to the matter of compensation discrimination.

An important policy dimension of the FLSA involves the question of whether a minimum wage will result in less overall employment. The economic argument turns on the neoclassical assumption that markets will use less labor if the cost of labor increases. This basic principle leads some theorists to assert that the proper level of a minimum wage is zero. Researchers have devoted considerable effort to this problem, and the evidence is mixed. In one famous study by economists David Card and Alan Krueger, the authors found that an increase in the minimum wage in New Jersey did not result in higher unemployment compared to Pennsylvania, which maintained its minimum wage at the same level.[14] Economists continue to debate the Card-Krueger study, but one fairly clear conclusion is that no definitive evidence shows that raising minimum wages reduces employment. As Card and Krueger summarized in a response to critiques of their work, "The increase in New Jersey's minimum wage probably had no effect on total employment in New Jersey's fast-food industry, and possibly had a small positive effect."[15]

A. Scope, Application, and Exemptions from Wage and Overtime Requirements

The FLSA had the same purpose as other New Deal economic legislation, which was to stabilize employment and provide the means for consumers to actively participate in commercial activity. By ensuring some level of income for work, it put a floor under labor markets. By discouraging long hours of work, it motivated employers to efficiently manage their workforce and maintain adequate levels of employment. Over the years, the minimum wage has fluctuated in terms of purchasing power because Congress must take action to raise the wage. If political forces are mobilized in favor of an increase, as during President Clinton's second term, the wage rises by whatever amount is specified. In 2011, the minimum wage is $7.25 per hour for covered workers. No further increases are scheduled.

The standard for coverage of the FLSA is a connection with interstate commerce. Congress intended by the law to regulate economic dealings across state lines and to prevent unfair competition through low wages. The U.S. Supreme Court upheld the law in the case of *United States v. Darby Lumber Co.* (1941). In this opinion, the Court discussed the Tenth Amendment, and explained that the federal government can regulate any activity that is encompassed in Article I of the Constitution; all the Tenth Amendment did was to express the truism that power not granted to the federal government is reserved to the states or the people. Because interstate commerce was ruled in *Gibbons v. Ogden* (1824) to be "plenary" and all-inclusive of economic activities, there was no limitation on that power under the FLSA. As Chief Justice John Marshall wrote in the 1824 case, "The wisdom and the discretion of Congress, their identity with the people, and the influence which their constituents possess at elections are, in this, as in many other instances, as that, for example, of declaring war, the sole restraints on which they have relied, to secure them from its abuse. They are the restraints on which the people must often rely solely, in all representative governments." In short, if Congress has extended its power too far under the commerce clause, the remedy is for citizens to change Congress, not for the Supreme Court to change the law.

According to the Wage and Hour Division of the Department of Labor, here are the major criteria to determine coverage of the law:

All employees of certain enterprises having workers engaged in interstate commerce, producing goods for interstate commerce, or handling, selling, or otherwise working on goods or materials that have been moved in or produced for such commerce by any person, are covered by FLSA.

A covered enterprise is the related activities performed through unified operation or common control by any person or persons for a common business purpose and:

1. whose annual gross volume of sales made or business done is not less than $500,000 (exclusive of excise taxes at the retail level that are separately stated); or
2. is engaged in the operation of a hospital, an institution primarily engaged in the care of the sick, the aged, or the mentally ill who reside on the premises; a school for mentally or physically disabled or gifted children; a preschool, an elementary or secondary school, or an institution of higher education (whether operated for profit or not for profit); or
3. is an activity of a public agency.

Domestic service workers such as day workers, housekeepers, chauffeurs, cooks, or full-time babysitters are covered if:

1. their cash wages from one employer in calendar year 2010 are at least $1,700 (this calendar year threshold is adjusted by the Social Security Administration each year); or
2. they work a total of more than 8 hours a week for one or more employers.

Although the law is broad in coverage, there are a number of exceptions regarding workers who may not fall under the minimum wage and overtime requirements. For employers, it is important to classify correctly those persons who can work overtime without extra compensation and are not subject to minimum wage laws. They are known as *exempt* employees, and they make up a category of workers who are typically regarded as "white collar," as opposed to "blue" or "pink" collar workers. The FLSA defines the exemption in the categories of executive, administrative, professional, computer expert, and outside sales employees as follows:

To qualify for the executive employee exemption, all of the following tests must be met:

- The employee must be compensated on a salary basis (as defined in the regulations) at a rate not less than $455 per week;
- The employee's primary duty must be managing the enterprise, or managing a customarily recognized department or subdivision of the enterprise;
- The employee must customarily and regularly direct the work of at least two or more other full-time employees or their equivalent; and
- The employee must have the authority to hire or fire other employees, or the employee's suggestions and recommendations as to the hiring, firing, advancement, promotion or any other change of status of other employees must be given particular weight.

To qualify for the administrative employee exemption, all of the following tests must be met:

- The employee must be compensated on a salary or fee basis (as defined in the regulations) at a rate not less than $455 per week;
- The employee's primary duty must be the performance of office or non-manual work directly related to the management or general business operations of the employer or the employer's customers; and
- The employee's primary duty includes the exercise of discretion and independent judgment with respect to matters of significance.

To qualify for the learned professional employee exemption, all of the following tests must be met:

- The employee must be compensated on a salary or fee basis (as defined in the regulations) at a rate not less than $455 per week;
- The employee's primary duty must be the performance of work requiring advanced knowledge, defined as work which is predominantly intellectual in character and which includes work requiring the consistent exercise of discretion and judgment;
- The advanced knowledge must be in a field of science or learning; and
- The advanced knowledge must be customarily acquired by a prolonged course of specialized intellectual instruction.

To qualify for the creative professional employee exemption, all of the following tests must be met:

- The employee must be compensated on a salary or fee basis (as defined in the regulations) at a rate not less than $455 per week;

- The employee's primary duty must be the performance of work requiring invention, imagination, originality, or talent in a recognized field of artistic or creative endeavor.

To qualify for the computer employee exemption, the following tests must be met:

- The employee must be compensated either on a salary or fee basis (as defined in the regulations) at a rate not less than $455 per week or, if compensated on an hourly basis, at a rate not less than $27.63 an hour;
- The employee must be employed as a computer systems analyst, computer programmer, software engineer or other similarly skilled worker in the computer field performing the duties described below;
- The employee's primary duty must consist of:

    1. The application of systems analysis techniques and procedures, including consulting with users, to determine hardware, software or system functional specifications;
    2. The design, development, documentation, analysis, creation, testing or modification of computer systems or programs, including prototypes, based on and related to user or system design specifications;
    3. The design, documentation, testing, creation or modification of computer programs related to machine operating systems; or
    4. A combination of the aforementioned duties, the performance of which requires the same level of skills.

To qualify for the outside sales employee exemption, all of the following tests must be met:

- The employee's primary duty must be making sales (as defined in the FLSA), or obtaining orders or contracts for services or for the use of facilities for which a consideration will be paid by the client or customer; and
- The employee must be customarily and regularly engaged away from the employer's place or places of business.

There are special provisions for police and fire personnel. The "work period" for overtime may be extended for up to 28 days, and the measuring period in hours depends on whether the employee works as a police or fire officer. The FSLA also contains a special provision for compensatory time off for specified public employees. According to the interpretation, "Under certain prescribed conditions, a State or local government agency may give compensatory time at a rate of not less than one and one-half hours for each overtime hour worked, in lieu of cash overtime compensation. Employees engaged in police and fire protection work may accrue up to 480 hours of compensatory time."

Other special cases under the FLSA include tipped employees and interns. Tipped employees may have their minimum wage offset by an amount that reflects earnings from tips. According to the Wage and Hour Division, "Tipped employees are those who customarily and regularly receive more than $30 a month in tips. Tips actually received by tipped employees may be counted as wages for purposes of the FLSA, but the employer must pay not less than $2.13 an hour in direct wages." The employee's total pay from tips and wages must be at least as much as the minimum wage, and the employer may be required to provide records of tips. In some cases, the tipped employee may enter into a tip pooling arrangement with other employees. The law specifically limits the persons who may participate in those agreements. The Wage and Hour fact sheet states, "Tipped employees may not be required to share their tips with employees who have not customarily and regularly participated in tip pooling arrangements, such as dishwashers, cooks, chefs, and janitors. Only those tips that are in excess of tips used for the tip credit may be taken for a pool." State laws may also regulate tip pooling. A group of baristas employed by Starbucks in California brought a class action claiming they were required to share tips with supervisors; the plaintiffs lost in the appeals court because the California law applied to tips given to individual employees rather than a "team" as a whole.[16]

With regard to interns, the Wage and Hour Division recognizes that some individuals may perform services in an organization, but do not fall under the minimum wage standards. The reason for this classification has to do with the difference between an employment relationship and a process of allowing individuals to learn about a business or occupation. The Department of Labor uses a series of factors to determine whether a person is, or is not, an employee subject to the FLSA. The primary criteria for creating an internship rather than employment are listed below:

- the training is similar to vocational school or higher education
- training benefits the trainee
- no regular employee is displaced and trainee works under close supervision
- there is no advantage to employer
- no expectation of job at end
- there is an understanding wages will not be paid

If these factors are satisfied, the intern can engage in any activities related to the assignment without falling under the minimum wage and overtime provisions.

The FLSA also regulates the employment of children under a certain age in certain occupations regarded as hazardous. The Wage Hour Division undertook a revision of child labor rules and published a final rule that became effective July 19, 2010. The Division explained that this is the first major attempt to modernize its child labor regulations in three decades, and it takes into account changes in work environments that ensure a worker's safety and confirms that some occupations are not safe for children. For example, the new rule permits persons under 16 years of age to work as lifeguards at a swimming facility, but "prohibits anyone under 16 from working as a dispatcher on elevated water slides or as a lifeguard at natural environment swimming facilities (lakes, rivers, ocean beaches, quarries, piers)." A comparison of the old and new rules is available at http://www.dol.gov/whd/cl/SidebySideReg3FinalRule.htm.

B. Integrating State and Federal Laws

States have legal authority to enact laws that go beyond the basic FLSA requirements, and many states have done so. The map below shows which states exceed the federal standards. In any case, the federal law applies to workers falling within its coverage, and employers in states with no minimum wage laws must comply with the national requirements. Many states have wage and hour laws that are specific to those states. Employers consequently must stay informed about both federal and state laws. To illustrate, Wal-Mart has paid out substantial damages in cases brought under state law. A class action in Minnesota cost the company "$54.25 million to settle a class-action lawsuit that alleged the discount giant cut workers' break time and didn't prevent employees from working off the clock in Minnesota." Other class-action suits likewise resulted in verdicts against the company for millions of dollars. "In Pennsylvania, workers won a $78.5 million judgment in 2006 for working off the clock and through rest breaks, and the company was hit with a $172 million verdict in California in 2005 for illegally denying lunch breaks." Another settlement in Colorado amounted to $50 million for alleged violations of state law.[17] Consequently, it is important to have knowledge of and comply with all applicable laws, whether state or federal. For a convenient summary of laws, the following Web site contains links to relevant legislation: http://www.eliinc.com/programs-solutions/wage-and-hour-FLSA-50statecomparison.cfm.

C. The Equal Pay Act

In 1963 Congress decided that employers should be prohibited from paying women workers less than men who were doing identical work. Toward that objective, Congress enacted section 6(d) as an amendment to the FLSA. This law is narrow in application, and requires the woman to prove that the work is the same as that done by a man—and not merely similar in nature. There are also four statutory defenses to an equal pay claim. Below is the text of the statute:

> No employer having employees subject to any provisions of this section shall discriminate, within any establishment in which such employees are employed, between employees on the basis of sex by paying wages to employees in such establishment at a rate less than the rate at which he pays wages to employees of the opposite sex in such establishment for equal work on jobs the performance of which requires equal skill, effort, and responsibility, and which are performed under similar working conditions, except where such

payment is made pursuant to (i) a seniority system; (ii) a merit system; (iii) a system which measures earnings by quantity or quality of production; or (iv) a differential based on any other factor other than sex: *Provided*, That an employer who is paying a wage rate differential in violation of this subsection shall not, in order to comply with the provisions of this subsection, reduce the wage rate of any employee.

The defenses are based on seniority, merit, quality or quantity of production, and a general provision allowing for differences based on any other factor, except sex. Employers can maintain a compensation system that incorporates common methods

Figure 3. Map of State Laws (Department of Labor)

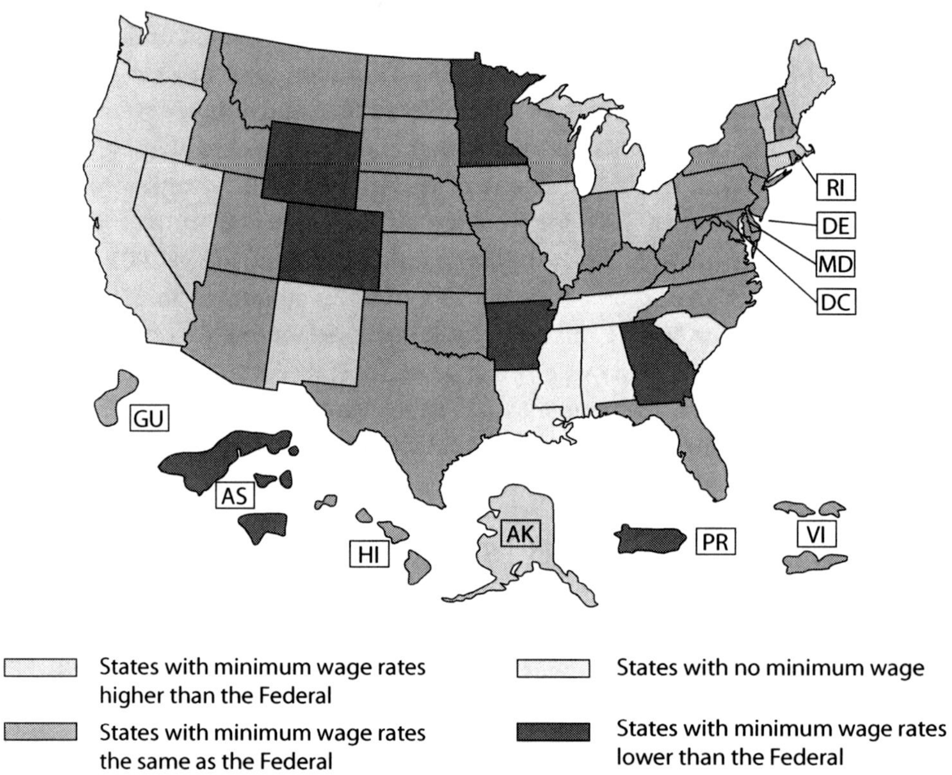

of evaluation, such as time on the job, performance, a bonus system, or some other measure. In addition, compensation that adjusts for labor market conditions satisfies the criterion as a factor "other than sex."

Consider a common example. In a university setting, more women tend to be employed as faculty in liberal arts colleges. More men tend to teach in schools of engineering. All faculty do essentially the same job of instructing college students, and the women professors may, in fact, spend more time doing research, interacting with students, and grading student work. The engineers tend to have significantly higher salaries than the liberal arts teachers. Is this a violation of the equal pay act? Or would it be a violation of the Civil Rights Act, which prohibits discrimination based on gender? The answer is that it violates neither.

When a similar case arose in 1985, the Ninth Circuit Court of Appeals rejected the argument that the state of Washington unlawfully paid women less than it paid men, even though the jobs were "comparable."[18] A consultant evaluated civil service pay scales and found that jobs done mostly by women were paid at about 20 percent less than jobs done mostly by men, when those jobs were rated as having equivalent worth to the employer. The plaintiffs relied on the theory that even if the jobs were not "equal" in terms of the EPA, the differentials made out a case of sex discrimination under the Civil Rights Act. In a decision by Judge Anthony Kennedy, now a member of the U.S. Supreme Court, the circuit court rejected the theory. Kennedy wrote:

> That concept [of equal pay] would be undermined if we were to hold that payment of wages according to prevailing rates in the public and private sectors is an act that, in itself, supports the inference of a purpose to discriminate. Neither law nor logic deems the free market system a suspect enterprise. Economic reality is that the value of a particular job to an employer is but one factor influencing the rate of compensation for that job. Other considerations may include the availability of workers willing to do the job and the effectiveness of collective bargaining in a particular industry. We recognized in [an earlier case] that employers may be constrained by market forces to set salaries under prevailing wage rates for different job classifications. We find nothing in the language of Title VII or its legislative history to indicate Congress intended to abrogate fundamental economic principles such as the laws of supply and demand or to prevent employers from competing in the labor market.

Accordingly, proof of a gender-based pay differential is not sufficient to maintain a discrimination claim. The Supreme Court ruled that a compensation claim may be brought under Title VII, but it explained that the defenses available under the EPA were also applicable to civil rights suits.[19] The result of the judicial interpretation of the two statutes has been generally to confine pay claims to the EPA standards.

In 2009 Representative Rosa DeLauro and Senator Hillary Rodham Clinton introduced the Paycheck Fairness Act (PFA) into Congress as a legislative means of strengthening remedies for pay discrimination. This bill was still pending during the 2010 midyear elections, but the Republican victory in the House of Representatives suggests that expansive workplace legislation is unlikely to be adopted in the near future. Regardless of the political climate, the proposed bill illustrates some of the problems women face in labor markets. According to the findings set forth in the bill's preamble, women now make up an important segment of the workforce, but inequities persist. The bill states: "Despite the enactment of the Equal Pay Act of 1963, many women continue to earn significantly lower pay than men for equal work. These pay disparities exist in both the private and governmental sectors. In many instances, the pay disparities can only be due to continued intentional discrimination or the lingering effects of past discrimination."

The proposed act specifies a number of steps to reduce pay disparities. The most important change in the law would modify the final defense in the EPA, which allows the employer to show compensation is based on any other factor other than sex. The PFA eliminates that language and substitutes the following: "The bona fide factor defense described in subparagraph (A)(iv) shall apply only if the employer demonstrates that such factor (i) is not based upon or derived from a sex-based differential in compensation; (ii) is job-related with respect to the position in question; and (iii) is consistent with business necessity." What the modification does is to shift the burden of proof to the employer to justify a compensation plan if the claimant shows it has a disparate impact on women. Returning to the case of the professors, if the women faculty in liberal arts showed they earned significantly less than engineering professors, the university would have to prove the compensation plan was "job related" and a matter of "business necessity." Such a showing would go beyond merely claiming that the market dictated the pay gap. Whether the PFA moves forward or not, the matter of gender equity remains an issue having serious implications.

D. The Davis-Bacon Act

The Davis-Bacon Act is similar in purpose to the minimum wage and other laws seeking to ensure that earnings are maintained at levels which provide adequate security for workers. It is confined to specific circumstances that involve federal contracting. As explained by the Wage and Hour Division:

> The Davis-Bacon and Related Acts, apply to contractors and subcontractors performing on federally funded or assisted contracts in excess of $2,000 for the construction, alteration, or repair (including painting and decorating) of public buildings or public works. Davis-Bacon Act and Related Act contractors and subcontractors must pay their laborers and mechanics employed under the contract no less than the locally prevailing wages and fringe benefits for corresponding work on similar projects in the area. The Davis-Bacon Act directs the Department of Labor to determine such locally prevailing wage rates. The Davis-Bacon Act applies to contractors and subcontractors performing work on federal or District of Columbia contracts. The Davis-Bacon Act prevailing wage provisions apply to the "Related Acts," under which federal agencies assist construction projects through grants, loans, loan guarantees, and insurance.

> There is no general requirement that workers be paid a set "market" rate for their labor. The statute applies only when the federal government engages in construction activities on public buildings or works.

The Act is sometimes criticized on the ground that it raises the cost of public construction activities and interferes with the normal function of labor markets. Following the damage to New Orleans in Hurricane Katrina, President George W. Bush issued a proclamation in September 2005 repealing the law for the rebuilding effort. Political opposition from Democrats led to Bush's reversal of the order only a month later, and the law has remained in full force since that time.

Questions

1. How should Congress determine the appropriate level of the minimum wage? If you were a member of Congress, would you vote to repeal the Fair Labor Standards Act? What reasoning supports your decision?
2. What is the purpose of the overtime law? Should it be based on earnings alone, so that a worker with a high hourly wage would not get overtime if a manager did not also?
3. Women now make up a majority of college students. Do they still need laws to protect their earnings?
4. Given the large deficits in the federal budget, would it be good policy to repeal the Davis-Bacon Act?

V. Social Security and Unemployment

A. Overview

Social Security (SS) came into existence in 1935. It aimed to protect a particularly vulnerable class of citizens—the elderly—from economic suffering. Over the next 70 years, the act was expanded to provide higher, and more extensive, levels of benefits. The evolution of SS gradually encompassed more participants, and expanded to include protections for survivors, the disabled, and former spouses. Under President Johnson, recipients of SS benefits also qualified for a health care program now known as Medicare. Each new element of SS added costs to the overall program, and Presidents Jimmy Carter and Ronald Reagan undertook measures to reform SS financing. When Reagan implemented changes in 1983, he predicted the SS program would remain stable for the next 50 years. Reagan was correct in his estimate. By 2013, SS revenues are projected to be less than its expenditures. Presently, demographics and economic conditions threaten the long-term stability of the system. A number of changes are under consideration at the national level, and some modifications will most likely take place to stabilize the program.

The Social Security Act of 1935 included a title dealing with unemployment insurance. This program was conceived as a joint state-federal undertaking and continues as such today. The unemployment rate in 2009 reached 10.2 percent and remained above 9 percent into the following year. The depletion of state funds and the problem of long-term unemployment led to several extensions of benefits, placing further pressures on the federal deficit. During the lame duck session of Congress in December 2010, benefits for about 2 million workers expired. The politics of the unemployment problem became a national issue, as discussed in the next section.

The table below describes the major phases of Social Security's evolution. According to most scholars, the addition of a survivor's benefit in 1939 marked the turning point that moved the program from a simple insurance concept to one of social welfare. By allowing a surviving spouse to collect benefits accrued by a wage earner, Social Security paid out money to individuals who needed it, rather than to individuals who had earned it. Stated another way, two workers who had identical earnings for an identical number of years should get identical SS benefits. But if one worker was married, he and his spouse would receive a higher benefit than his unmarried colleague. The result is not equitable to the individuals, but it is appropriate for providing resources to a family unit.

Table 2. Major Social Security Legislation

Law	Date Enacted	Major Features
The Social Security Act	August 14, 1935	Established individual retirement benefits.
The 1939 amendments	August 10, 1939	Added dependents and survivors' benefits, and made benefits more generous for early participants. Financing at issue.
The 1950 amendments	August 28, 1950	Adjusted, on a major scale, coverage and financing. Increased benefits for the first time. Provided for gratuitous wage credits for military service.
The 1960 amendments	September 13, 1960	Disability benefits at any age.
The 1972 Debt-Ceiling Bill	July 1, 1972	Added automatic annual cost-of-living adjustments.
The 1977 amendments	December 20, 1977	Raised taxes and scaled back benefits. Long-range solvency at issue.

Table 2. Major Social Security Legislation		
Law	**Date Enacted**	**Major Features**
The 1983 amendments	April 20, 1983	Raised taxes and scaled back benefits. Long-range and short-range solvency at issue.
Senior Citizens Freedom to Work Act of 2000	April 7, 2000	Eliminated the retirement earnings test for those at the full retirement age.
SOURCE: Congressional Research Service (CRS) Report RL30920, Major Decisions in the House and Senate on Social Security, 1935–2009.		

B. Social Security Benefits

The Social Security system relies on a payroll tax on employers and employees to provide benefits for individual recipients in the program. This method of funding is known as "pay-go," because it uses incoming revenues to pay current liabilities. As SS evolved, payroll taxes increased to pay for increased benefits. The rates were at a relatively low combined amount of 9.3% in 1981. After the reforms of the Reagan administration, the rates jumped to 14% in 1984, and then to the current level of 15.3% effective in 1990. Congress has declined to enact further tax increases, but it may be forced to do so in the near future to maintain adequate SS funding. The 2010 Trustees Report explained the financing mechanism with the following question and answer:

> **How Are Social Security and Medicare Financed?** For Old Age, Survivors, and Disability Insurance and Hospital Insurance, the major source of financing is payroll taxes on earnings that are paid by employees and their employers. The self-employed are charged the equivalent of the combined employer and employee tax rates. During 2009, an estimated 156 million people had earnings covered by Social Security and paid payroll taxes; for Medicare the corresponding figure was 160 million. The payroll tax rates are set by law and for OASDI apply to earnings up to an annual maximum ($106,800 in 2010) that ordinarily increases with the growth in the nationwide average wage. When the cost-of-living adjustment (COLA) for December of any year is zero, which occurred in December 2009 and is projected for December 2010, the maximum taxable amount of earnings is not increased for the following year. This constraint will lower OASDI tax income in 2010 and 2011. In contrast, HI taxes are paid on total earnings. The payroll tax rates (in percent) for 2010 are:

	OASI	DI	OASDI	HI	Total
Employees	5.30	0.90	6.20	1.45	7.65
Employers	5.30	0.90	6.20	1.45	7.65
Combined total	10.60	1.80	12.40	2.90	15.30

Starting in 2013, the Affordable Care Act imposes an additional HI tax equal to 0.9 percent of earnings over $200,000 for individual tax return filers and on earnings over $250,000 for joint return filers.

According to the report, the 2010 health care legislation will stabilize expenditures under the hospital insurance component of SS for a decade more than previously predicted. The projected savings are associated with cost controls enacted by the new laws. Despite that, other elements of SS face shortfalls in the near term, and require congressional action in the near future. That issue is discussed more fully after a brief explanation of how SS calculates benefits.

The simplest concept behind SS is that an individual makes required contributions to the program and receives a payment based on the contribution. That concept, however, includes a number of refinements aimed at wealth redistribution, from high earners to low earners. The process by which redistribution is accomplished is an objective one, meaning that the formula applies to all recipients, but the formula itself is complicated and subject to manipulation. It starts with a beneficiary's "primary insurance amount." This figure is derived from earnings in the "base years" adjusted for inflation, and then inserted in a mathematical formula which produces a dollar amount. The SSA gives detailed guidance for estimating a retirement benefit at its Web site, http://www.ssa.gov/policy/docs/statcomps/supplement/2009/apnd.html. The material below is taken from this page.

Step 1—Determining the Number of Computation Years

For workers born from 1934 through 1947, the number of computation years is 35.

Step 2—Wage Indexing of Earnings

The following description and examples are provided for persons who wish to compute the index factors and indexed earnings. The indexing year is the year a person attains age 60. Beneficiaries born on January 1 are deemed to have attained age 60 on December 31 of the prior year.

The average wage for the indexing year is divided by the average wage in each prior year to obtain the factor for each prior year. For example, for a person attaining age 62 in 2009, the indexing year is 2007. The average annual wage for 2007 was $40,405.48. The average annual wage for 1990 was $21,027.98. The amount $40,405.48 divided by $21,027.98 yields a factor of 1.9215103.

The worker's actual earnings covered under Social Security in that year, up to the maximum earnings creditable, are multiplied by the indexing factor to obtain the indexed earnings (see Worksheet 1). For example, actual covered earnings of $10,000 in

1990, multiplied by 1.9215103, result in indexed earnings of $19,215.10; actual earnings of $51,300 (the maximum creditable) result in indexed earnings of $98,573.47.

Step 3—Computing the Average Indexed Monthly Earnings (AIME)

After the earnings in each year have been indexed, they are used in computing average indexed monthly earnings. The years of highest indexed earnings corresponding to the number of computation years are selected and totaled. This total is then divided by the number of months in the computation years. The result, rounded to the nearest lower dollar, is the average indexed monthly earnings.

For example, for a person attaining age 62 in 2009, the highest 35 years of indexed earnings are used. If the sum of these earnings equals $400,000, the AIME is $952 ($400,000 divided by 420 = $952.38, rounded to $952).

Step 4—Computing the Primary Insurance Amount (PIA)

The PIA, the amount from which all Social Security benefits payable on a worker's earnings record are based, is computed by applying a formula to the AIME. The formula consists of brackets in which three percentages are applied to amounts of AIME. The dollar amounts defining the brackets are called *bend points*, and the bend points are different for each calendar year of attainment of age 62. The PIA is rounded to the nearest lower 10 cents.

For retired workers who attained age 62 in 2009, the bend points are $744 and $4,483. Thus the formula is 90 percent of the first $744 of AIME; plus 32 percent of the next $3,739 of AIME; plus 15 percent of AIME above $4,483. The following are examples of PIA computations for such workers with different AIME amounts.

Example 1—**AIME of $300**
PIA is $270
Based on: 90 percent of $300

Example 2—**AIME of $952**
PIA is $736.16 rounded to $736.00
Based on: 90 percent of $744 ($669.60); plus
32 percent of $208 ($66.56)

Example 3—**AIME of $5,000**
PIA is $1,943.63 rounded to $1,943.60
Based on: 90 percent of $744 ($669.60); plus
32 percent of $3,739 ($1,196.48); plus
15 percent of $517 ($77.55)

The above calculations are applicable to workers who attain age 62 in 2009. For workers who attained age 62 in prior years, the bend points will be different, and the

PIA must be increased to reflect cost-of-living adjustments between the year of attainment of age 62 and 2009. After the PIA is calculated for the year of attainment of age 62, cost-of-living increases are applied for each year through 2008. The result is the current 2009 PIA.

For example, a worker who attained age 62 in 2006 would receive cost-of-living adjustments for the years 2006–2008. The adjustments are cumulative, with each step rounded to the next lower dime. If the PIA at age 62 was $700, the cost-of-living adjustments would be

2006: $700 multiplied by 1.033 = $723.10
2007: $723.10 multiplied by 1.023 = $739.70
2008: $739.70 multiplied by 1.058 = $782.60
$782.60 would be the PIA effective December 2008.

Step 5—Computation of the Monthly Benefit

The full PIA is payable to a worker who retires at the full retirement age (FRA). In 2000, the FRA, scheduled to be gradually raised to age 67 for workers attaining age 62 in 2022, began to be phased in.

To compare SS with an insurance concept, consider the SS formula in relation to an annuity. In the latter case, an individual may agree to purchase an annuity from a private investment company. She gives the company a certain amount of money, which the company invests. The company uses actuarial tables to predict how long the worker will live, and then calculates how much it will pay from the date of retirement until death. For example, if she stops work at age 67, the insurer may guarantee a yearly income of some designated amount for the remainder of life. If the worker wants to protect her surviving spouse, the insurer will adjust the annuity downward to reflect an additional risk. If the recipient lives longer than the insurer planned, the insurer takes a loss on the policy. Over time, though, the actuarial calculations will favor the insurer, just as the gambling odds favor a casino.

Now look at the way SS determines an award. It uses contributions to the system as one factor, but it adjusts those contributions by "indexing" them for inflation. It may also drop some years of lower earnings from the calculation to arrive at an "average indexed monthly earning," or AIME. Next, the AIME is used to figure the "primary insurance amount," or PIA, which is then processed through a series of "bend points" to reach a dollar figure for the monthly payment. The examples given above illustrate three different earnings records, and show that lower earners have proportionately greater replacement rates for their earnings history. In addition, awards are adjusted upward for a cost-of-living factor.

Further, the SS program provides benefits to recipients other than the retired worker. As noted, if the worker has a family, she may be entitled to a benefit based on the number of dependents and limited by a maximum family benefit determined by a PIA formula, but not to exceed 150% of the worker's PIA. A former spouse of an insured worker may claim on the worker's record if the marriage lasted more than ten years and the spouse has reached the age of 62. Other cases include dependent children or grandchildren under 18 or 19 if attending secondary school. The disability component of SS provides benefits for persons who are unable to engage in substantial gainful work in the national economy and for their dependents. Again, there is a maximum amount available, which is less than the family maximum for old age and survivors. The amount of earnings credit needed to qualify for disability varies according to the beneficiary's age at the time of disability.

C. SS Financing and the Future of the Program

The "baby boom" generation beginning in 1946 and whose members are reaching retirement in 2010 is numerically larger than preceding or following generations. As a result, the baby boomers created a large surplus in the SS trust funds. The funds will be paid down as the generation retires, and the smaller number of current workers will be supporting a larger number of retirees. The resulting demographic conditions will lead to shortfalls in SS financing. The 2010 Report of the SSA Trustees provides a chart illustrating the trends in SS financing. It shows that the old age and survivors' component will begin paying out more than it takes in beginning around 2040. The HI fund will be exhausted in 2030, a decade later than predicted in the 2009 report, and which is explained by the federal health care legislation enacted in 2010. The most serious financing shortfall occurs in the DI fund, which will reach exhaustion in 2017.

According to the August 2010 report of the Social Security Board of Trustees, the fiscal prospects for Medicare have "improved substantially" as a result of the recent health care reforms. Consequently, the Hospital Insurance Trust Fund, for example, will remain solvent for 12 years longer than projected in 2009. Conversely, the recession had a negative impact on SS revenues, which affected other areas of the program. Supplemental medical insurance, enacted during George W. Bush's second term, is particularly vulnerable. The trustees said that "the aging population will result in SMI costs growing rapidly from 1.9 percent of GDP in 2009 to 3.5 percent of GDP in 2040; about three-quarters of these costs will be financed from general revenues and about one-quarter from premiums paid by beneficiaries." Overall, the report warns, "The long-run financial challenges facing Social Security and those that remain for Medicare should be addressed soon."

The urgency of the SS system funding was reflected in a recent interview by the well-known economist Laurence Kotlikoff. He asserted, "The U.S. is bankrupt. Neither spending more nor taxing less will help the country pay its bills. What it can and must do is radically simplify its tax, health-care, retirement and financial systems, each of which is a complete mess."[20] President Barack Obama's bipartisan commission on fiscal strategy issued a report in December 2010, which recommended a number of changes in SS, including raising the retirement age and the taxable wage base. The report generated massive media coverage and political controversy. In order to place

Figure 4. Trends in Funding

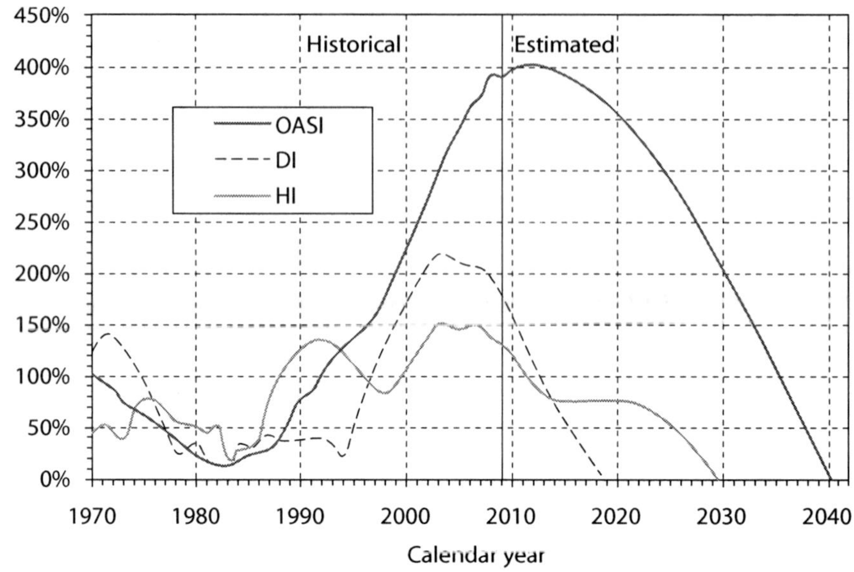

the recommendations before Congress, a supermajority of committee members had to vote to approve the plan. It failed to gain enough support to form a basis for legislation, but it did bring issues such as retirement and the deficit to the forefront of national debate.[21] At the same time, other types of retirement plans suffered from the deteriorating economic conditions.

D. The Second Pillar of Retirement: Employment-Based Plans

Defined Benefit Pensions

Social Security is not designed to provide for all of an individual's needs in retirement. For that reason, a retirement benefit has become a common feature of the employment relationship. Unions established through collective bargaining a type of pension known as the "defined benefit" plan, which many large nonunion employers also adopted. In simplest terms, an employee works for a set number of years, reaches a designated age, and receives a fixed payment of money at given dates. Assume, for example, that a person starts work at a General Motors plant at age 20. He works for a period of time, say 30 years, and is 50 years of age. The pension plan is based on the "rule of 80," a combination of age and service. The plan might pay $50 per month per year of service. Consequently, the pensioner would have a monthly income of $1,500, in addition to a Social Security benefit.

The defined benefit pension imposes a duty on the employer to accumulate enough money to provide payments when due. The fund's liabilities are determined by actuarial methods, and federal laws regulate the amounts an employer must maintain for fund solvency. If the employer declares bankruptcy and cannot pay the pension, a federally created private insurance company may take over the plan. The Pension Benefit Guaranty Corporation (PBGC) collects insurance premiums from private sector employers with defined benefit plans, and provides a safety net for workers who might otherwise lose all their retirement income. The PBGC issued its annual report in November 2010.[22] Here is a statement from the report that explains the PBGC's purpose and functions:

> Even as a fledgling economic recovery slowly takes hold, Americans face uncertainty: uncertainty about the economy; uncertainty that their companies and their jobs will last beyond the next paycheck; and uncertainty about when and how government efforts to help will work.
>
> Throughout this uncertainty, ***PBGC continues to help***. Thirty-six years ago Congress set us up to protect and insure pension plans, and make sure workers' benefits get paid. That remains our mission:
>
> - ***We work with companies to keep their pension plans.*** Last year PBGC staff negotiated with dozens of companies, both in bankruptcy and otherwise, to preserve their plans. Partly as a result 250,000 people will keep their pension plans that otherwise might not.
> - ***When plans do fail, we step in and make sure benefits keep getting paid.*** We work to ensure that retirees get the full benefits provided by law—on time. Over the years we've become responsible for almost 1.5 million people in 4,200 failed plans. Every month, on average, we pay $467 million for pensions for 801,000 retirees. PBGC is also responsible for future payments to almost 700,000 who have not yet retired. During FY 2010, we assumed responsibility for 109,000 additional workers and retirees in 172 failed plans.
> - ***We implement pension laws, and work with the President and Congress to improve them.*** In FY 2010 we worked with both the private sector and other government agencies to implement the funding provisions provided by the Pension Protection Act of 2006, and, working with other agencies, helped Congress revise it. We will continue to provide policymakers with the information they need to decide if and when future changes are necessary.
>
> We currently protect the retirement hopes of 44 million Americans in more than 27,500 ongoing pension plans. When a PBGC-insured plan cannot keep its pension promises, PBGC makes sure the plan's participants get their benefits, up to the limits of federal pension law.

The PBGC faces actuarial shortfalls over the long term, just as the Social Security system does. According to the report, the corporation paid out $5.6 billion during the fiscal year in cases where the employer's plan was not able to meet its obligations.

Actuarial analysis showed a deficit of $21.6 billion for single-employer plans, which was due in part to economic conditions and to inadequate plan funding. Another factor was that the PBGC premiums were too low to meet its obligations. The trustees summarized the situation as follows: "Since our obligations are paid out over decades, we have more than sufficient funds to pay benefits for the foreseeable future. Nonetheless, we cannot ignore PBGC's future financial condition any more than we would that of the pension plans we insure."

Defined Contribution Pensions

Because defined benefit pensions place the risk of solvency on the employer, they are declining relative to the other type of plan, the defined contribution retirement plan. This type of plan is often referred to as a "401(k)" retirement program. The designation is taken from the section of the Internal Revenue Code that permits a deferral of income tax on contributions to a plan meeting IRS requirements. The 401(k) concept was initially aimed at high-level executives who could shelter part of their salary by this method. It has become the primary retirement savings vehicle for American workers. The Department of Labor provides the following explanation of the 401(k) plan:

> **What Are 401(k) Plans?**
>
> Your employer may establish a defined contribution plan that is a cash or deferred arrangement, usually called a 401(k) plan. A participant can elect to defer receiving a portion of their salary which is instead contributed on their behalf, before taxes, to the 401(k) plan. Sometimes the employer may match their contributions. There are special rules governing the operation of a 401(k) plan. For example, there is a dollar limit on the amount a participant may elect to defer each year. ... Other limits may apply to the amount that may be contributed on a participant's behalf. For example, if the participant is highly compensated, they may be limited depending on the extent to which rank and file employees participate in the plan. An employer must advise participants of any limits that may apply to them.
>
> Although a 401(k) plan is a retirement plan, participants may be permitted access to funds in the plan before retirement. For example, if a participant is an active employee, the plan may allow them to borrow from the plan. Also, the plan may permit a withdrawal on account of hardship, generally from the funds the participant contributed. The sponsor may want to encourage participation in the plan, but it cannot make participants' elective deferrals a condition for the receipt of other benefits, except for matching contributions.

As the quoted material indicates, the employer may decide to offer a contribution along with the contribution of the employee. Employers can develop rules about their contributions to ensure that the employee has a certain length of service before the employer contribution "vests" or becomes the property of the employee. If conditions change, the employer can reduce or eliminate any matching at the employer's discretion. One advantage of a defined contribution plan is that it can be moved or "rolled over" from one place of employment to another. If the employee loses her job, she may cash in a 401(k) to access the funds. Doing so, however, involves tax liability.

The Employment Benefits Research Institute (EBRI) compiled data on pension plans for the years 1979 to 2008. They found that among private sector participants in a retirement plan, 62% had a defined benefit plan only in 1979 and 7% did in 2008. For the defined contribution (401(k) type) plans, 16% had only such a plan in 1979, while 67% did in 2008.[23] EBRI published a December 2010 analysis of retirement plans, and found that 59 percent of all workers over 16 years of age had an employer who sponsored a pension plan, and 45 percent of that number actually participated in the plan.[24] Most workers were offered a defined contribution plan, rather than a defined benefit pension. The risk of having insufficient funds for retirement in a defined contribution plan is borne by the employee.

To sum up, American workers face difficult choices about retirement. Those choices are likely to become more problematic as the federal government takes up budgetary measures to lower the record deficit going forward.

E. Unemployment Insurance

In October 2009 the unemployment rate in the United States rose just above 10 percent for the first time since late 1982, when it peaked at 10.8 percent of the working population. The figure below, downloaded from the Bureau of Labor Statistics (BLS) Web site, shows the historical fluctuations in unemployment rates since the end of World War II. In President Reagan's first term, both unemployment and inflation concerned policymakers, and Reagan implemented a policy of monetary restriction that gradually controlled inflation through high unemployment. Once the economy recovered, unemployment fell into the early 1990s. The election of Bill Clinton in 1992 commenced a period in which employment and incomes rose for the next ten years. The economic crisis precipitated a dramatic increase in unemployment, which continued through 2010.

Most problematically, unemployment in Obama's first two years in office featured very long periods in which individuals could not find work. The *New York Times* reported, "This country has some of the highest levels of long-term unemployment—out of work longer than six months—it has ever recorded. Meanwhile, job growth has been, and looks to remain, disappointingly slow, indicating that those out of work for a while are likely to remain so for the foreseeable future."[25] Economists debated whether the causes of long term unemployment were "structural" or "demand" in nature. Structural unemployment occurs when workers do not have the necessary skills to compete for new jobs, either because the jobs have disappeared or because technology has made

Figure 5. Unemployment Rates

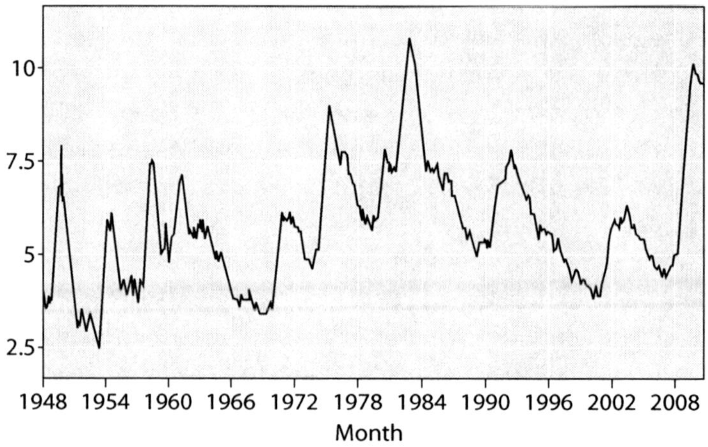

their skills obsolete. Unemployment caused by a lack of demand in the economy may be reduced by stimulus measures that encourage businesses to increase production. In past recessions, unemployment fell quickly when economic activity rebounded. The issue is important for formulating appropriate policy responses.

Unemployment benefits are normally paid for 26 weeks, but the federal government provided funds to states for extended benefits. In many cases, claimants received benefits up to 99 months in duration, after which their eligibility expired. The "99ers" included persons who had been regularly employed for years, but were unable to find any type of employment despite their searches. According to the BLS, "The number of persons jobless for a year or more rose from 645,000 in the second quarter of 2007 to 4.5 million in the second quarter of 2010. The group's share of total unemployment jumped from 9.5 percent to a record high of 30.9 percent."[26] Workers in their 50s and 60s were pessimistic about their chances of ever regaining a foothold in the economy.

During the lame duck session of Congress in November and December 2010, extended benefits played a prominent role in a compromise package of legislation that involved the Bush-era tax cuts, along with various other spending and revenue measures. The Bush administration enacted a 10-year tax plan that gave high earners a lower rate than during either the Reagan or Clinton eras. Those cuts were scheduled to expire at the end of 2010 for all taxpayers. Democrats argued that the middle class should continue to pay the Bush rates, but Republicans insisted that all taxpayers should continue with existing schedules. Republicans succeeded in keeping all the tax rates in place until 2012, and Democrats succeeded in extending unemployment benefits and passing a payroll tax cut for workers. According to the administration, the compromise measures would provide additional stimulus to the economy without significantly adding to the deficit.[27]

1. How the Unemployment Insurance System Encourages State Participation

Unemployment insurance originated as Title III part of the 1935 Social Security Act, and is a joint state and federal venture. The Tenth Amendment to the U.S. Constitution grants all powers not expressly given to the federal government. The Roosevelt administration favored an arrangement that involved states in the administration of unemployment benefits. The members of the Committee on Economic Security considered a wholly federal plan, but rejected that approach in favor of the joint project advocated by Roosevelt. As enacted, the Social Security legislation featured a tax-offset mechanism that encouraged states to develop their own programs, and avoided issues of federal constitutional power. Upholding the constitutionality of UI in *Steward Machine Co. v. Davis* (1937), the Supreme Court noted that states were not forced to participate in the UI program, but did so voluntarily. The explanation for the states' "voluntary" participation is that a state may decline to have a UI program, but there are important consequences for doing so.

Under the Federal Unemployment Tax Act, the federal government presently imposes on employers a payroll tax of 6.2 percent on a wage base of $7,000. This tax is owed directly to the federal government. Employers, however, may be given an offset credit of 5.4 percent if they are covered by, and pay into, an approved state plan. Under the state plans, the tax an employer actually pays is based on the employer's experience rating, which is determined by the benefits charged against the employer's account. Consequently, depending on the employer's ability to avoid claims, the employer may pay a lower tax—or even no tax—to the state fund. Regardless of the employer's actual tax liability to the state, the employer is given the full 5.4 percent offset for any taxes due under the federal law. As a result, there are powerful incentives for states to provide an unemployment insurance program; if they did not do so, employers in that state would be liable for the full tax to the federal government. Justice Cardozo made the point with a nice rhetorical flourish, when he dismissed the argument that the Tenth Amendment forbids the federal government from "coercing" the states to have an unemployment insurance system. He said, "Who then is coerced through the operation of this statute? Not the taxpayer. He pays in fulfillment of the mandate of the local legislature. Not the state. Even now, she does not offer a suggestion that, in passing the unemployment law, she was affected by duress. For all that appears, she is satisfied with her choice, and would be sorely disappointed if it were now to be annulled."[28] All 50 states currently have unemployment insurance programs in place. The following declaration of legislative policy from the California statutes explains the purpose and function of unemployment insurance.[29]

UNEMPLOYMENT INSURANCE CODE SECTIONS 100–102

100. As a guide to the interpretation and application of this division the public policy of this State is declared as follows:

> Experience has shown that large numbers of the population of California do not enjoy permanent employment by reason of which their purchasing power is unstable. This is detrimental to the interests of the people of California as a whole.
>
> The benefit to all persons resulting from public and private enterprise is realized in the final consumption of goods and services. It is contrary to public policy to permit the supply of consumption goods and services at prices which do not provide against that harm to the population consequent upon periods of unemployment of those who contribute to the production and distribution of such goods and services.
>
> Experience has shown that private charity and local relief cannot alone prevent the effects of unemployment. Experience has shown that if the State awaits the coming of excessive unemployment it can neither create immediately the organization necessary to orderly, economical and effective relief nor bear the financial burden of relief without disrupting its whole system of ordinary revenues and without jeopardizing its credit.
>
> The Legislature therefore declares that in its considered judgment the public good and the general welfare of the citizens of the State require the enactment of this measure under the police power of the State, for the compulsory setting aside of funds to be used for a system of unemployment insurance providing benefits for persons unemployed through no fault of their own, and to reduce involuntary unemployment and the suffering caused thereby to a minimum.
>
> It is the intent of the Legislature that unemployed persons claiming unemployment insurance benefits shall be required to make all reasonable effort to secure employment on their own behalf.

2. *Qualifications, Reductions, and Benefits*

Because UI (unemployment insurance) is intended to provide short-term protection for workers, it has several important conditions that must be satisfied. First, workers must demonstrate an attachment to the workforce through an earnings history, usually consisting of specified dollar amounts earned during the "base year" preceding their application for benefits. Second, the worker must be unemployed "through no fault of his own," and workers who quit work or are fired for misconduct may be denied part or all of their benefits. Third, the worker must be able to work and be available for work. Individuals injured on the job, for example, are covered under workers' compensation programs, rather than UI. Individuals who have withdrawn from the labor force, such as a person who enrolls in a full-time course of education or training, will not be available for work. UI programs impose an obligation on recipients to accept "suitable work" that is offered to them. Suitable work may vary, depending on the length of unemployment and the individual's skills and past earnings history. A software engineer should not be forced to take a job in the fast food industry or lose unemployment benefits so long as there is a reasonable expectation that she will find work commensurate with her level of expertise.

The requirement that a worker be unemployed "through no fault of his own" is a standard interpreted under state law. Each jurisdiction creates statutory law and case interpretation dealing with employee misconduct that will result in no or reduced benefits. The point is important, because employers can reduce their costs of unemployment if there are few charges against their account. For example, if an employer fires an employee for being rude to a customer, the employee may file for benefits and state that she was separated due to lack of work. The unemployment administrator will contact the employer, who can state other reasons for the termination. The state agency resolves the issue through various levels of appeal, which may eventually lead to judicial determination. The employee's incentive is to receive benefits until he finds a job, and the employer's incentive is to protect the solvency of her fund. Remember that if an employer has a reserve in the insurance fund, the state may reduce the amount of tax the employer pays. The state of California provides the following information on its Web site.[30]

> An individual is disqualified for unemployment compensation benefits if the director finds that he or she left his or her most recent work voluntarily without good cause or that he or she has been discharged for misconduct connected with his or her most recent work. An individual is presumed to have been discharged for reasons other than misconduct in connection with his or her work and not to have voluntarily left his or her work without good cause unless his or her employer has given written notice to the contrary to the department ... setting forth facts sufficient to overcome the presumption. The presumption provided by this section is rebuttable.

The UI system also requires that a claimant undertake a regular job search. Using California law as an example again, the requirement is that "a person must be physically able to work, available for work and actively looking for work each week benefits are claimed." To monitor the job search, the claimant must verify the job search by submitting a form every two weeks to the Department. "If the information on the form shows that the individual did not meet eligibility requirements, the Department will schedule a telephone interview. Based on the information obtained, benefits may be reduced or denied. An individual who disagrees with our decision to reduce or deny benefits may file an appeal." Consequently, the process of obtaining UI benefits entails some very specific requirements. Unemployed workers who fail to comply with the guidelines may lose benefits or be subject to future penalties.

3. A Note on Extended Benefits

During the lame duck session of Congress in late 2010, legislators reached a compromise on the important issues of taxation and unemployment. The Obama administration agreed to support an extension of all federal tax rates due to expire at the end of the year, including the rates paid by earners in the upper income brackets. Congressional Democrats favored repeal of those rates and a reinstatement of the higher rates of the Clinton era. Republicans agreed to an extension of unemployment benefits, provided Democrats would keep tax rates at existing levels for an additional two years. The impact for unemployed workers is explained in the statement from the California state government below. The excerpt explains how unemployment benefits are arranged in tiers to provide extended coverage for long-term unemployment.

New Developments on Federal Unemployment Extensions (Updated January 18, 2011)

Updated: Number of individuals who have run out of benefits is more than 304,000

The U.S. Congress has approved, and President Obama has signed, a sweeping tax package that includes a reauthorization of federal unemployment extension benefits for another 13 months. While the legislation does not add anything further to the current maximum of up to 99 weeks of benefits available, it does add more time for eligible unemployed workers to be able to collect those maximum benefits while trying to secure a new job.

In anticipation of Congressional action, the Employment Development Department (EDD) was already taking steps to ensure we are ready to file and pay extended benefits to eligible claimants who were in danger of interruptions in their unemployment checks. A total of more than 250,000 customers who would have normally expected a check during the week of December 20th were in danger of missing that payment unless Congress acted by December 18th.

Approximately 23,000 of those customers had recently run out of their current level of unemployment benefits and were prevented from moving into any further extension claim. The EDD has already filed their next extension claim and sent out claim forms. Now that extensions are reauthorized, these customers should complete their claim forms and return them to EDD as they normally would per the date noted on their form. Once received, it takes EDD a day or so to process the forms and issue payments to eligible customers.

The remaining 235,000 people of the total customers impacted are those with a payable balance remaining on the separate extension known as the FED-ED here in California. Without further Congressional action, the week ending December 11th was the last payable week of FED-ED benefits. The Department has continued to send claim forms to these customers in anticipation of the program being reauthorized. Customers should now complete those claim forms as they normally would and return them according to the date noted on the form. Payments can then be issued for eligible claimants without interruption.

NEW FILING DEADLINES FOR FEDERAL EXTENSION BENEFITS

For more than two years, an unprecedented offering of federal unemployment extension benefits has provided additional financial support to unemployed workers hit hard in this long, harsh recession. In addition to the up to 26 weeks of regular UI benefits offered any time an eligible worker becomes unemployed, up to 73 weeks of additional benefits have been available through four different tiers of extension benefits and a separate extension of benefits known as the FED-ED extension. All together, up to 99 weeks of unemployment benefits have been available to help support unemployed workers, their families, and their communities.

Here is a breakdown of the new filing deadlines for federal extension benefits now that the program has been extended for another 13 months:

CURRENT UI EXTENDED BENEFIT DURATION & CLAIM DEADLINES

UI Benefits Provided During This Recession

UI Claims	Maximum Weeks of Benefits Provided	Deadline for Starting This Type of UI Claim
Regular UI Claim	Up to 26 weeks of benefits	Once someone becomes unemployed
1st Tier of Federal Extension	Up to 20 weeks of benefits	December 25, 2011
2nd Tier of Federal Extension	Up to 14 weeks of benefits	January 1, 2012
3rd Tier of Federal Extension	Up to 13 weeks of benefits	January 1, 2012
4th Tier of Federal Extension	Up to 6 weeks of benefits	January 1, 2012
Separate FED-ED Extension	Up to 20 weeks of benefits	January 8, 2012
POTENTIAL TOTAL MAXIMUM BENEFITS	**Up to 99 weeks of benefits**	

This chapter describes the basic elements of the American safety net. Out of the grave economic conditions of the Great Depression came the foundation for modern social protections. As we enter into the second decade of the 21st century, those foundations rest on shifting and unstable ground. Federal spending approaches unsustainable levels, but high levels of unemployment continue to threaten our future prosperity. Inequality in the United States in 2010 was greater than at any time since 1929. Political solutions appear stymied by conflicting views about deficits and employment. A resurgence of New Deal economic programs to stimulate growth is unlikely, but it is equally likely that imposing greater austerity in spending will inflict more deprivation on many citizens. Below are some points for consideration and discussion.

Questions

1. What evidence supports Keynes's view that government intervention may be necessary to generate economic activity?
2. How does collective bargaining promote economic growth, or does it?
3. Is the financing system for Social Security the best option? Should workers pay more into the system, or should employers pay more?
4. How could Social Security be privatized?
5. What changes would you make in Social Security in order to stabilize the system, and why?
6. Should Medicare coverage be extended to all people in the United States? Or should Medicare be taken out of the Social Security system?
7. What options are available to workers who have exhausted unemployment benefits?
8. Should unemployment be limited to the base of 26 weeks regardless of economic conditions?
9. Most citizens in early 2011 thought that the main problem in the country was the lack of jobs. What can the federal government do about that? What did Roosevelt do in the New Deal?

Suggested Exercises

1. Watch the 2011 film produced by HBO called *Too Big to Fail*. Are there any heroes in the drama? Does the film help you to understand Bernanke's argument about the Great Depression?
2. Form two teams and debate the merits of the proposed Employee Free Choice Act. One team should take the position that the bill must be passed in order to have real prosperity in this country.

3. In a team, prepare a presentation that convinces someone to vote for union representation at a hypothetical company. Hold a vote to determine whether or not you were successful in the presentation.
4. Research the realities of public sector unionism. Write a paper discussing your findings and conclusions. Conclude with a recommendation about changing your state's laws.
5. Analyze the overtime provisions of the Fair Labor Standards Act. Make a presentation explaining the law to a group of students.
6. Research the overtime laws in your state, and write a paper summarizing them. Discuss any litigation in which employees received back-pay awards, and why.
7. Compare the political positions of Republicans and Democrats with respect to changing the Social Security program. Hold a debate on the subject.
8. Analyze the two kinds of pension plans that can be used by employers. Write a paper that explains them, and what the advantages and disadvantages are of each one for employees and employers.
9. Look up current and historical data on unemployment, and give a presentation on trends in the United States. Examine rates in other countries, and offer explanations for any differences. Conclude by making recommendations for modifying the U.S. system.

Notes

1. Paul Krugman, *New York Times*, Oct. 25, 2010. Online: http://www.nytimes.com/2010/10/25/opinion/25krugman.html?th&emc=th/.
2. Alan Blinder & Mark Zandi, How the Great Recession Was Brought to an End (July 27, 2010), p. 2. Online: http://www.economy.com/mark-zandi/documents/End-of-Great-Recession.pdf.
3. Remarks by Federal Reserve governor Ben S. Bernanke at the H. Parker Willis Lecture in Economic Policy, Washington and Lee University, Lexington, Virginia, March 2, 2004. The speech is available on a government Web site: http://www.federalreserve.gov/boarddocs/speeches/2004/200403022/default.htm.
4. John Maynard Keynes, *The General Theory of Employment, Interest and Money* (Basingstoke, UK: Palgrave, 2007 [1936]).
5. Raymond Hogler, "Exclusive Representation and the Wagner Act: The Structure of Federal Collective Bargaining Law," *Labor Law Journal*, 58 (fall 2007), pp. 157–69.
6. Frank Levy and Peter Temin, "Institutions and Wages in Post–World War II America," in *Labor in the Era of Globalization*, ed. Clair Brown, Barry Eichengreen, and Michael Reich (New York: Cambridge University Press, 2010), p. 16.
7. Jacob Hacker and Paul Pierson, *Winner Take All Politics: How Washington Made the Rich Richer—And Turned Its Back on the Middle Class* (New York: Simon & Schuster, 2010).

8. Raymond Hogler and Steven Shulman, "The Law, Economics, and Politics of Right to Work: An Analysis of Colorado's Labor Peace Act," *University of Colorado Law Review*, vol. 70, no. 3 (summer 1999), pp. 871–952.
9. Raymond Hogler, Steven Shulman, and Stephan Weiler, "Right-to-Work Legislation, Social Capital, and Variations in State Union Density," *The Review of Regional Studies*, 34, no. 1 (2004), pp. 95–111.
10. Union density figures were drawn from the following sources: Richard Freeman, "Spurts in Union Growth: Defining Moments and Social Processes," in *The Defining Moment: The Great Depression and the American Economy in the Twentieth Century.* Ed. M. Bordo, C. Goldin, and E. White (Chicago: University of Chicago Press, 1997), pp. 265–96; "Working Life" at http://www.workinglife.org/wiki/Union+Membership:+Public+Sector+(1948-2004); Barry Hirsch and Donald Macpherson, Union Membership and Coverage Database. www.unionstats.com.
11. For further information on public unions, see generally Benjamin Aaron, Joyce M. Najita, and James L. Stern, *Public-Sector Bargaining,* Washington, DC: BNA Books (2nd ed., 1988); Joseph Slater, *Public Workers: Government Employee Unions, the Law, and the State, 1900–1962.* Ithaca, NY: ILR Press, 2004.
12. Steven Greenhouse, "Strained States Turning to Laws to Curb Labor Unions," *New York Times*, Jan. 4, 2011, p. A1.
13. "(Government) workers of the world unite." *The Economist*, Jan. 8–14, 2011, pp. 21–23.
14. David Card and Alan B. Krueger, *Myth and Measurement: The New Economics of the Minimum Wage*, Princeton University Press, 1995.
15. David Card and Alan B. Krueger, "Minimum Wages and Employment: A Case Study of the Fast-Food Industry in New Jersey and Pennsylvania: Reply," *American Economic Review*, Dec. 2000, pp. 1396-1420.
16. *Chau v. Starbucks Corp.*, 174 Cal.App.4th 688 (2009).
17. CBS News Online Report, Dec. 9, 2009. Retrieved Nov. 2010 from http://www.cbsnews.com/stories/2008/12/09/business/main4657472.shtml.
18. *American Federation of State, County, and Municipal Employees v. Washington*, 770 F.2d 1401(1985).
19. *County of Washington v. Gunther*, 452 U.S. 161 (1981).
20. Laurence Kotlikoff, "U.S. Is Bankrupt and We Don't Even Know It," Bloomberg News, online at: http://www.bloomberg.com/news/2010-08-11/u-s-is-bankrupt-and-we-don-t-even-know-commentary-by-laurence-kotlikoff.html.
21. For commentary, see http://www.washingtonpost.com/wp-dyn/content/article/2010/12/03/AR2010120307027.html. The proposal had the support of 11 members, but a vote of 14 in favor was needed to advance the plan to Congress.
22. The report is available at: http://www.pbgc.gov/about/ar2010.html.
23. See the EBRI chart at http://www.ebri.org/publications/benfaq/index.cfm?fa=retfaq14.
24. Craig Copeland, "Retirement Plan Participation: Survey of Income and Program Participation (SIPP) Data, 2009," *EBRI Notes,* 31, no. 11, November 2010.
25. Catherine Rampel, "Unemployed, and likely to stay that way," *New York Times*, Dec. 3, 2010, p. B1.

26. See BLS, http://www.bls.gov/opub/ils/pdf/opbils87.pdf.
27. http://www.whitehouse.gov/taxcut.
28. *Steward Machine Co. v. Davis*, 301 U.S. 548 (1937).
29. The text of the statute is available at http://law.justia.com/california/codes/2009/uic/100-102.html.
30. See http://www.edd.ca.gov/Unemployment/Eligibility.htm.

3. Safety and Health: Regulation of the Workplace and Individual Health Care

I. The Occupational Safety and Health Act (OSHA)

The Occupational Safety and Health Act, or OSHA, was enacted in 1970. The bill followed a long period of Democratic control in Congress and the liberal politics of the Kennedy-Johnson administration. Richard Nixon, a Republican, defeated the Democratic presidential candidate, Hubert Humphrey, in the 1968 elections. Nixon faced a Congress dominated by Democrats, who presented him with a health and safety bill, which he signed into law. OSHA thus represents the culmination of a political era in employment regulation. It was strongly opposed by the business community, which criticized the further expansion of governmental authority into business operations. Organized labor, on the other hand, viewed the event as a landmark victory in the struggle for workplace safety reform.

OSHA is straightforward in its design and implementation. The act sets out safety and health guidelines known as "standards." It then prescribes a method of enforcement through inspections, citations, and penalties, illustrated by the figure below. Within this general framework, OSHA addresses a number of specific issues, such as the content of the standards, the adequacy of inspections, and the effectiveness of penalties. This section begins with an overview of the law, and then considers in more detail each of OSHA's operative principles.

Figure 1. How OSHA Works

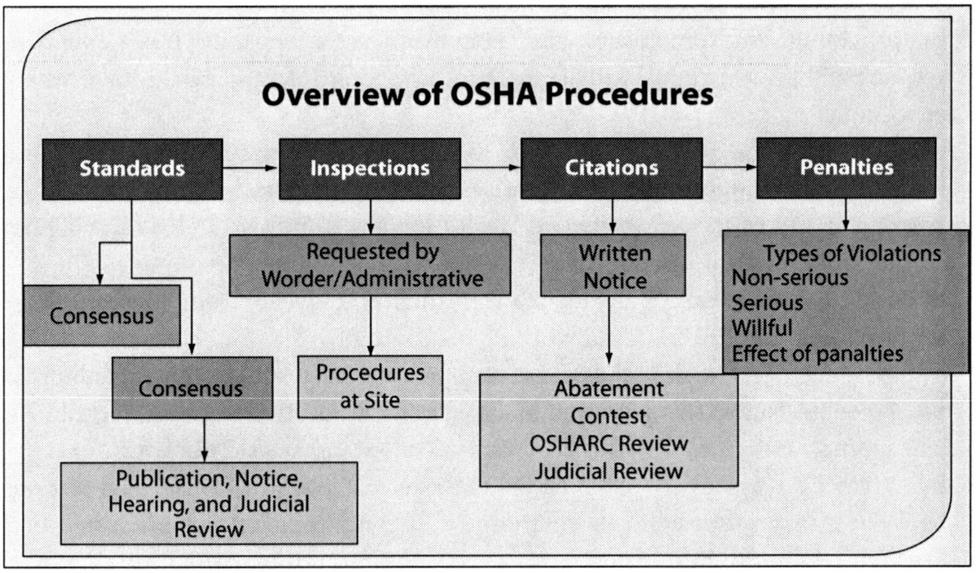

A. Findings and Purposes of OSHA

Congress articulated an elaborate and detailed explanation of its objective for the occupational safety and health legislation. An excerpt from the statute is quoted below. Congress listed 13 ways in which safety and health might be assured to workers on the job. They included various motivations for employers and employees to participate in creating safe workplaces, a regulatory regime to oversee the law, and means of developing knowledge about safety and health issues. As you consider the congressional goals, you should think about the relative success, or lack of success, which we have achieved through this massive legislative undertaking. Here is the statutory introduction to the OSH Act:

a. The Congress finds that personal injuries and illnesses arising out of work situations impose a substantial burden upon, and are a hindrance to, interstate commerce in terms of lost production, wage loss, medical expenses, and disability compensation payments.
b. The Congress declares it to be its purpose and policy, through the exercise of its powers to regulate commerce among the several States and with foreign nations and to provide for the general welfare, to assure so far as possible every working man and woman in the Nation safe and healthful working conditions and to preserve our human resources—

1. by encouraging employers and employees in their efforts to reduce the number of occupational safety and health hazards at their places of employment, and to

stimulate employers and employees to institute new and to perfect existing programs for providing safe and healthful working conditions;

2. by providing that employers and employees have separate but dependent responsibilities and rights with respect to achieving safe and healthful working conditions;
3. by authorizing the Secretary of Labor to set mandatory occupational safety and health standards applicable to businesses affecting interstate commerce, and by creating an Occupational Safety and Health Review Commission for carrying out adjudicatory functions under the Act;
4. by building upon advances already made through employer and employee initiative for providing safe and healthful working conditions;
5. by providing for research in the field of occupational safety and health, including the psychological factors involved, and by developing innovative methods, techniques, and approaches for dealing with occupational safety and health problems;
6. by exploring ways to discover latent diseases, establishing causal connections between diseases and work in environmental conditions, and conducting other research relating to health problems, in recognition of the fact that occupational health standards present problems often different from those involved in occupational safety;
7. by providing medical criteria which will assure insofar as practicable that no employee will suffer diminished health, functional capacity, or life expectancy as a result of his work experience;
8. by providing for training programs to increase the number and competence of personnel engaged in the field of occupational safety and health; affecting the OSH Act since its passage in 1970 through January 1, 2004.
9. by providing for the development and promulgation of occupational safety and health standards;
10. by providing an effective enforcement program which shall include a prohibition against giving advance notice of any inspection and sanctions for any individual violating this prohibition;
11. by encouraging the States to assume the fullest responsibility for the administration and enforcement of their occupational safety and health laws by providing grants to the States to assist in identifying their needs and responsibilities in the area of occupational safety and health, to develop plans in accordance with the provisions of this Act, to improve the administration and enforcement of State occupational safety and health laws, and to conduct experimental and demonstration projects in connection therewith;
12. by providing for appropriate reporting procedures with respect to occupational safety and health which procedures will help achieve the objectives of this Act and accurately describe the nature of the occupational safety and health problem;
13. by encouraging joint labor-management efforts to reduce injuries and disease arising out of employment.

OSHA also imposes an obligation on employers and employees under Section 5 of the Act, which describes the "general duty" to maintain a safe workplace:

Each employer—

1. shall furnish to each of his employees employment and a place of employment which are free from recognized hazards that are causing or are likely to cause death or serious physical harm to his employees;
2. shall comply with occupational safety and health standards promulgated under this Act.
    b. Each employee shall comply with occupational safety and health standards and all rules, regulations, and orders issued pursuant to this Act which are applicable to his own actions and conduct.

B. Coverage of the Law

Note that OSHA is based on the federal power to regulate interstate commerce. As we have seen, this power is very broad, and exceptions to the scope of the statute are ones imposed by Congress, not by the Constitution. Accordingly, the OSH Act applies to the extent that Congress thought politically expedient, and it exempted some activities and some entities from the law's application.

Generally, the act covers private sector employees in the United States and its protectorates. It *does not* apply to workers in the public sector. States are free to adopt safety measures or not and to participate in the federal regulatory process if they so prefer. Congress intended that states would take an active role in protecting workers, and the law allows states to develop their own programs for both private and public workers and to coordinate with the federal agency. Under Section 18 of the federal law, states with approved plans may receive up to one-half of their operating expenses through a federal subsidy. Presently, 22 states have such plans covering both the private and public workforce. Four states cover only their public employees. According to the OSHA Web site, state plans must be consistent with national principles. The federal requirements are as follows:

> States must set job safety and health standards that are "at least as effective as" comparable federal standards. (Most States adopt standards identical to federal ones.) States have the option to promulgate standards covering hazards not addressed by federal standards.
>
> A State must conduct inspections to enforce its standards, cover public (State and local government) employees, and operate occupational safety and health training and education programs. In addition, most States provide free on-site consultation to help employers identify and correct workplace hazards. Such consultation may be provided either under the plan or through a special agreement under section 21(d) of the Act.

More information is available at:
http://www.osha.gov/dcsp/osp/faq.html#oshaprogram

C. Setting Standards

1. Consensus Standards

When OSHA came into effect in 1970, many employers already had workplace safety programs featuring national voluntary standards for creating safe conditions for workers. Those programs relied on practices certified by such organizations as the American National Standards Institute and others that described the best way to engage in certain activities. ANSI is still an important part of the business environment, and the organization describes its activities in the following way on its Web site (http://www.ansi.org/about_ansi/overview/overview.aspx?menuid=1):

> The Institute oversees the creation, promulgation and use of thousands of norms and guidelines that directly impact businesses in nearly every sector: from acoustical devices to construction equipment, from dairy and livestock production to energy distribution, and many more. ANSI is also actively engaged in accrediting programs that assess conformance to standards—including globally-recognized cross-sector programs such as the ISO 9000 (quality) and ISO 14000 (environmental) management systems.

The existence of recognized and widespread safety standards allowed OSHA to incorporate a body of existing rules into the statutory framework, and OSHA may still use that procedure. When OSHA proposed its "Walking-Working Surfaces and Personal Protective Equipment rule," the American Society of Safety Engineers urged OSHA to adopt the ANSI standard, rather than develop another rule. The group explained, "A voluntary consensus standard is a documented agreement established by a consensus of subject matter experts and approved by a recognized body that provides rules, guidelines or characteristics to ensure that materials, products, processes and services are fit for their purpose. Voluntary consensus standards developed by industry in accordance with ANSI's procedures for due process, openness and consensus subsequently are often adopted by the government as part of the regulatory framework."[1] Obviously, coordination between the federal agency and private groups is advantageous to everyone affected by safety issues. It also allows for the effective use of resources in providing safety standards.

2. Promulgation by the OSH Administration

For safety issues that present new risks and problems, such as those emerging in the 1980s with HIV/AIDS, new approaches are needed to adequately protect workers. Under such circumstances, OSHA may develop a standard which it then implements according to administrative rules. First, OSHA must publish the proposed standard and give affected parties an opportunity to comment on the proposed rule. After that process, OSHA may modify its standard, rescind it, or implement it as drafted. The standard can then be challenged in court to determine such matters as OSHA's scope of authority, the legal basis of the rule, or other related questions. If a court approves the rule, it goes into effect, and becomes binding on all designated parties. Some further examples will show how the process works.

In one of its most controversial rules, OSHA issued a standard regulating the permissible amount of cotton dust to which workers could be exposed while working in a mill, because it caused a lung condition known as byssinosis. The cotton dust standard reached the Court in *American Textile Manufacturers v. Donovan,* 452 U.S. 490 (1981). Writing for the Court, Justice Brennan upheld OSHA's rule that the manufacturers had to reduce the levels of dust to the lowest amount that was feasible. OSHA argued that the law required the government to "enact the most protective standard possible to eliminate a significant risk of material health impairment, subject to the constraints of economic and technological feasibility," and the Supreme Court agreed with this argument. Consequently, the benefits of employee health outweighed economic impacts on the manufacturers, so long as the standard was feasible, or "capable of being achieved."

Although the textile industry strenuously opposed the standard, it had little long-term effect. Global economic forces led to the offshoring of textile manufacturing, primarily to low-wage areas where safety factors played a smaller role. That process has continued into the 2010s. A safety consulting firm recently posted the following comment on its Web site blog under the title "Is OSHA Killing the American Dream?":[2]

> While no one wants to come home in a body bag after a day of work and no one condones bad safety practices, the question is, how much compliance is too much compliance? In today's economy it's difficult to run a shop, keep up with payroll, and accommodate all of OSHA's requirements while others in that industry outsource to foreign countries and enjoy lax labor laws.

The argument goes to an important issue in health and safety, which is the extent to which costs of safety and health should be balanced against the loss of jobs and economic development. This question will be addressed more fully at the end of this chapter.

To consider another contemporary example of an OSHA standard, the agency was confronted in the 1980s with the problem of HIV-AIDS, which is a blood-borne pathogen capable of causing death. OSHA issued an emergency standard to deal temporarily with the problem, and through the standard-setting process, arrived at the "Bloodborne Pathogens and Needlestick Prevention" regulation. OSHA found that "Needlestick injuries and other sharp-related injuries which expose workers to bloodborne pathogens continues to be an important public health concern. Workers in many different occupations are at risk of exposure to bloodborne pathogens, including Hepatitis B, Hepatitis

C, and HIV/AIDS." The standard requires that certain safety precautions be followed, along with improved equipment and record-keeping procedures. OSHA provides informational and instructional materials dealing with the standard at the following Web site: http://www.osha.gov/SLTC/bloodbornepathogens/index.html.

D. Enforcement[3]

Inspections

The OSHA standards are enforced through a process of inspections, citations, and penalties. The procedures for an OSHA inspection are relatively straightforward. To begin with, OSHA prioritizes its inspection activity according to a system aimed at reaching the most hazardous activities. Its first priority, for example, deals with an "imminent danger situations," which could lead to death or serious physical harm to workers. In such cases, OSHA will request an immediate correction of the problem or removing workers from exposure to the harm. The imminent danger priority is followed by incidents involving the death or hospitalization of an employee, complaints about hazardous conditions, referrals from state agencies or individuals, follow-up inspections to ensure that previous conditions have been abated, and programmed inspections based on evidence of a high-hazard industries or workplaces.

Normally, an OSHA inspection is conducted without notice. When the OSHA compliance officer arrives at the inspection site, the employer may ask for a valid warrant and the officer's credentials before proceeding with the inspection. The officer conducts a preliminary meeting to explain the purpose of the inspection. The employer can appoint a representative to accompany the officer, and employees are also entitled to have a representative during the inspection. The officer has authority to walk around the premises, speak with employees, point out any violations, review records, and ensure that required OSHA posters are in place. The inspection concludes with a closing conference that covers such matters as violations, proposed penalties, and any other relevant safety and health issues. OSHA claims that it has improved its inspection record over the past few years and has become more effective in administering the law and achieving its goals. The tables below are OSHA's statistics about inspections and compliance.

> "OSHA Inspection Activity: Focused and Efficient"
> By proactively targeting the industries and employers that experience the greatest number of workplace injuries and illnesses, OSHA continues to maintain its high level of annual inspection activity. In FY 2009, OSHA conducted 39,004 total inspections. This year's significant enforcement actions included 120 inspections; each resulting in a total proposed monetary penalty of more than $100,000. OSHA conducted 24,316 programmed inspections and 14,688 unprogrammed inspections, including employee complaints,

accidents, and referrals. The number of fatality investigations decreased by 28.5%; a significant decrease over the past five fiscal years, thus demonstrating OSHA's firm commitment to reducing the number of workplace fatalities.

Figure 2. Inspections

OSHA Inspection Statistics	FY2005	FY2006	FY2007	FY2008	FY2009	%Change - 2009
Total Inspection	38,714	38,579	39,324	38,667	39,004	75%
Total Programmed Inspections	21,404	21,506	23,035	23,041	24,316	13.6%
Total Unprogrammed Inspections	17,310	17,073	16,289	15,626	14,688	-15.1%
Fatality Investigations	1,114	1,081	1,043	936	797	-28.5%
Complaints	7,716	7,376	7,055	6,708	6,661	-13.7%
Referrals	7,787	5,019	5,007	4,880	4,375	-8.6%
Other	4,693	3,597	3,184	3,102	2,855	-39.2%

Hazards Identified: Total Violations Decrease; Serious Violations Increase
While total injury and illness rates continue to decline, OSHA continues to direct enforcement resources to those establishments with the highest incidence of serious hazards. In FY 2009, 87,663 violations of OSHA's standards and regulations were found in the nation's workplaces, a 2.8% increase since FY 2005. The total number of serious and repeat violations issued increased by 10.9% and 17.5%, respectively, over the past five years. The total number of willful violations issued significantly decreased since FY 2005, decreasing by 46.3%.

Figure 3. Violations

OSHA Violation Statistics	FY2005	FY2006	FY2007	FY2008	FY2009	%Change 2005–2009
Total Violations	85,307	83,913	88,846	87,687	87,663	2.8%
Total Serious Violations	61,018	61,337	67,176	67,052	67,668	10.9%
Total Willful Violations	747	479	415	517	401	–46.3%

Citations and Penalties

If an inspection reveals any violation of a standard, OSHA may issue a citation which will set forth the violations, propose a penalty, and set a time for the abatement of the condition. OSHA characterizes the violations according to different categories. Those categories are other-than-serious, serious, willful, repeated, and failure to abate. The amount of the penalty ranges from up to $7,000 for each serious violation, and up to $70,000 for each willful or repeated violation. The penalties may be reduced for various mitigating circumstances, such as whether the employer acted in good faith, the extent of the employer's past history with OSHA, and the size of the business. If the violation is willful, the penalty will not be adjusted. The statutory language of section 9 is as follows:

> a) If, upon inspection or investigation, the Secretary or his authorized representative believes that an employer has violated a requirement of section 5 of this Act, of any standard, rule or order promulgated pursuant to section 6 of this Act, or of any regulations prescribed pursuant to this Act, he shall with reasonable promptness issue a citation to the employer. Each citation shall be in writing and shall describe with particularity the nature of the violation, including a reference to the provision of the Act, standard, rule, regulation, or order alleged to have been violated. In addition, the citation shall fix a reasonable time for the abatement of the violation. The Secretary may prescribe procedures for the issuance of a notice in lieu of a citation with respect to de minimis violations which have no direct or immediate relationship to safety or health.
>
> (b) Each citation issued under this section, or a copy or copies thereof, shall be prominently posted, as prescribed in regulations issued by the Secretary, at or near each place a violation referred to in the citation occurred.
>
> (c) No citation may be issued under this section after the expiration of six months following the occurrence of any violation.

OSHA fines can be substantial, depending on the nature of the violation. In October 2009 OSHA proposed a penalty of $87,430,000 against BP Products North America, Inc. The violations occurred at a BP oil refinery in Texas City, Texas, following an explosion that killed a number of workers. The OSHA press release is reprinted below.[4] Note how OSHA explains the amounts imposed in this case:

> **U.S. Department of Labor's OSHA Issues Record-Breaking Fines to BP**
>
> **WASHINGTON**—The U.S. Department of Labor's Occupational Safety and Health Administration (OSHA) today announced it is issuing $87,430,000 in proposed penalties to BP Products North America Inc. for the company's failure to correct potential hazards faced by employees. The fine is the largest

in OSHA's history. The prior largest total penalty, $21 million, was issued in 2005, also against BP.

Safety violations at BP's Texas City, Texas, refinery resulted in a massive explosion—with 15 deaths and 170 people injured—in March of 2005. BP entered into a settlement agreement with OSHA in September of that year, under which the company agreed to corrective actions to eliminate potential hazards similar to those that caused the 2005 tragedy. Today's announcement comes at the conclusion of a six-month inspection by OSHA, designed to evaluate the extent to which BP has complied with its obligations under the 2005 agreement and OSHA standards.

"When BP signed the OSHA settlement from the March 2005 explosion, it agreed to take comprehensive action to protect employees. Instead of living up to that commitment, BP has allowed hundreds of potential hazards to continue unabated," said Secretary of Labor Hilda L. Solis. "Fifteen people lost their lives as a result of the 2005 tragedy, and 170 others were injured. An $87 million fine won't restore those lives, but we can't let this happen again. Workplace safety is more than a slogan. It's the law. The U.S. Department of Labor will not tolerate the preventable exposure of workers to hazardous conditions."

For noncompliance with the terms of the settlement agreement, the BP Texas City Refinery has been issued 270 "notifications of failure to abate" with fines totaling $56.7 million. Each notification represents a penalty of $7,000 times 30 days, the period that the conditions have remained unabated. OSHA also identified 439 new willful violations for failures to follow industry-accepted controls on the pressure relief safety systems and other process safety management violations with penalties totaling $30.7 million.

"BP was given four years to correct the safety issues identified pursuant to the settlement agreement, yet OSHA has found hundreds of violations of the agreement and hundreds of new violations. BP still has a great deal of work to do to assure the safety and health of the employees who work at this refinery," said acting Assistant Secretary of Labor for OSHA Jordan Barab.

The BP Texas City Refinery is the third largest refinery in the United States with a refining capacity of 475,000 barrels of crude per day. It is located on a 1,200-acre facility in Texas City, southeast of Houston in Galveston County.

A willful violation exists where an employer has knowledge of a violation and demonstrates either an intentional disregard for the requirements of the Occupational Safety and Health (OSH) Act of 1970, or shows plain indifference to employee safety and health. A penalty of up to $70,000 may be assessed for each willful violation.

A notification of failure to abate can be issued if an employer fails to correct a cited condition and the citation is a final order of the Occupational Safety and Health Review Commission. A penalty of up to $7,000 may be assessed for each day that the violation remains uncorrected.

E. OSHA in Operation: The Death of a Wal-Mart Security Officer

In a tragic accident, a security officer working at a Wal-Mart store in New York was trampled to death on "Black Friday" (the day after Thanksgiving) in 2008. OSHA cited the store for a violation of the act's general duty clause, Section 5(a), which is quoted above. There is no standard for crowd control, and OSHA chose to issue a citation for the store's failure to address a recognized safety problem that could have been prevented. OSHA fined the store $7,000 for a serious violation. Wal-Mart litigated the case before the Occupational Safety and Health Review Commission (OSHRC). Administrative Law Judge Covette Rooney upheld the OSHA finding.[5]

Under OSHA's general duty clause, the agency must prove that the particular hazard was one that could cause serious injury or death, that the employer was aware of the hazard, and that it was a preventable one. As part of its evidence, OSHA argued that "during the 2008 Blitz Day Respondent's employees at the Store were exposed to 'struck by' hazards, including employees being struck by glass, doors and customers as a result of [Wal-Mart's] failure to take sufficient measures to protect its employees from crowd crush, crowd surge, or crowd trampling." Any measures the company did take were "completely inadequate" to protect employees against the crowd surge. Wal-Mart had actual knowledge of the hazard based on "the events that took place upon the opening of the Store's doors for the 2004, 2005, 2006 and 2007 Blitz Day events, including customers knocking doors off while entering and causing broken glass to fall on employees, customers falling and being injured, employees being pinned against the store so they could not move, employees being pushed and stepped on by customers." The events were documented by internal company communications and similar incidents at stores across the country. Wal-Mart could have dealt with the safety problem by various methods, including giving employees training to deal with crowd control as suggested by the company's own consultant. Those methods were effective, as proved by Wal-Mart's successful safety measures used in the 2009 Black Friday sales.[6]

According to the *New York Times,* Wal-Mart vigorously challenged the $7,000 fine and agency representatives claimed that "the company had spent more than $2 million on legal fees in the case. OSHA officials said federal employees had to devote more than 4,700 hours of legal work in response to Wal-Mart's effort to block the $7,000 fine." A Wal-Mart spokesman said the company planned to continue its appeal.[7] OSHA issued a press release in the case, reprinted here:

U.S. Department of Labor's OSHA Applauds Decision Upholding Citation against Wal-Mart Stores Inc. in Crowd-Management Fatality Case

WASHINGTON—The U.S. Department of Labor's Occupational Safety and Health Administration today applauded a ruling by Chief Administrative Law Judge Covette Rooney of the independent Occupational Safety and Health Review Commission upholding the citation and full penalty issued to Wal-Mart Stores Inc. for inadequate crowd management following a November 2008 trampling death of a worker at one of the company's retail locations in New York.

"This is a win for both workers and consumers. It's only fitting that today, the 100th anniversary of the deadly Triangle Shirtwaist Factory fire in New York City where 146 workers lost their lives, a judge affirmed OSHA's right to protect the safety and health of workers from clearly recognized hazards," said Assistant Secretary of Labor for Occupational Safety and Health Dr. David Michaels. "Today's ruling supports OSHA's position that, even in the absence of a specific rule or standard, employers are still legally responsible for providing a place of employment free of recognized hazards that are likely to cause serious injury or death. If not properly managed by retailers, a large crowd poses a significant threat to the lives of workers and customers."

In May 2009, OSHA cited Wal-Mart Stores Inc. for inadequate crowd management, concluding an investigation launched after a worker was trampled to death on Nov. 28, 2008, at a Wal-Mart store in Valley Stream, N.Y. The worker was knocked to the ground and crushed by a crowd of about 2,000 shoppers surging into the store for its annual "Blitz Friday" holiday sales event. OSHA's inspection found that the store's workers were at risk of being crushed by the crowd due to the store's failure to implement reasonable and effective crowd management practices. Those practices would have provided the store's workers with the necessary training and tools to safely manage a large crowd of shoppers.

Under the Occupational Safety and Health Act's general duty clause, OSHA issued Wal-Mart Stores Inc. one serious citation for exposing workers to the recognized hazards of asphyxiation or being crushed by a crowd. The citation carried a proposed fine of $7,000, the maximum penalty amount for a serious violation allowed under the law. A violation is serious when death or serious physical harm is likely to result from a hazard about which the employer knew or should have known.

"During the course of OSHA's investigation, the company implemented crowd control measures storewide, and the National Retail Federation also promoted those practices to its members," said Michaels. "We praise that action, and urge all retailers to implement crowd management practices ahead of future sales events likely to draw large crowds."

Wal-Mart Stores Inc. disputed the May 2009 OSHA citation before the OSHRC, an independent federal agency created to decide contests of citations or penalties resulting from inspections of American workplaces by OSHA. An employer who is cited by OSHA for an alleged workplace health or safety violation(s) can contest the citation(s) and have the case heard by a commission administrative law judge, who ultimately issues a decision. Wal-Mart Stores Inc. has 20 days from the date Rooney's decision is docketed with OSHRC to appeal to its commissioners, whose members are presidential appointees. *Source: http://www.oshrc.gov/foia/SecLabWalMart/09-1013_SecretaryPostTrialBrief_AppA.pdf*

F. No-Discrimination Clause

Section 11 of OSHA protects employees against retaliation for exercising their rights under OSHA. The statute provides:

> (1) No person shall discharge or in any manner discriminate against any employee because such employee has filed any complaint or instituted or caused to be instituted any proceeding under or related to this Act or has testified or is about to testify in any such proceeding or because of the exercise by such employee on behalf of himself or others of any right afforded by this Act.

One of the most controversial cases to arise under OSHA was decided by the U.S. Supreme Court in 1980. The case involved the Whirlpool Corporation, which manufactures household appliances. At its plant in Marion, Ohio, employees worked under a steel net, which protected them from falling objects as they were transported across the facility. Workers routinely walked out onto the netting to retrieve items that had fallen. Two employees were ordered to perform that job, but they objected because the screen was unsafe. In fact, employees had fallen through the mesh on previous occasions, and one employee died as a result of the fall. When they refused to perform the work, their supervisor instructed them to punch out and leave for the day. They were later issued written warnings for insubordination.

The Court ruled in *Whirlpool Corp. v. Marshall* (445 U.S. 1) that under a specific set of circumstances, employees might be protected in their refusal to perform work as directed and upheld an OSHA regulation to that effect. The Court noted that OSHA set forth a detailed scheme by which employees could bring a safety issue to the attention of their employer or to OSHA. In the Court's words:

> Upon receipt of an employee inspection request stating reasonable grounds to believe that an imminent danger is present in a workplace, OSHA must conduct an inspection. In the event this inspection reveals workplace conditions or practices that "could reasonably be expected to cause death or serious

> physical harm immediately or before the imminence of such danger can be eliminated through the enforcement procedures otherwise provided by" the Act, the OSHA inspector must inform the affected employees and the employer of the danger and notify them that he is recommending to the Secretary that injunctive relief be sought. At this juncture, the Secretary can petition a federal court to restrain the conditions or practices giving rise to the imminent danger. By means of a temporary restraining order or preliminary injunction, the court may then require the employer to avoid, correct, or remove the danger or to prohibit employees from working in the area.

Despite those general provisions, the Court recognized that a unique situation might arise in which the employee was "ordered by his employer to work under conditions that the employee reasonably believes pose an imminent risk of death or serious bodily injury, and the employee has reason to believe that there is not sufficient time or opportunity either to seek effective redress from his employer or to apprise OSHA of the danger." Where the employee exercised a good-faith refusal to submit to an imminent threat of death or serious injury, the employer could not take discriminatory action against the employee.

In its opinion, the Court conceded that Congress rejected a "strike with pay" provision in OSHA that would have required employers to pay workers who refused to perform unsafe work, but the employees in this case received no pay and were not entitled to it. Rather, the employer punished them for exercising their rights by putting a written warning in their records. The Court also discussed Congress's debate regarding a plant shutdown because of safety issues. This case, they wrote, did not involve a threatened OSHA closure of a place of business. Congress did not give OSHA such powers, and workers could not invoke the law to accomplish that same result. Consequently, the legislative history had little relevance to the given case.

The *Whirlpool* decision illustrates the scope of OSHA and the extent to which workers can engage in self-help to protect themselves. Where workers are represented by a union, the collective bargaining contract typically offers broader protections in matters of safety. Coal miners, for example, usually have rights to request a meeting with a safety officer and a union steward if the worker believes conditions are abnormally unsafe, but even those safeguards may not be sufficient. In April 2010, miners at the Upper Big Branch mine in Montcoal, West Virginia, encountered high levels of methane gas in their work area. The gas exploded, killing 25 miners. Massey Coal Company, which owned the site, took little notice of safety complaints, according to mine employees. One subcontractor said that "workers had regularly been told to work 12-hour shifts when eight hours is the industry standard. He also said that live wires had been left exposed and that an accumulation of coal dust and methane was routinely ignored."[8] Obviously, safety issues have not been eliminated from many workplaces.

G. Are the Benefits of OSHA Worth the Costs?

One of the important issues about public policy involves the assessment of risk. To evaluate policies, a cost-benefit analysis may provide useful information about how we deal with a problem. If, for example, we believe that human activity is driving climate change and such change will have negative consequences for the planet, how much should we spend to ameliorate the problem? The growing field of behavioral economics suggests that our cognitive filters influence the information we get from experts in the field.

By any reasonable standard, there is persuasive evidence of human impact on climate conditions. Despite that, there is also widespread disagreement whether we should limit the emissions of cars and coal plants through international agreements. People respond to the issues based on individualized views of the world. A current example is the way communities react to red-light cameras, which provide surveillance at intersections and result in traffic citations. There is evidence that those cameras reduce accidents, and particularly fatal accidents, but some citizens criticize them because they are too intrusive and represent another case of the "nanny state." The same analysis can be applied to OSHA.

Cass Sunstein, a well-known legal scholar, discussed this point in a paper that analyzed why public policy is distorted by common human misapprehensions about risk.[9] He pointed out, among a number of examples, that the OSHA standard dealing with procedures for safeguarding machines against being turned on while someone is working on them—the "lockout-tagout" standard—costs approximately $70.9 million for every premature death averted. Does the cost of preventing a single death justify the expenditure of $70 million? Sunstein goes on to discuss some of the obstacles to formulating good policy: "It is true but obvious to say that people lack information and that their lack of information can lead to an inadequate or excessive demand for regulation, or a form of 'paranoia and neglect.'" What is less obvious, he continues, is that the common distortions affecting risk perception often lead to laws that are not adequately based on fact. Because people have a tendency to exaggerate risks or to miscalculate the benefits of risk reduction, they impose poor choices on political leaders. Consequently, he concludes, "The government currently allocates its limited resources poorly, and it does so partly because it is responsive to ordinary judgments about the magnitude of risks. A government that could insulate itself from misinformed judgments could save tens of thousands of lives and tens of billions of dollars annually."

The debate over OSHA costs and benefits was brought into focus in 2011 debates about the federal budget. House Republicans proposed numerous cuts in the federal regulatory programs. Their justification was that excessive government spending needed to be curtailed, and federal intervention into workplaces simply added further costs to businesses. A story on National Public Radio in March 2011 reported, "Congressional Republicans are promising to scrub the government for what they say are 'job killing' regulations. One of their primary targets is the Occupational Safety and Health Administration, or OSHA."[10] Republicans initially tried to cut $61 billion from the overall budget, and OSHA was targeted for a reduction of $99 million. The rationale for the cuts was straightforward and consistent with criticisms of OSHA over the past 40 years. According to one Republican representative, "Over the last two years, OSHA has not only attempted to implement several policy changes that would have profound impact on the workplace; it has become an administration more focused on punishment than prevention." He asserted that OSHA's job is to prevent injuries, "not simply shame an employer once a tragedy has occurred on the job site."

Whether OSHA will be defunded at levels demanded by conservatives remains to be seen. If the 2012 elections result in a marked political shift either to the left or the right, OSHA's fate will hinge on that outcome. In any case, demands for less government spending and attempts to reduce the deficit require politicians to carefully consider how scarce resources are allocated. OSHA, meanwhile, continues to expand its efforts to adequately protect workers. The agency recently proposed guidelines to safeguard hearing loss by imposing obligations on employers to implement whatever steps are feasible in reducing noise. It announced, "Accordingly, OSHA now proposes to consider administrative or engineering controls economically feasible when the cost of implementing such controls will not threaten the employer's ability to remain in business, or if such a threat to viability results from the employer's failure to meet industry safety and health standards."[11] OSHA extended its deadline for comments until March 2011, after which the agency said it would review the feedback and consider further action. Some experts in the field of audiology supported the approach and argued that the United States is far behind other countries in noise controls.[12] The debate will certainly continue over regulation versus employment.

Questions

1. In the congressional debates on OSHA, one congressman said that there were more game wardens in the United States than workplace inspectors. Is that a convincing argument about the need for safety at work?
2. Consider the figure showing the operational structure of OSHA. Are there any ways to improve the design of the program?
3. Congress said that the purpose of the act was "to provide for the general welfare, to assure so far as possible every working man and woman in the Nation safe and healthful working conditions." Do you think this goal is stated too broadly? What should it say?
4. How does OSHA integrate activities of the states and the federal government? Why are states given an opportunity to create their own programs? Do you think states have an incentive to vigorously enforce safety and health laws?
5. Should Congress raise the amount of fines under OSHA? How much should they be?

6. Why is Wal-Mart pursuing its appeal of the OSHA citation in the security officer death case? Do you think Wal-Mart's strategy is a good or bad one, in terms of its corporate image?
7. Should OSHA's budget be reduced to help lower the deficit?

II. Will the United States Have a National Health Insurance Program?

The well-known Swedish furniture manufacturer, IKEA, has an international reputation for its products and employee-relations programs. It has expanded into global markets and maneuvered successfully through the 2008–2009 recession by a combination of low prices and quality furniture. When IKEA moved into the U.S. market, it opened a plant in Danville, Virginia. Residents of the area welcomed the company and anticipated there would be a number of good jobs available to the town's residents, which suffered from the loss of other manufacturing activity and high levels of unemployment. Unfortunately, IKEA turned out to be a low-wage, anti-union company like many of its American counterparts.

According to a story in the *Los Angeles Times*, IKEA received about $12 million in incentives to locate the plant in Danville.[13] The Americans make products identical to those made in Sweden, but, the report notes: "The big difference is that the Europeans enjoy a minimum wage of about $19 an hour and a government-mandated five weeks of paid vacation. Full-time employees in Danville start at $8 an hour with 12 vacation days—eight of them on dates determined by the company." IKEA also hires about one third of its workforce through temporary agencies, and pays lower wages and no benefits. When the Danville workers contacted the Machinists' union about an organizing drive, IKEA hired one of the most notorious anti-union law firms in the United States to combat the union effort. One of the union staff members remarked, "It's ironic that IKEA looks on the U.S. and Danville the way that most people in the U.S. look at Mexico." Perhaps most ironically, Europeans have a system of health care offered to all citizens, but Americans have yet to attain this basic entitlement.

Part of the explanation for the lack of a national health care program lies in the unique structure of American employment relations. As noted in earlier chapters of this book, America is "exceptional" in that many work-related benefits are negotiated between employees and their employer, rather than being part of a government system. Swedish workers at IKEA plants enjoy mandatory paid vacations, family leave with pay, generous unemployment benefits, and secure pension plans, along with guaranteed health care provided by national legislation. Famous political figures in the United States advocated similar laws, but those efforts failed to attract sufficient support. After his 1945 inauguration, for example, President Harry S. Truman launched a vigorous campaign for health insurance. According to the Truman Library, the plan "called for the creation of a national health insurance fund to be run by the federal government. This fund would be open to all Americans, but would remain optional. Participants would pay monthly fees into the plan, which would cover the cost of any and all medical expenses that arose in a time of need. The government would pay for the cost of services rendered by any doctor who chose to join the program. In addition, the insurance plan would give a cash balance to the policy holder to replace wages lost due to illness or injury."[14] Truman's proposal was attacked by the American Medical Association as a "Socialist" plan, and characterized Truman's staff as "followers of the Moscow party line."

On March 23, 2010, Congress passed the Patient Protection and Affordable Care Act (PPACA), a fulfillment of President Obama's campaign promise to enact a national health care system. The November 2010 elections led to a Republican majority in the House of Representatives, and many of the incoming representatives claimed that their election constituted a mandate to repeal "Obamacare," as they referred to the PPACA. House Republicans actually passed a repeal measure in January 2011, describing health care reform as a "job killer." An independent analysis rated this claim as "false."[15] Moreover, given the Democratic majority in the Senate and a Democratic president, the prospects for successful repeal before 2012 are little more than ideological theatrics. Opposition to the program, however, could undermine its effectiveness over the long term. What is clear is that the United States spends more on health care—about 16 percent of our gross domestic product—than any other nation, and costs are persistently above increases in the consumer price index. Health care expenditures are increasing globally as a result of greater longevity, advances in medical technology, and the economic downturn of 2008. The Organization for Economic Cooperation and Development (OECD) issued an excellent recent summary of those trends.[16]

The PPACA has provisions that become effective over a period of years. The official government Web site at healthcare.gov offers a good summary of what the bill contains and the effective dates.[17] A number of provisions have been implemented, including limits on insurers' ability to reject preexisting health conditions and rescind coverage for individuals. Future changes deal with affordability and access to health care, such as the formation of insurance exchanges to be implemented in January 2014. According to the Web site, "Starting in 2014 if your employer doesn't offer insurance, you will be able to buy insurance directly in an Exchange—a new transparent and competitive insurance marketplace where individuals and small businesses can buy affordable and qualified health benefit plans. Exchanges will offer you a choice of health plans that meet certain benefits and cost standards. Starting in 2014, Members of Congress will be getting their health care insurance through Exchanges, and you will be able to buy your insurance through Exchanges too."

If the Obama plan withstands attacks from its conservative opponents, it will profoundly affect U.S. employment relations. No longer will workers seek out jobs because they offer health insurance, and employers will no longer compete on a tilted playing field that favors large firms and attractive worker demographics that reduce insurance risk. Likewise, global corporations such as IKEA will not engage in a race to the bottom by locating in a country where the provision of health insurance is just another optional cost of doing business.

Questions

1. Should the U.S. Congress simply extend Medicare to all Americans? Should it be funded the same way that it is funded under Social Security?
2. How can a country like Sweden afford a national health care system for its citizens, but the United States cannot? Which country spends more in terms of gross domestic product on health care? Why is that?
3. Which parts of the PPACA are the most objectionable? Least objectionable?
4. Congressman Paul Ryan (R, WI) was hailed as a visionary thinker for his proposed budget in early 2011. Democrats attacked the plan as a repeal of Medicare. In a special election in May 2011, a Democrat won in a traditionally Republican district in upstate New York by focusing on the Medicare issue. Does this example suggest that most Americans want a national health care program, as opposed to private insurance? What is your opinion on that issue, and why?

Suggested Exercises

1. Research BP's safety record and write a paper about it, including the drilling rig incident in the Gulf. Conclude by recommending what OSHA could effectively do to regulate companies like BP.
2. Research the OSHA standard on musculoskeletal work disorders that was signed into law by President Clinton. Write a report describing what the standard was designed to do, how it accomplished its objectives, and what happened to it. Discuss the politics of the standard, and evaluate the issue in terms of policy.
3. Engage in a debate about OSHA. The proposition for debate should be, "OSHA does not generate benefits that justify its costs."
4. Prepare a presentation on the health care bill passed in 2010. Describe its main features and dates of implementation. Include in the presentation an evaluation of the political implications of the legislation for Republicans and Democrats.
5. Research the background of national health care proposals in this country, beginning with the Truman administration. Write an argumentative essay taking a position either in favor of a national program or opposed to it. Use historical examples to support your position.

Notes

1. http://ehstoday.com/standards/concensus/asse-osha-consensus-slips-falls-rule-7766/
2. http://ohsonline.com/blogs/the-ohs-wire/2010/10/is-osha-killing-the-american-dream.aspx

3. The information in this section is drawn from the OSHA Fact Sheet describing the inspection and citation process. It is posted http://www.osha.gov/OshDoc/data_General_Facts/factsheet-inspections.pdf
4. The document is available at the following site: http://www.osha.gov/pls/oshaweb/owadisp.show_document?p_table=NEWS_RELEASES&p_id=16674
5. OSHA issued a press release in the case, available at the following site: http://www.osha.gov/pls/oshaweb/owadisp.show_document?p_table=NEWS_RELEASES&p_id=19500
6. For a collection of documents in the case, see http://www.oshrc.gov/foia/SecLabWalMart/09-1013_SecretaryPostTrialBrief_AppA.pdf
7. Steven Greenhouse, Judge Upholds $7,000 Fine in Trampling at Wal-Mart. *New York Times*, March 25, 2011. Online: http://www.nytimes.com/2011/03/26/business/26osha.html
8. Ian Urbina and Michael Cooper, "Deaths at West Virginia Mine Raise Issues About Safety," *New York Times*, April 7, 2010, p. A1.
9. Cass R. Sunstein, Cognition and Cost-Benefit Analysis, John M. Olin Law and Economics Working Paper no. 85, 2nd series, University of Chicago, available online at http://papers.ssrn.com/sol3/search.taf
10. Brian Naylor, "OSHA Budget Cut Plan Spotlights Regulatory Debate," National Public Radio, March 1, 2011. Online at http://www.npr.org/2011/03/01/134177079/GOP-Looks-To-Make-Cuts-At-OSHA
11. The text of the document is on the OSHA Web site at: http://www.osha.gov/pls/oshaweb/owadisp.show_document?p_table=FEDERAL_REGISTER&p_id=21857
12. See, for example, the blog posting on the American Speech-Language-Hearing Association Web site at http://blog.asha.org/2011/03/08/osha-policies-on-noise-control-and-what-you-can-do-to-help/
13. Nathaniel Popper, "IKEA's U.S. factory churns out unhappy workers," *Los Angeles Times*, April 10, 2011. Online: http://articles.latimes.com/2011/apr/10/business/la-fi-ikea-union-20110410/2.
14. Harry S. Truman Library, http://www.trumanlibrary.org/anniversaries/healthprogram.htm.
15. Politicfact.com, http://www.politifact.com/truth-o-meter/statements/2011/jan/20/eric-cantor/health-care-law-job-killer-evidence-falls-short/
16. For a report, see Organization for Economic Cooperation and Development (OECD), at http://www.oecd.org/document/11/0,3746,en_21571361_44315115_45549771_1_1_1_1,00.html
17. http://www.healthcare.gov/law/timeline/index.html

4. Civil Rights Laws and Unlawful Discrimination against Employees

I. Introduction

In April 2011 a Republican Party committee member in Orange County, California, distributed an e-mail that contained a family photo showing President Barack Obama as the offspring of two apes. The picture was captioned, "Now you know why no birth certificate." The party operative, Marilyn Davenport, denied that it had any racist implications. She said, "In no way did I even consider the fact he's half black when I sent out the e-mail. In fact, the thought never entered my mind until one or two other people tried to make this about race."[1] A blogger who wrote about this incident disagreed and observed: "President Obama has received far more death threats than any president before him, the Republicans have made it their mission in life to obstruct anything he tries to do, he's received a level of hatred and animosity that seems to accuse him of working to destroy the free world, and no one seems to think there's anything odd about this."[2]

Should a cartoon depicting an African American as an ape be considered racist? Winthrop Jordan, the leading historian on the subject of white cultural attitudes toward blacks, published a 1968 study that comprehensively analyzes the ways in which whites created a social and legal apparatus to justify the system of slavery. One of his chapters is titled "The Bodies of Men," and it examines the treatment of Africans in terms of physical differences. On the one hand, Christians believed that the "great chain of being" categorically differentiated humans above all animals. At the same time, classifying Africans as closer to apes made it possible to reduce the cognitive dissonance that permeated slavery. In a poignant description, Jordan offers this explanation:

> Even in an age thoroughly accustomed to the hovering omnipresence of early death, the enormous toll of Negro life must have caused many white men to withdraw in silent horror, to refuse to admit identity with a people they were methodically slaughtering year after year. The cruelties of slavery inevitably produced a sense of disassociation. To the horrified witness of a scene of torture, the victim becomes a "poor devil," a "mangled creature. He is no longer a man. He can no longer be human because to credit him with one's own human attributes would be too horrible."[3]

By reducing blacks to a "lower order," whites could rationalize the injustice and indignity that necessarily accompanied enslavement and ownership of other human beings. So, by depicting a U.S. president as an ape, Obama's political opponents can simultaneously degrade his presidency and undermine his legitimacy. The e-mail photo is reprinted on numerous Web sites; you can judge the picture for yourself.[4] You can also reach your own conclusions about whether we have arrived at a "post-racial" society.

A related development adds to the discussion about race. During his publicity campaign touting himself as a possible presidential candidate in early 2011, Donald Trump made Obama's American citizenship (or asserted lack of it) the centerpiece of his platform. Critics accused Trump of legitimizing the "birther" wing of the conservative movement, thereby adding further racist elements to our political system. Trump maintained that he had investigators on location in Hawaii to provide evidence in support of his position, but, in fact, President Obama produced the "long form" of his birth certificate in a nationally televised news conference. When Trump subsequently dropped out of the race to pursue his television program, his political career ended for the moment. If someone like Donald Trump can so conveniently and successfully depict a U.S. president as some kind of "foreign" operative, it speaks volumes about our society.

Adding to racial friction, one of the interesting turns in antidiscrimination law involves the phenomenon of "reverse discrimination," where an innocent third party is injured by an attempt to overcome the effects of discrimination. The U.S. Supreme Court in 2009 decided that the City of New Haven had intentionally discriminated against a white firefighter when it refused to promote him, even though he had the top score on a qualifying exam. The New Haven city council concluded that the test had a disparate impact on black candidates, and it therefore rejected the test as a criterion for advancement.[5] The Court's decision rejecting the city council's efforts was only the latest ambiguous pronouncement on an issue that is now more than three decades old. Justice Thurgood Marshall, who was the first African American appointed to the Supreme Court, wrote a concurring opinion in the 1978 case of *Bakke v. Regents of the University of Californ*ia summarizing the history of race relations in this country.[6] His opinion offers a succinct account of how law, politics, and social mores interacted to the disadvantage of blacks in this country and justified the practice of giving some groups preferential treatment to remedy past inequalities. Here is part of his opinion. It is a trenchant summary of race relations in this country.

MR. JUSTICE MARSHALL

> I agree with the judgment of the Court only insofar as it permits a university to consider the race of an applicant in making admissions decisions. I do not agree that petitioner's admissions program violates the Constitution. For it must be remembered that, during most of the past 200 years, the Constitution, as interpreted by this Court, did not prohibit the most ingenious and pervasive forms of discrimination against the Negro. Now, when a State acts to remedy the effects of that legacy of discrimination, I cannot believe that this same Constitution stands as a barrier.
>
> Three hundred and fifty years ago, the Negro was dragged to this country in chains to be sold into slavery. Uprooted from his homeland and thrust into bondage for forced labor, the slave was deprived of all legal rights. It was unlawful to teach him to read; he could be sold away from his family and friends at the whim of his master; and killing or maiming him was not a crime. The system of slavery brutalized and dehumanized both master and slave.
>
> The denial of human rights was etched into the American Colonies' first attempts at establishing self-government. When the colonists determined to seek their independence from England, they drafted a unique document cataloguing their grievances against the King and proclaiming as 'self-evident' that 'all men are created equal' and are endowed 'with certain unalienable Rights,' including those to 'Life, Liberty and the pursuit of Happiness.' The self-evident truths and the unalienable rights were intended, however, to apply only to white men. An earlier draft of the Declaration of Independence, submitted by Thomas Jefferson to the Continental Congress, had included among the charges against the King that '[h]e has waged cruel war against human nature itself, violating its most sacred rights of life and liberty in the persons of a distant people who never offended him, captivating and carrying them into slavery in another hemisphere, or to incur miserable death in their transportation thither.'
>
> The Southern delegation insisted that the charge be deleted; the colonists themselves were implicated in the slave trade, and inclusion of this claim might have made it more difficult to justify the continuation of slavery once the ties to England were severed. Thus, even as the colonists embarked on a course to secure their own freedom and equality, they ensured perpetuation of the system that deprived a whole race of those rights.
>
> The implicit protection of slavery embodied in the Declaration of Independence was made explicit in the Constitution, which treated a slave as being equivalent to three-fifths of a person for purposes of apportioning

representatives and taxes among the States. Art. I, § 2. The Constitution also contained a clause ensuring that the 'Migration or Importation' of slaves into the existing States would be legal until at least 1808, Art. I, § 9, and a fugitive slave clause requiring that, when a slave escaped to another State, he must be returned on the claim of the master, Art. IV, § 2. In their declaration of the principles that were to provide the cornerstone of the new Nation, therefore, the Framers made it plain that 'we the people,' for whose protection the Constitution was designed, did not include those whose skins were the wrong color. As Professor John Hope Franklin has observed, Americans 'proudly accepted the challenge and responsibility of their new political freedom by establishing the machinery and safeguards that insured the continued enslavement of blacks.'

The individual States likewise established the machinery to protect the system of slavery through the promulgation of the Slave Codes, which were designed primarily to defend the property interest of the owner in his slave. The position of the Negro slave as mere property was confirmed by this Court in *Dred Scott v. Sanford,* 19 How. 393 (1857), holding that the Missouri Compromise—which prohibited slavery in the portion of the Louisiana Purchase Territory north of Missouri—was unconstitutional because it deprived slave owners of their property without due process. The Court declared that, under the Constitution, a slave was property, and '[t]he right to traffic in it, like an ordinary article of merchandise and property, was guaranteed to the citizens of the United States. …' The Court further concluded that Negroes were not intended to be included as citizens under the Constitution, but were 'regarded as beings of an inferior order … altogether unfit to associate with the white race, either in social or political relations; and so far inferior that they had no rights which the white man was bound to respect. …'

The status of the Negro as property was officially erased by his emancipation at the end of the Civil War. But the long-awaited emancipation, while freeing the Negro from slavery, did not bring him citizenship or equality in any meaningful way. Slavery was replaced by a system of 'laws which imposed upon the colored race onerous disabilities and burdens, and curtailed their rights in the pursuit of life, liberty, and property to such an extent that their freedom was of little value.' *Slaughter-House Cases,* 16 Wall. 36, 70 (1873). Despite the passage of the Thirteenth, Fourteenth, and Fifteenth Amendments, the Negro was systematically denied the rights those Amendments were supposed to secure. The combined actions and inactions of the State and Federal Governments maintained Negroes in a position of legal inferiority for another century after the Civil War.

The Southern States took the first steps to re-enslave the Negroes. Immediately following the end of the Civil War, many of the provisional legislatures passed Black Codes, similar to the Slave Codes, which, among other things, limited the rights of Negroes to own or rent property and permitted imprisonment for breach of employment contracts. Over the next several decades, the South managed to disenfranchise the Negroes in spite of the Fifteenth Amendment by various techniques, including poll taxes, deliberately complicated balloting processes, property and literacy qualifications, and, finally, the white primary.

Congress responded to the legal disabilities being imposed in the Southern States by passing the Reconstruction Acts and the Civil Rights Acts. Congress also responded to the needs of the Negroes at the end of the Civil War by establishing the Bureau of Refugees, Freedmen, and Abandoned Lands, better known as the Freedmen's Bureau, to supply food, hospitals, land, and education to the newly freed slaves. Thus, for a time, it seemed as if the Negro might be protected from the continued denial of his civil rights, and might be relieved of the disabilities that prevented him from taking his place as a free and equal citizen. That time, however, was short-lived. Reconstruction came to a close, and, with the assistance of this Court, the Negro was rapidly stripped of his new civil rights. In the words of C. Vann Woodward, 'By narrow and ingenious interpretation [the Supreme Court's] decisions over a period of years had whittled away a great part of the authority presumably given the government for protection of civil rights.'

The Court began by interpreting the Civil War Amendments in a manner that sharply curtailed their substantive protections. *See, e.g., Slaughter-House Cases, supra; United States v. Reese,* 92 U.S. 214 (1876); *United States v. Cruikshank,* 92 U.S. 542 (1876). Then, in the notorious *Civil Rights Cases,* 109 U.S. 3 (1883), the Court strangled Congress' efforts to use its power to promote racial equality. In those cases, the Court invalidated sections of the Civil Rights Act of 1875 that made it a crime to deny equal access to 'inns, public conveyances, theatres and other places of public amusement.' According to the Court, the Fourteenth Amendment gave Congress the power to proscribe only discriminatory action by the State. The Court ruled that the Negroes who were excluded from public places suffered only an invasion of their social rights at the hands of private individuals, and Congress had no power to remedy that. 'When a man has emerged from slavery, and, by the aid of beneficent legislation, has shaken off the inseparable concomitants of that state,' the Court concluded, 'there must be some stage in the progress of his elevation when he takes the rank of a mere citizen, and ceases to be the special favorite of the laws. ...' As Mr. Justice Harlan noted in dissent, however, the Civil War Amendments and Civil Rights Acts did not make the Negroes the 'special favorite' of the laws, but instead 'sought to accomplish in reference to that race ...—what had already been done in every State of the Union for the white race—to secure and protect rights belonging to them as freemen and citizens; nothing more.'

The Court's ultimate blow to the Civil War Amendments and to the equality of Negroes came in *Plessy v. Ferguson,* 163 U.S. 537 (1896). In upholding a Louisiana law that required railway companies to provide 'equal but separate' accommodations for whites and Negroes, the Court held that the Fourteenth Amendment was not intended 'to abolish distinctions based upon color, or to enforce social, as distinguished from political, equality, or a commingling of the two races upon terms unsatisfactory to either.' Ignoring totally the realities of the positions of the two races, the Court remarked: 'We consider the underlying fallacy of the plaintiff's argument to consist in the assumption that the enforced separation of the two races stamps the colored race with a badge of inferiority. If this be so, it is not by reason of anything found in the act, but solely because the colored race chooses to put that construction upon it.'

Mr. Justice Harlan's dissenting opinion recognized the bankruptcy of the Court's reasoning. He noted that the 'real meaning' of the legislation was 'that colored citizens are so inferior and degraded that they cannot be allowed to sit in public coaches occupied by white citizens.' He expressed his fear that, if like laws were enacted in other States, 'the effect would be in the highest degree mischievous.' Although slavery would have disappeared, the States would retain the power 'to interfere with the full enjoyment of the blessings of freedom; to regulate civil rights, common to all citizens, upon the basis of race; and to place in a condition of legal inferiority a large body of American citizens. ...'

The fears of Mr. Justice Harlan were soon to be realized. In the wake of *Plessy*, many States expanded their Jim Crow laws, which had, up until that time, been limited primarily to passenger trains and schools. The segregation of the races was extended to residential areas, parks, hospitals, theaters, waiting rooms, and bathrooms. There were even statutes and ordinances which authorized separate phone booths for Negroes and whites, which required that textbooks used by children of one race be kept separate from those used by the other, and which required that Negro and white prostitutes be kept in separate districts. In 1898, after *Plessy,* the Charlestown News and Courier printed a parody of Jim Crow laws: 'If there must be Jim Crow cars on the railroads, there should be Jim Crow cars on the street railways. Also on all passenger boats. ... If there are to be Jim Crow cars, moreover, there should be Jim Crow waiting saloons at all stations, and Jim Crow eating houses. ... There should be Jim Crow sections of the jury box, and a separate Jim Crow dock and witness stand in every court—and a Jim Crow Bible for colored witnesses to kiss.' The irony is that, before many years had passed, with the exception of the Jim Crow witness stand, 'all the improbable applications of the principle suggested by the editor in derision had been put into practice—down to and including the Jim Crow Bible.'

Nor were the laws restricting the rights of Negroes limited solely to the Southern States. In many of the Northern States, the Negro was denied the right to vote, prevented from serving on juries, and excluded from theaters, restaurants, hotels, and inns. Under President Wilson, the Federal Government began to require segregation in Government buildings; desks of Negro employees were curtained off; separate bathrooms and separate tables in the cafeterias were provided; and even the galleries of the Congress were segregated. When his segregationist policies were attacked, President Wilson responded that segregation was 'not humiliating, but a benefit,' and that he was 'rendering [the Negroes] more safe in their possession of office, and less likely to be discriminated against.'

The enforced segregation of the races continued into the middle of the 20th century. In both World Wars, Negroes were, for the most part, confined to separate military units; it was not until 1948 that an end to segregation in the military was ordered by President Truman. And the history of the exclusion of Negro children from white public schools is too well known and recent to require repeating here. That Negroes were deliberately excluded from public graduate and professional schools—and thereby denied the opportunity to become doctors, lawyers, engineers, and the like is also well established. It is, of course, true that some of the Jim Crow laws (which the decisions of this Court had helped to foster) were struck down by this Court in a series of decisions leading up to *Brown v. Board of Education*, 347 U.S. 483 (1954). *See, e.g., Morgan v. Virginia*, 328 U.S. 373 (1946); *Sweatt v. Painter*, 339 U.S. 629 (1950); *McLaurin v. Oklahoma State Regents*, 339 U.S. 637 (1950). Those decisions, however, did not automatically end segregation, nor did they move Negroes from a position of legal inferiority to one of equality. The legacy of years of slavery and of years of second-class citizenship in the wake of emancipation could not be so easily eliminated.

II

The position of the Negro today in America is the tragic but inevitable consequence of centuries of unequal treatment. Measured by any benchmark of comfort or achievement, meaningful equality remains a distant dream for the Negro. [Justice Marshall cites various statistics to support his point.]

III

I do not believe that the Fourteenth Amendment requires us to accept that fate. Neither its history nor our past cases lend any support to the conclusion that a university may not remedy the cumulative effects of society's discrimination by giving consideration to race in an effort to increase the number and percentage of Negro doctors.

A

This Court long ago remarked that 'in any fair and just construction of any section or phrase of these [Civil War] amendments, it is necessary to look to the purpose which we have said was the pervading spirit of them all, the evil which they were designed to remedy. ...' *Slaughter-House Cases*, 16 Wall. at 72. It is plain that the Fourteenth Amendment was not intended to prohibit measures designed to remedy the effects of the Nation's past treatment of Negroes. The Congress that passed the Fourteenth Amendment is the same Congress that passed the 1866 Freedmen's Bureau Act, an Act that provided many of its benefits only to Negroes. Although the Freedmen's Bureau legislation provided aid for refugees, thereby including white persons within some of the relief measures, the bill was regarded, to the dismay of many Congressmen, as 'solely and entirely for the freedmen, and to the exclusion of all other persons. ...' Cong.Globe, 39th Cong., 1st Sess., 544 (1866) (Indeed, the bill was bitterly opposed on the ground that it 'undertakes to make the negro in some respects ... superior ..., and gives them favors that the poor white boy in the North cannot get' (remarks of Sen. McDougall). The bill's supporters defended it not by rebutting the claim of special treatment, but by pointing to the need for such treatment: 'The very discrimination it makes between "destitute and suffering" negroes and destitute and suffering white paupers proceeds upon the distinction that, in the omitted case, civil rights and immunities are already sufficiently protected by the possession of political power, the absence of which in the case provided for necessitates governmental protection.' (remarks of Rep. Phelps).

Despite the objection to the special treatment the bill would provide for Negroes, it was passed by Congress. President [Andrew] Johnson vetoed this bill, and also a subsequent bill that contained some modifications; one of his principal objections to both bills was that they gave special benefits to Negroes. Rejecting the concerns of the President and the bill's opponents, Congress overrode the President's second veto. Cong.Globe, 39th Cong., 1st Sess., 3842, 3850 (1866).

Since the Congress that considered and rejected the objections to the 1866 Freedmen's Bureau Act concerning special relief to Negroes also proposed the Fourteenth Amendment, it is inconceivable that the Fourteenth Amendment was intended to prohibit all race-conscious relief measures. It 'would be a distortion of the policy manifested in that amendment, which was adopted to prevent state legislation designed to perpetuate discrimination on the basis of race or color,' *Railway Mail Assn. v. Corsi*, 326 U.S. 88, 94 (1945), to hold that it barred state action to remedy the effects of that discrimination. Such a result would pervert the intent of the Framers by substituting abstract equality for the genuine equality the Amendment was intended to achieve.

IV

While I applaud the judgment of the Court that a university may consider race in its admissions process, it is more than a little ironic that, after several hundred years of class-based discrimination against Negroes, the Court is unwilling to hold that a class-based remedy for that discrimination is permissible. In declining to so hold, today's judgment ignores the fact that for several hundred years, Negroes have been discriminated against not as individuals, but rather solely because of the color of their skins. It is unnecessary in 20th-century America to have individual Negroes demonstrate that they have been victims of racial discrimination; the racism of our society has been so pervasive that none, regardless of wealth or position, has managed to escape its impact. The experience of Negroes in America has been different in kind, not just in degree, from that of other ethnic groups. It is not merely the history of slavery alone, but also that a whole people were marked as inferior by the law. And that mark has endured. The dream of America as the great melting pot has not been realized for the Negro; because of his skin color, he never even made it into the pot.

These differences in the experience of the Negro make it difficult for me to accept that Negroes cannot be afforded greater protection under the Fourteenth Amendment where it is necessary to remedy the effects of past discrimination. In the *Civil Rights Cases, supra*, the Court wrote that the Negro emerging from slavery must cease 'to be the special favorite of the laws.' 109 U.S. at 25. We cannot, in light of the history of the last century, yield to that view. Had the Court, in that decision and others, been willing to 'do for human liberty and the fundamental rights of American citizenship what it did … for the protection of slavery and the rights of the masters of fugitive slaves,' 109 U.S. at 53 (Harlan, J., dissenting), we would not need now to permit the recognition of any 'special wards.'

Most importantly, had the Court been willing in 1896, in *Plessy v. Ferguson*, to hold that the Equal Protection Clause forbids differences in treatment based on race, we would not be faced with this dilemma in 1978. We must remember, however, that the principle that the 'Constitution is colorblind' appeared only in the opinion of the lone dissenter. The majority of the Court rejected the principle of color blindness, and for the next 60 years, from *Plessy* to *Brown v. Board of Education*, ours was a Nation where, by law, an individual could be given 'special' treatment based on the color of his skin.

It is because of a legacy of unequal treatment that we now must permit the institutions of this society to give consideration to race in making decisions about who will hold the positions of influence, affluence, and prestige in America. For far too long, the doors to those positions have been shut to Negroes. If we are ever to become a fully integrated society, one in which the color of a person's skin will not determine the opportunities available to him or her, we must be willing to take steps to open those doors. I do not believe that anyone can truly look into America's past and still find that a remedy for the effects of that past is impermissible.

It has been said that this case involves only the individual, Bakke, and this University. I doubt, however, that there is a computer capable of determining the number of persons and institutions that may be affected by the decision in this case. For example, we are told by the Attorney General of the United States that at least 27 federal agencies have adopted regulations requiring recipients of federal funds to take '*affirmative action* to overcome the effects of conditions which resulted in limiting participation ... by persons of a particular race, color, or national origin.' I cannot even guess the number of state and local governments that have set up affirmative action programs, which may be affected by today's decision.

I fear that we have come full circle. After the Civil War, our Government started several 'affirmative action' programs. This Court, in the *Civil Rights Cases* and *Plessy v. Ferguson*, destroyed the movement toward complete equality. For almost a century, no action was taken, and this nonaction was with the tacit approval of the courts. Then we had *Brown v. Board of Education* and the Civil Rights Acts of Congress, followed by numerous affirmative action programs. Now, we have this Court again stepping in, this time to stop affirmative action programs of the type used by the University of California."

Justice Marshall cited data concerning racial disparities in employment and earnings. In March 2011, as the effects of the Great Recession still lingered, the percentage unemployment rate by race, age, and gender is shown in the following chart:

Figure 1. Unemployment Rates

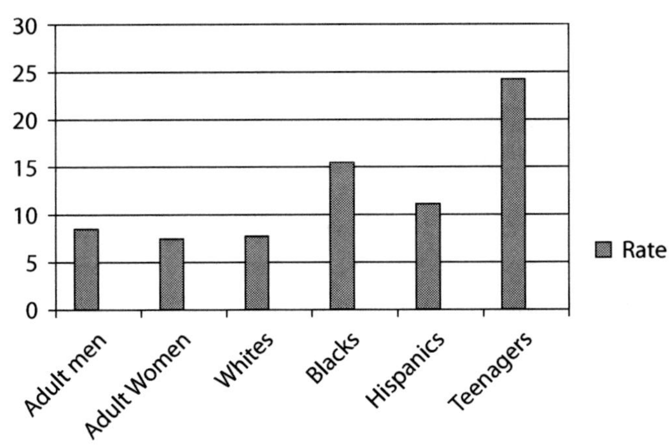

Differences in income show similar disparities, with white men earning more than women and racial minorities.[7] As Justice Marshall argued, racial differences in our economy and society have hardly disappeared.

Questions

1. What was the holding in the *Dred Scott* case? What part of the Constitution did the case interpret? Does Justice Marshall say the Court's decision was wrong in that case?
2. What was the holding in the *Civil Rights Cases*? Was that case right or wrong? Has the case been overruled?
3. What was the holding in *Plessy v. Ferguson*? How did that case affect race relations in this country?
4. Why does Justice Marshall think it is "inconceivable" that the Fourteenth Amendment would prevent preferential treatment for African Americans? In a recent case, Justice Clarence Thomas said that preferential treatment serves to "stigmatize" blacks. How do you think Justice Marshall would respond to that statement?
5. Do you think President Obama got preferential treatment at the Harvard Law School when he was elected editor of the law review there? Do you think former president George W. Bush got preferential treatment when he was admitted to Yale? (His father, George H. Bush, graduated from the school.)
6. Should any "innocent" individual in this country be forced to give up some right to make up for past discrimination against a race? If so, under what circumstances?

II. The Civil Rights Acts of 1964 and 1991

As a result of the civil rights movement of the early 1960s led by Martin Luther King Jr. and others, Congress enacted legislation in 1964 to outlaw the practice of segregation condoned under *Plessy v. Ferguson*. The campaign started under President John Kennedy, who was elected in 1960. After Kennedy's assassination in 1963, President Lyndon Johnson continued the drive. Johnson was particularly effective in gaining congressional support for the bill, despite the opposition of Southern legislators, and he signed it into law on July 2, 1964. The law very broadly prohibited discrimination on the basis of race and other factors in housing, accommodation, and employment. The section of the bill affecting employment is set out in Title VII of the act. For that reason, the prohibition against discrimination in the workplace is sometimes referred to simply as "Title VII."

As with the earlier civil rights laws, the United States Supreme Court has played an important role in interpreting Title VII. Several early decisions created rules about race discrimination that still apply today; those decisions will be taken up in more detail below. In its 1989 term, the Court decided six cases that dramatically altered the scope and effect of Title VII. Those decisions were so bizarre that Congress swiftly acted to overrule them. The result was a set of amendments to Title VII known as the Civil Rights Act of 1991. While it was engaged in correcting the Court's spurt of irrationality, Congress went on to strengthen some parts of the law and to add additional protections. The result is the current set of rules governing relations of race, gender, religion, age, and disabilities in the workplace. The table below summarizes the development of the law between 1964 and 2008.

Legislation	Summary of Provisions
Title VII, Civil Rights Act of 1964	Illegal to discriminate against someone on the basis of race, color, religion, national origin, or sex.
Age Discrimination in Employment Act, 1967	Unlawful to fail or refuse to hire or to discharge any individual or otherwise discriminate against any individual with respect to his compensation, terms, conditions, or privileges of employment, because of such individual's age.
Civil Rights Act of 1991	Amends Title VII and the ADA to permit jury trials and compensatory and punitive damage awards in intentional discrimination cases; caps damage amounts by size of firm.
Americans with Disabilities Act of 1992	Illegal to discriminate against a qualified person with a disability in the private sector and in state and local governments; also requires that employers reasonably accommodate the known physical or mental limitations of an otherwise qualified individual with a disability who is an applicant or employee, unless doing so would impose an undue hardship on the operation of the employer's business.
The Genetic Information Nondiscrimination Act of 2008	Prohibits discrimination on the basis of genetic information, with respect to health insurance and employment.

A. Coverage and Claim Procedures

Whether or not an employer falls under the various laws enforced by the EEOC depends on the specific statutory regulation. As a general rule for private businesses, a complaint that involves "race, color, religion, sex (including pregnancy), national origin, age (40 or older), disability or genetic information, the business is covered by the laws we enforce if it has 15 or more employees who worked for the employer for at least twenty calendar weeks (in this year or last)." State and local governmental entities are covered if they have 15 employees, and all employees of the federal government are covered.

The first step in bringing a claim of discrimination is to file a complaint with the Equal Employment Opportunity Commission (EEOC), which is responsible for administering the laws summarized above, and, as noted in a previous chapter, the Equal Pay Act. Filing with the EEOC is necessary to have a claim heard in court, because Congress wanted the federal agency to resolve issues, if possible, before an individual filed a lawsuit. Here is the EEOC statement on how to file a claim:

> You may file a charge of employment discrimination at the EEOC office closest to where you live, or at any one of the EEOC's 53 field offices (http://www.eeoc.gov/field/index.cfm.). Your charge, however, may be investigated at the EEOC office closest to where the discrimination occurred. If you are a U.S. citizen working for an American company overseas, you should file your charge with the EEOC field office closest to your employer's corporate headquarters.
>
> Where the discrimination took place can determine how long you have to file a charge. The 180 calendar day filing deadline is extended to 300 calendar days if a state or local agency enforces a state **or** local law that prohibits employment discrimination on the same basis. The rules are slightly different for age discrimination charges. For age discrimination, the filing deadline is only extended to 300 days if there is a **state** law prohibiting age discrimination in employment and a state agency or authority enforcing that law. The deadline is **not** extended if **only** a local law prohibits age discrimination.
>
> Many states and localities have agencies that enforce laws prohibiting employment discrimination. EEOC refers to these agencies as Fair Employment Practices Agencies (FEPAs). EEOC and some FEPAs have worksharing agreements in place to prevent the duplication of effort in charge processing. According to these agreements, if you file a charge with either EEOC or a FEPA, the charge also will be automatically filed with the other agency. This process, which is defined as dual filing, helps to protect charging party rights under both federal and state or local law.

The EEOC requires that a charge be filed either in person or by mail. The agency will not accept electronic filing of charges, but it does have information online that will assist employees in deciding if their issue belongs with the EEOC. The link is at https://egov.eeoc.gov/eas/. For filings in person, the individual can contact one of the EEOC offices. Workers can also contact the EEOC by telephone for further assistance with charges. If filing by mail is preferred, the EEOC requires the following information:

- Your name, address, and telephone number
- The name, address, and telephone number of the employer (or employment agency or union) you want to file your charge against
- The number of employees employed there (if known)
- A short description of the events you believe were discriminatory (for example, you were fired, demoted, harassed)
- When the events took place
- Why you believe you were discriminated against: for example, because of your race, color, religion, sex (including pregnancy), national origin, age (40 or older), disability, or genetic information
- Your signature

Once a charge is filed, the EEOC may suggest mediation of the dispute. The agency describes mediation as an impartial process that benefits all parties. According to the EEOC Web site, "The decision to mediate is completely voluntary. If either party turns down mediation, the charge will be forwarded to an investigator. If both parties agree to mediate, we will schedule a mediation, which will be conducted by a trained and experienced mediator. If the parties do not reach an agreement at the mediation, the charge will be investigated like any other charge. A written signed agreement reached during mediation is enforceable in court just like any other contract." Among other benefits, a resolution may be reached in a fairly short time compared to an investigation and decision.

As noted, filing a charge is generally a requirement for getting into a court. The EEOC explains the law as follows:[8]

> If you plan to file a lawsuit alleging discrimination on the basis of race, color, religion, sex (including pregnancy), national origin, age (40 or older), disability, genetic information, or retaliation, you first have to file a charge with one of our field offices (unless you plan to bring your lawsuit under the Equal Pay Act, which allows you to go directly to court without filing a charge). We will give you what is called a "Notice-of-Right-to-Sue" at the time we dismiss your charge, usually, after completion of an investigation. However, we may dismiss for other reasons, including failure to cooperate in an investigation. This notice gives you permission to file a lawsuit in a court of law. Once you receive a Notice-of-Right-to-Sue, you must file your lawsuit within 90 days.
>
> If you plan to file an age discrimination lawsuit, you won't need a Notice of Right-to-Sue to file in court. You can file any time after 60 days have passed from the day you filed your charge (but no later than 90 days after you receive notice that our investigation is concluded). If you plan to file a lawsuit under the Equal Pay Act, you don't have to file a charge or obtain a Notice of Right-to-Sue before filing. Rather, you can go directly to court, provided you file

your suit within two years from the day the discrimination took place (3 years if the discrimination was willful).

Keep in mind, though, Title VII also makes it illegal to discriminate based on sex in the payment of wages and benefits. If you have an Equal Pay Act claim, there may be advantages to also filing under Title VII. In order to pursue a Title VII claim in court, you must have filed a charge with EEOC and received a Notice of Right-to-Sue.

Once the EEOC procedures have been satisfied, a claimant can litigate under any bases covered in the statutes. The law provides that a prevailing plaintiff can recover attorneys' fees in any case on the theory that the individual is acting to benefit others by enforcing the statute.

The EEOC maintains records of their cases for every law they enforce. Their most recent update shows EEOC activity from fiscal year 1997 through fiscal year 2010.[9] For the category of "all charges," the agency handled 80,680 cases in 1997, and that amount increased to 99,922 in 2010. During the latest year, most cases involved race discrimination, which consisted of 35,890 charges for 35.9 % of the caseload. That was followed by sex discrimination at 29.1%; disability discrimination at 25.2%; and age discrimination at 23.3%. To some extent, charges follow economic conditions and decline when unemployment is low. When unemployment reaches above 10 percent, as it did in 2010, charges likewise go up. The chart below depicts the fluctuation in the EEOC caseload for the 1997–2010 reporting period.

Figure 2. Number of Charges Filed

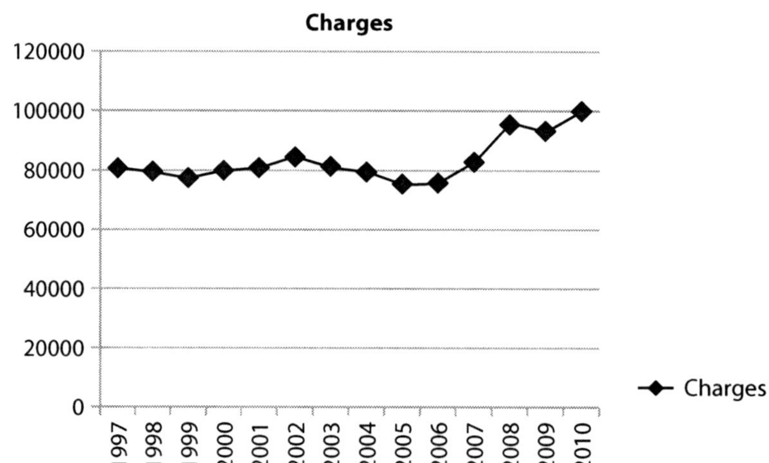

B. Theories of Discrimination

Disparate Treatment

One of the obvious ways an employer might discriminate is to treat someone in a protected class differently from other workers. The structure of a disparate treatment lawsuit is fairly straightforward, in terms of evidence and burdens of proof. There are four steps to the basic process.

> *Step 1.* The plaintiff proves that an adverse job or hiring decision affected him or her.
> *Step 2.* The plaintiff proves a "prima facie" case of discrimination, based on his or her protected status, such as race or gender.
> *Step 3.* The employer "articulates a legitimate, nondiscriminatory reason" for the decision.
> *Step 4.* The plaintiff proves that the employer's reason is "pretextual."

If a party fails to carry the assigned burden of proof at any step, the opposing party wins the lawsuit. In the 1991 Civil Rights Act, Congress added a further refinement to the procedure. Some cases may involve what is called a "mixed motive," where the employer did engage in unlawful discrimination but claims that the same result would have been reached even in the absence of the plaintiff's protected status.

The case excerpt below involves an African American employee named Stalter who worked at Wal-Mart and was discharged for theft. Employees at the store sometimes left opened containers of food on a table in the break room, and the general understanding was that the item could be consumed by anyone in the room. The employee ate a handful of taco chips from a bag belonging to another employee who was not in the room at the time. After his termination, Stalter filed a charge with the EEOC, received the right-to-sue letter, and proceeded to federal district court. The district court ruled against him, finding that theft was a legitimate reason for termination. The Seventh Circuit disagreed and reversed the lower court. The appellate court's opinion is a lucid example of how antidiscrimination suits are litigated.[10]

> The district court assumed for the purposes of Wal-Mart's summary judgment motion that Stalter met his burden of establishing a prima facie case of racial discrimination. Wal-Mart met its burden of articulating a legitimate, non-discriminatory reason, according to the district court, by explaining that it terminated Stalter for theft, and not because of his race. This explanation shifted the burden back to Stalter to show that the reason stated was a pretext for race discrimination. Stalter argued to the district court that Wal-Mart's stated reason was pretextual, as evidenced by (1) Wal-Mart's failure to investigate his claim of racial harassment by Sowinski and Ellenbecker; (2)

Wal-Mart's use of the theft provision in circumstances where it clearly should not apply; and (3) Wal-Mart's more favorable treatment of Ellenbecker, a Caucasian employee, who committed another form of gross misconduct near the time of the taco chip incident. The district court rejected each of these arguments, finding that there was no evidence that Stalter had informed Wal-Mart that Ellenbecker's and Sowinski's mistreatment of him was race-based, that Stalter did technically commit theft under Wal-Mart's policy, and that lying to a supervisor was readily distinguishable from and less serious than theft. The district court therefore granted summary judgment in favor of Wal-Mart.

On appeal, Stalter raises as evidence of pretext: (1) that Wal-Mart did not actually believe that Stalter engaged in theft; (2) that the punishment was grossly excessive in relation to the offense committed; (3) that Wal-Mart treated a Caucasian employee who had committed a similar offense much more leniently; and (4) that Wal-Mart failed to respond to Stalter's complaints of racial harassment by co-workers. Wal-Mart, in turn, contends that Stalter has not even made out a prima facie case of racial discrimination, much less shown that Wal-Mart's proffered reason for the termination was pretext.

Stalter seeks to prove his case under the *McDonnell Douglas* burden shifting method. See *McDonnell Douglas Corp. v. Green*, 411 U.S. 792 (1973). To make out a prima facie case under this framework, Stalter must show that he is a member of a protected class, that he suffered an adverse employment action, that he was meeting his employer's legitimate performance expectations, and that his employer treated similarly situated employees who were not in the protected class more favorably.

To defeat summary judgment on the prima facie case, Stalter need only demonstrate that there is a genuine issue of material fact regarding these factors. No one disputes that Stalter, an African-American person, is in a protected class, and suffered an adverse employment action when he was terminated. Stalter raises a genuine issue of material fact on the remaining two prongs with evidence that he received a satisfactory performance review shortly before his firing, and with evidence that Wal-Mart counseled a Caucasian employee who committed a similar offense instead of terminating her. Wal-Mart makes much of the difference between theft and lying, but its policy for gross misconduct encompasses both, and Wal-Mart's dispute with Stalter's evidence cannot be resolved on summary judgment. Stalter therefore carries his burden on the prima facie case.

Under *McDonnell Douglas*, the burden then shifts back to Wal-Mart to state a legitimate, non-discriminatory reason for the firing. Wal-Mart claims that it fired Stalter not because of his race, but because he committed theft, and that company policy regarding gross misconduct such as theft, requires immediate dismissal. Stalter believes that Wal-Mart's argument fails at this point because part of meeting the legitimate, nondiscriminatory reason criteria is that the stated reason be credible. According to Stalter, Wal-Mart could not have believed that he committed theft based on the statement of the alleged victim, who did not care that her property had been taken. Stalter's argument really applies to the third part of the *McDonnell Douglas* test, whether the plaintiff can show that the employer's stated reason for the termination is a pretext for race discrimination. Certainly if Wal-Mart believed that Stalter committed theft, that would be a legitimate, non-discriminatory reason to fire him.

Under the *McDonnell Douglas* framework, the burden then shifts back to Stalter to show that Wal-Mart's reason is pretextual. Stalter may show pretext by producing evidence that Wal-Mart's ostensible justification is unworthy of credence. "[A] plaintiff may accomplish this showing with evidence tending to prove that the employer's proffered reasons are factually baseless, were not the actual motivation for the discharge in question, or were insufficient to motivate the discharge" [case citation omitted].

Stalter maintains that Wal-Mart could not have reasonably believed that he committed theft, especially in light of the statement of the alleged victim of the theft that he should "forget about it" and that she considered it "no big deal." He also points out that the punishment of termination was grossly excessive in light of the alleged infraction of eating a handful of taco chips without permission, also casting doubt on Wal-Mart's true motive. Moreover, he asserts that Wal-Mart treated a similarly situated Caucasian employee who committed a similar offense much more leniently. Finally, he maintains that Wal-Mart's failure to investigate his claims of harassment by other employees indicates that Wal-Mart's true motive was race-based. With the exception of this last bit of evidence, we believe that Stalter raises more than sufficient evidence to impugn the genuineness of Wal-Mart's motives. We discount the last fact, that Wal-Mart failed to investigate his claim of harassment, because Stalter conceded at oral argument that he never told Wal-Mart that the harassment was race-related. Wal-Mart's failure to investigate the claim cannot therefore be construed as race-related.

However, Stalter's other claims are more than adequate to call into question the sincerity of Wal-Mart's claim that it terminated him for theft. Wal-Mart's policy did not define theft, but any common understanding of the term would include a wrongful taking or a taking without permission, a definition [the management official], embraced at his deposition. Wal-Mart was well aware that the chips were left in an open bag on the countertop of the break room and that the owner of the chips did not object to their taking. Stalter produced evidence that food left in the break room in this fashion was considered abandoned and was fair game for anyone who wished to eat it. Wal-Mart claims that food left on tables was abandoned but that food left on the countertop was not considered abandoned by employees. This is a classic dispute of material fact, best left to the finder of fact to resolve, and on summary judgment, we construe the facts in Stalter's favor. Under Stalter's version of events, Wal-Mart knew that Stalter had Ellenbecker's implied permission to take the chips because of the placement of the open bag in the break room. Wal-Mart also knew that Ellenbecker did not actually object to Stalter's taking of the chips.

Wal-Mart claims it was sincere in its application of its theft policy, but we think this is much like the employer's claim in *Williams v. Bristol-Myers Squibb Co.*, 85 F.3d 270, 275 (7th Cir. 1996). There the employer claimed it terminated an older worker for falsifying records, when the company's code could not be reasonably read to support that interpretation. The employee had not falsified the record in question but had merely failed to notice that the record contained an unauthorized signature. We found that the company's insistence that the employee's action was identical to the actions of other employees terminated for falsification (employees who clearly met the definition) was "so perverse as to cast additional doubt on its good faith." Here Wal-Mart claims that it terminated seven other employees, not in the protected group, for theft. Wal-Mart was unable to tell us at oral argument what these employees took, except to say that some of the terminations were for theft of time, i.e. conducting personal business on company time, and some for theft of property. These actions clearly fit within a reasonable understanding of the term "theft." Eating a handful of Doritos from an open bag on a countertop in the lunchroom is well outside of this domain, and a jury is certainly free to believe that this was not the true reason Wal-Mart fired Stalter.

More compelling is the severity of the punishment in relation to the alleged offense. It bears repeating that Stalter ate a handful of chips belonging to an employee who considered the incident "no big deal" and conveyed that sentiment to the company as well as to Stalter. This strikes us as swatting a fly with a sledge hammer. That Wal-Mart felt compelled to terminate Stalter for this offense does not pass the straight-face test, especially in light of two additional facts: first, Wal-Mart did not terminate a Caucasian employee who also committed gross misconduct by failing to report to work as scheduled and then lying to her supervisor twice about the reason she was absent. Second, Wal-Mart claims that its policy was mandatory, that it was obliged to terminate an employee for any theft, no matter how slight the offense. This claim is belied both by the fact that Wal-Mart did not terminate the Caucasian employee for conduct that came under the very same provision of its policy, the gross misconduct provision, and by the fact that the provision is actually permissive. The policy reads:

There are, however, certain actions of misconduct which may result in immediate termination—Coaching for Improvement will not be used to address

> gross misconduct. These actions include, but are not limited to, the following examples:
>
> - Theft
> - Dishonesty/Compromised Integrity
>
> Later in the policy, Wal-Mart states that "Dishonesty in any form will result in immediate termination." Thus, Wal-Mart's policy did not require termination for theft, and Stalter was terminated. The policy did require termination for dishonesty, yet the Caucasian employee was merely "counseled" and allowed to keep her job. A jury could certainly infer from these facts that Wal-Mart's claim of theft was a pretext for Stalter's termination, and that the leniency extended to the Caucasian worker was evidence that race played a role in Stalter's termination.

As the appeals court makes clear, Wal-Mart's actions were suspect at best. The circuit court sent the case back to the district level for a trial to a jury. Based on the evidence cited in the opinion, the plaintiff might well convince a jury that race discrimination occurred.

Questions

1. If you were a juror in this case, would you find in favor of the plaintiff on his claims?
2. The court has no difficulty rejecting Wal-Mart's interpretation of its policy against theft. How should their policy be revised to justify a discharge for theft?
3. Assume a grocery store has a policy that says theft will be punished by discharge. An employee eats a grape from a display and a supervisor sees the event. Theft? Discharge?
4. If Stalter had been a white man, would this case turn out the same? Why or why not? If the difference is between white and black, is it fair to protect one worker and not another from arbitrary treatment?

Disparate Impact

The second theory of unlawful employer activity is much different than the simple notion of an employer intentionally acting to disadvantage an employee because of the employee's protected status. Disparate impact refers to a fair and neutral employment policy that adversely affects some group of persons, even though the employer had no intent to discriminate. For example, assume a correctional facility offers to hire guards for work in the prison. The facility posts a newspaper advertisement about the positions, and the ad specifies that all applicants must be at least 6' in height and 200 pounds in weight. This requirement does not single out any race or gender, but, in practice, many more men can meet the qualification than women. Why is this unlawful? The landmark case of *Griggs v. Duke Power Company* in 1971 changed the way American businesses hired workers.[11] In deciding this case, the Supreme Court explained the rule by using a fable. The decision is set forth in part below.

[CHIEF JUSTICE BURGER wrote the unanimous opinion of the Court.]

> We granted the writ in this case to resolve the question whether an employer is prohibited by the Civil Rights Act of 1964, Title VII, from requiring a high school education or passing of a standardized general intelligence test as a condition of employment in or transfer to jobs when (a) neither standard is shown to be significantly related to successful job performance, (b) both requirements operate to disqualify Negroes at a substantially higher rate than white applicants, and (c) the jobs in question formerly had been filled only by white employees as part of a longstanding practice of giving preference to whites.
>
> The District Court found that prior to July 2, 1965, the effective date of the Civil Rights Act of 1964, the Company openly discriminated on the basis of race in the hiring and assigning of employees at its Dan River plant. The plant was organized into five operating departments: (1) Labor, (2) Coal Handling, (3) Operations, (4) Maintenance, and (5) Laboratory and Test. Negroes were employed only in the Labor Department where the highest paying jobs paid less than the lowest paying jobs in the other four "operating" departments in which only whites were employed. Promotions were normally made within each department on the basis of job seniority. Transferees into a department usually began in the lowest position.
>
> In 1955 the Company instituted a policy of requiring a high school education for initial assignment to any department except Labor, and for transfer from the Coal Handling to any "inside" department (Operations, Maintenance, or Laboratory). When the Company abandoned its policy of restricting Negroes to the Labor Department in 1965, completion of high school also was made a prerequisite to transfer from Labor to any other department. From the time the high school requirement was instituted to the time of trial, however, white employees hired before the time of the high school education requirement continued to perform satisfactorily and achieve promotions in the "operating" departments. Findings on this score are not challenged.
>
> The Company added a further requirement for new employees on July 2, 1965, the date on which Title VII became effective. To qualify for placement

in any but the Labor Department it became necessary to register satisfactory scores on two professionally prepared aptitude tests, as well as to have a high school education. Completion of high school alone continued to render employees eligible for transfer to the four desirable departments from which Negroes had been excluded if the incumbent had been employed prior to the time of the new requirement. In September 1965 the Company began to permit incumbent employees who lacked a high school education to qualify for transfer from Labor or Coal Handling to an "inside" job by passing two tests: the Personnel Test, which purports to measure general intelligence, and the Bennett Mechanical Comprehension Test. Neither was directed or intended to measure the ability to learn to perform a particular job or category of jobs. The requisite scores used for both initial hiring and transfer approximated the national median for high school graduates.

The District Court had found that while the Company previously followed a policy of overt racial discrimination in a period prior to the Act, such conduct had ceased. The District Court also concluded that Title VII was intended to be prospective only and, consequently, the impact of prior inequities was beyond the reach of corrective action authorized by the Act.

The Court of Appeals was confronted with a question of first impression, as are we, concerning the meaning of Title VII. After careful analysis a majority of that court concluded that a subjective test of the employer's intent should govern, particularly in a close case, and that in this case there was no showing of a discriminatory purpose in the adoption of the diploma and test requirements. On this basis, the Court of Appeals concluded there was no violation of the Act.

The Court of Appeals reversed the District Court in part, rejecting the holding that residual discrimination arising from prior employment practices was insulated from remedial action. The Court of Appeals noted, however, that the District Court was correct in its conclusion that there was no showing of a racial purpose or invidious intent in the adoption of the high school diploma requirement or general intelligence test, and that these standards had been applied fairly to whites and Negroes alike. It held that, in the absence of a discriminatory purpose, use of such requirements was permitted by the Act. In so doing, the Court of Appeals rejected the claim that because these two requirements operated to render ineligible a markedly disproportionate number of Negroes, they were unlawful under Title VII unless shown to be job related. We granted the writ on these claims.

The objective of Congress in the enactment of Title VII is plain from the language of the statute. It was to achieve equality of employment opportunities and remove barriers that have operated in the past to favor an identifiable group of white employees over other employees. Under the Act, practices, procedures, or tests neutral on their face, and even neutral in terms of intent, cannot be maintained if they operate to "freeze" the status quo of prior discriminatory employment practices.

The Court of Appeals' opinion, and the partial dissent, agreed that, on the record in the present case, "whites register far better on the Company's alternative requirements" than Negroes. This consequence would appear to be directly traceable to race. Basic intelligence must have the means of articulation to manifest itself fairly in a testing process. Because they are Negroes, petitioners have long received inferior education in segregated schools and this Court expressly recognized these differences in *Gaston County v. United States*, 395 U.S. 285 (1969). There, because of the inferior education received by Negroes in North Carolina, this Court barred the institution of a literacy test for voter registration on the ground that the test would abridge the right to vote indirectly on account of race. Congress did not intend by Title VII, however, to guarantee a job to every person regardless of qualifications. In short, the Act does not command that any person be hired simply because he was formerly the subject of discrimination, or because he is a member of a minority group. Discriminatory preference for any group, minority or majority, is precisely and only what Congress has proscribed. What is required by Congress is the removal of artificial, arbitrary, and unnecessary barriers to employment when the barriers operate invidiously to discriminate on the basis of racial or other impermissible classification.

Congress has now provided that tests or criteria for employment or promotion may not provide equality of opportunity merely in the sense of the fabled offer of milk to the stork and the fox. On the contrary, Congress has now required that the posture and condition of the job-seeker be taken into account. It has, to resort again to the fable, provided that the vessel in which the milk is proffered be one all seekers can use. The Act proscribes not only overt discrimination but also practices that are fair in form, but discriminatory in operation. The touchstone is business necessity. If an employment practice which operates to exclude Negroes cannot be shown to be related to job performance, the practice is prohibited.

On the record before us, neither the high school completion requirement nor the general intelligence test is shown to bear a demonstrable relationship to successful performance of the jobs for which it was used. Both were adopted, as the Court of Appeals noted, without meaningful study of their relationship to job-performance ability. Rather, a vice president of the Company testified, the requirements were instituted on the Company's judgment that they generally would improve the overall quality of the work force.

The evidence, however, shows that employees who have not completed high school or taken the tests have continued to perform satisfactorily and make progress in departments for which the high school and test criteria are now used. The promotion record of present employees who would not be able to meet the new criteria thus suggests the possibility that the requirements may not be needed even for the limited purpose of preserving the avowed policy of advancement within the Company. In the context of this case, it is unnecessary to reach the question whether testing requirements that take into account capability for the next succeeding position or related future promotion might be utilized upon a showing that such long-range requirements fulfill a genuine business need. In the present case the Company had made no such showing.

The Court of Appeals held that the Company had adopted the diploma and test requirements without any "intention to discriminate against Negro employees." We do not suggest that either the District Court or the Court of Appeals erred in examining the employer's intent; but good intent or absence of discriminatory intent does not redeem employment procedures or testing mechanisms that operate as "built-in headwinds" for minority groups and are unrelated to measuring job capability.

The Company's lack of discriminatory intent is suggested by special efforts to help the undereducated employees through Company financing of two-thirds the cost of tuition for high school training. But Congress directed the thrust of the Act to the consequences of employment practices, not simply the motivation. More than that, Congress has placed on the employer the burden of showing that any given requirement must have a manifest relationship to the employment in question. …

Nothing in the Act precludes the use of testing or measuring procedures; obviously they are useful. What Congress has forbidden is giving these devices and mechanisms controlling force unless they are demonstrably a reasonable measure of job performance. Congress has not commanded that the less qualified be preferred over the better qualified simply because of minority origins. Far from disparaging job qualifications as such, Congress has made such qualifications the controlling factor, so that race, religion, nationality, and sex become irrelevant. What Congress has commanded is that any tests used must measure the person for the job and not the person in the abstract.

[The judgment of the Court of Appeals is reversed.]

The *Griggs* decision created an industry to satisfy the Court's assertion that "The touchstone is business necessity. If an employment practice which operates to exclude Negroes cannot be shown to be related to job performance, the practice is prohibited." If a protected class proves statistically that it has been "excluded" from a job, then unless it can "be shown to be related to job performance," the employer must abandon the policy. Note that the Court does not say who must prove job relatedness, but the law places the burden of proof on the employer.

Assume a fairly simple example. A police department gives a written examination for promotion. The test asks questions about legal rules and proper police procedures. Overall, 90 out of 100 white officers had a passing grade, but only 25 blacks out of 50 passed. The difference between a 90 percent and 50 percent pass rate establishes disparate impact. If the police department wants to use the test, what must it do to prove job relatedness? The answer depends on the nature of the test and the validation strategy. For example, a firefighter might be asked to perform physical tasks, such as unrolling a hose, climbing a ladder, and carrying a heavy weight out of a building. This is known as "content" validation, because it is based on the actual duties of the job. A written test, in contrast, uses a "criterion" validation strategy, because it measures certain criteria that psychologists can show will predict job success, such as "analytical ability."

In one of its 1989 cases trying to change existing civil rights laws, the Supreme Court attempted to undo the rules in the *Griggs* case. The decision in *Wards Cove v. Antonio*, which involved the fishing industry in Alaska, changed the language requiring an employer to prove business necessity for a policy having an adverse impact. Instead, the Court said, the employer's only obligation was to present a reasonable explanation for its policy. To quote Justice White for the majority, "Though we have phrased the query differently in different cases, it is generally well established that, at the justification stage of such a disparate impact case, the dispositive issue is whether a challenged practice serves, in a significant way, the legitimate employment goals of the employer."[12] White insisted that any greater burden imposed on employers would result in hiring quotas not consistent with the act. Congress corrected the Court's view by rejecting the *Wards Cove* analysis by name and reinstating the formula stated in *Griggs*. Consequently, the rule of *Griggs* is still the rule.

In September 2010 the EEOC issued guidelines dealing with validation under the different validation techniques.[13] Below is some material taken from those guidelines. Note that the EEOC is simply describing some of the tests that employers might use. The agency does not say that all of the tests are always legal.

Examples of employment tests and other selection procedures, many of which can be administered online, include the following:

- Cognitive tests assess reasoning, memory, perceptual speed and accuracy, and skills in arithmetic and reading comprehension, as well as knowledge of a particular function or job;
- Physical ability tests measure the physical ability to perform a particular task or the strength of specific muscle groups, as well as strength and stamina in general;
- Sample job tasks (e.g., performance tests, simulations, work samples, and realistic job previews) assess performance and aptitude on particular tasks;
- Medical inquiries and physical examinations, including psychological tests, assess physical or mental health;
- Personality tests and integrity tests assess the degree to which a person has certain traits or dispositions (e.g., dependability, cooperativeness, safety) or aim to

predict the likelihood that a person will engage in certain conduct (e.g., theft, absenteeism);

- Criminal background checks provide information on arrest and conviction history;
- Credit checks provide information on credit and financial history;
- Performance appraisals reflect a supervisor's assessment of an individual's performance; and
- English proficiency tests determine English fluency.

The EEOC also published a document that advised employers on testing procedures titled "Uniform Guidelines on Employee Selection Procedures," which was subsequently made a part of the Code of Federal Regulations.[14] A portion of that document is reprinted below and gives a general summary of the validation process.

Sec. 1607.5 General standards for validity studies.

A. Acceptable types of validity studies. For the purposes of satisfying these guidelines, users may rely upon criterion-related validity studies, content validity studies or construct validity studies, in accordance with the standards set forth in the technical standards of these guidelines, section 14 below. New strategies for showing the validity of selection procedures will be evaluated as they become accepted by the psychological profession.

B. Criterion-related, content, and construct validity. Evidence of the validity of a test or other selection procedure by a criterion-related validity study should consist of empirical data demonstrating that the selection procedure is predictive of or significantly correlated with important elements of job performance. See section 14B below. Evidence of the validity of a test or other selection procedure by a content validity study should consist of data showing that the content of the selection procedure is representative of important aspects of performance on the job for which the candidates are to be evaluated. See 14C below. Evidence of the validity of a test or other selection procedure through a construct validity study should consist of data showing that the procedure measures the degree to which candidates have identifiable characteristics which have been determined to be important in successful performance in the job for which the candidates are to be evaluated. See section 14D below.

C. Guidelines are consistent with professional standards. The provisions of these guidelines relating to validation of selection procedures are intended to be consistent with generally accepted professional standards for evaluating standardized tests and other selection procedures, such as those described in the Standards for Educational and Psychological Tests prepared by a joint committee of the American Psychological Association, the American Educational Research Association, and the National Council on Measurement in Education (American Psychological Association, Washington, DC, 1974) (hereinafter "A.P.A. Standards") and standard textbooks and journals in the field of personnel selection.

Questions

1. What were the job requirements at issue in *Griggs*? Can a reasonable inference be drawn that such requirements were useful to the employer in selecting applicants for the job? Would a "reasonable inference" be sufficient to withstand the legal challenge here?
2. According to the Court, what test of employer intent was utilized by the court of appeals? What finding did the lower courts reach relative to intent?
3. By what reasoning did the Supreme Court reverse the lower courts' conclusions on the issue of intent? In your answer, consider the following statutory language, which the Court quotes in footnote 1 of its opinion:

> Sec. 703. (a) It shall be an unlawful employment practice for an employer … (2) to limit, segregate, or classify his employees in any way which would deprive or tend to deprive any individual of employment opportunities or otherwise adversely affect his status as an employee, because of such individual's race, color, religion, sex, or national origin … (h) Notwithstanding any other provision of this title, it shall not be an unlawful employment practice for an employer … to give and to act upon the results of any professionally developed ability test provided that such test, its administration or action upon the results is not designed, intended or used to discriminate because of race, color, religion, sex or national origin …

4. What words in the statute have reference to the employer's intent? What language supports the Court's conclusion that "Congress has placed on the employer the burden of showing that any given requirement must have a manifest relation to the employment in question?" What is the effect of shifting the burden of demonstrating job relatedness?
5. The heart of the *Griggs* opinion is its assertion that Congress intended to proscribe "not only overt discrimination but also practices that are fair in form, but discriminatory in operation." What reasoning is offered to support that very important conclusion? What precedent or legislative history does the Court rely on?
6. *Griggs* stands for the proposition that employment policies having an "adverse impact" on a protected group may be unlawful. How did the plaintiffs in *Griggs* demonstrate adverse impact? In general, what method should be used to prove adverse impact?

7. Under *Griggs*, a plaintiff must first establish adverse impact. According to the opinion, how may an employer defend against liability, even if adverse impact is shown?
8. In the introductory section of its guidelines on employee selection procedures, the EEOC says of test validation:

> Validation has become highly technical and complex, and yet is constantly changing as a set of concepts in industrial psychology. … There are three concepts which can be used to validate a selection procedure. … They are (1) criterion-related validity, (2) content validity, and (3) construct validity. In criterion-related validity, a selection procedure is justified by a statistical relationship between scores on the text or other selection procedure and measures of job performance. In content validity, a selection procedure is justified by showing that it representatively samples significant parts of the job, such as a typing test for a typist. Construct validity involves identifying the psychological trait (the construct) which underlies successful performance on the job and then devising a selection procedure to measure the presence and degree of the construct. An example would be a test of "leadership ability."

9. Assume that you wanted to devise a pencil-and-paper test for applicants for an entry-level welder position. What measures of job performance might you attempt to test for on the basis of criterion-related validity?
10. The EEOC notes that a typing test for a typist illustrates the content approach to validation. Can you think of others? How would you develop a test for firefighters? What if a valid job qualification based on content, such as a physical performance examination, eliminates all women applicants? Should we have fire departments that are segregated on the basis of gender?
11. Regarding construct validity, most authorities agree that construct validity is very difficult to prove. What might explain that conclusion? Do you perceive any relation between this point and the usefulness of handwriting analysis as a selection procedure? Do you think selecting employees based on their handwriting would violate Title VII?
12. In *Griggs*, the Court held that the requirement of a high school education resulted in unlawful discrimination. How should an employer's efforts to hire educated, experienced workers be accommodated? For example, should a PhD or equivalent degree be required for college instructors, even though it adversely impacts racial minorities and women?

C. Reverse Discrimination and Affirmative Action

As noted above, Donald Trump began his truncated political career by demanding that President Obama prove his American citizenship. Obama did in fact produce the "long form" birth certificate to settle the matter. Immediately afterward, Trump switched his attack to Obama's academic credentials. Trump publicly speculated how Obama managed to gain admittance to such prestigious schools as Columbia and Harvard Law School. The underlying motif of those questions had to do with public attitudes toward "preferences" presumably granted to some groups in our society to create a more level playing field. The civil rights laws did not mandate affirmative action; in fact, most members of Congress who spoke on the subject made clear that the laws were intended to eliminate discrimination in the future, not to eliminate the past effects of discrimination. The Supreme Court made up its own set of rules as the issue was presented, and it continues to do so. Even though the law is still under construction, a fairly solid foundation exists on which employers can build policies to promote "diversity" as they think appropriate.

1. Doing Business with the Government: Contracts with Affirmative Action Plans

Different anti-discrimination laws cover different types of employment relations. The one clear principle about "reverse discrimination" is that the federal government cannot monitor a private sector employer and order them to hire more women and minorities to achieve a "balanced" workforce. There are many variations on this theme, however. Consider a private sector employer who *wants* to hire minority workers for legitimate business reasons. Another case involves hiring by a public sector employer. To what extent can they make race- or gender-conscious decisions? Can an employer flatly discriminate against a man in order to hire female food servers, as happens at Hooters restaurants? Finally, how does the federal government get the authority to require private sector firms to have, and comply with, an "affirmative action" plan? This section addresses the last question, followed by longer and more complex discussions of the other questions.

The reason the federal government can require an employer to maintain an appropriately diverse workforce arises out of the government's power to write contracts with firms who do business with the government. In other words, if someone wants to sell beef to the government, the company may have to enter into an agreement to hire a certain number of underrepresented workers, such as women. The Office of Federal Contract Compliance Programs (OFCCP) is the agency responsible for creating and administering such agreements. In 2011 the agency announced a settlement with a beef packing company which had failed to hire enough women. The press release is printed below.[15]

U.S. Labor Department Settles Gender-Discrimination Case with Green Bay Dressed Beef on behalf of 970 Female Applicants for $1.65 million

GREEN BAY, Wis. Federal contractor Green Bay Dressed Beef LLC will pay $1.65 million in back wages, interest, and benefits to 970 women who were

> subjected to systemic discrimination by the company. The settlement follows an investigation by the U.S. Department of Labor's Office of Federal Contract Compliance Programs, which found that the women were rejected for general laborer positions at the company's Green Bay plant in 2006 and 2007.
>
> "This is the 21st century in the United States of America. There is no such thing as a 'man's job,'" said Secretary of Labor Hilda L. Solis. "I am pleased that my department has been able to work out a resolution with Green Bay Dressed Beef, and that the settlement not only compensates the victims of discrimination but also provides jobs for many of these women."
>
> In addition to financial compensation, the beef supplier will extend a total of 248 offers of employment to affected women as positions become available. The company already has hired more than 60 of the women in the original class.
>
> During a scheduled compliance review, OFCCP determined that the company had violated Executive Order 11246, which prohibits federal contractors from discriminating on the basis of gender in their employment practices. Under the terms of the conciliation agreement worked out between the Labor Department and the contractor, the $1.65 million will be divided among the affected women who return timely notifications. The company also has agreed to undertake extensive self-monitoring and corrective measures to ensure that all employment practices fully comply with the law and will immediately correct any discriminatory practices.
>
> Two of Green Bay Dressed Beef's largest clients are the U.S. Department of Agriculture and the U.S. Department of Defense as one of the largest suppliers of beef products for the federal school lunch program and one of the leading providers of beef products to American military personnel worldwide.
>
> In addition to Executive Order 11246, OFCCP's legal authority exists under Section 503 of the Rehabilitation Act of 1973 and the Vietnam Era Veterans' Readjustment Assistance Act of 1974. As amended, these three laws hold those who do business with the federal government, both contractors and subcontractors, to the fair and reasonable standard that they not discriminate in employment on the basis of gender, race, color, religion, national origin, disability or status as a protected veteran. For general information, call OFCCP's toll-free helpline at 800-397-6251. Additional information is also available at http://www.dol.gov/ofccp.

As the bulletin makes clear, anyone dealing with the federal government may be required to comply with affirmative action guidelines. Secretary Solis claims that employing more women in a packing plant serves some legitimate government interest. Does the press release set forth a convincing explanation of what that interest might be? What interest would women have in working in a packing house (formerly known as a "slaughterhouse")?

2. Private Sector Preferential Treatment: Weber v. United Steelworkers

In 1978 the Supreme Court made a landmark ruling about reverse discrimination in the private sector. Put simply, the Court held that employers have broad discretion to give minorities preferential hiring treatment. The rationale for that conclusion is unconvincing. The law says clearly that any discrimination on the basis of race is illegal. If white people are considered a "race," it seems inescapable that employers could not legally discriminate against them. Justice Rehnquist wrote a powerful dissent in this case, part of which is included in the excerpt below. Compare the logic of the majority and the dissent in terms of persuasiveness.

[MR. JUSTICE BRENNAN delivered the opinion of the Court:]

> Challenged here is the legality of an affirmative action plan—collectively bargained by an employer and a union—that reserves for black employees 50% of the openings in an in-plant craft training program until the percentage of black craft workers in the plant is commensurate with the percentage of blacks in the local labor force. The question for decision is whether Congress, in Title VII of the Civil Rights Act of 1964, left employers and unions in the private sector free to take such race-conscious steps to eliminate manifest racial imbalances in traditionally segregated job categories. We hold that Title VII does not prohibit such race-conscious affirmative action plans.
>
> In 1974, petitioner United Steelworkers of America (USWA) and petitioner Kaiser Aluminum & Chemical Corp. (Kaiser) entered into a master collective bargaining agreement covering terms and conditions of employment at 15 Kaiser plants. The agreement contained, inter alia, an affirmative action plan designed to eliminate conspicuous racial imbalances in Kaiser's then almost exclusively white craft workforces. Black craft hiring goals were set for each Kaiser plant equal to the percentage of blacks in the respective local labor forces. To enable plants to meet these goals, on-the-job training programs were established to teach unskilled production workers—black and white—the skills necessary to become craft workers. The plan reserved for black employees 50% of the openings in these newly created in-plant training programs.
>
> This case arose from the operation of the plan at Kaiser's plant in Gramercy, La. Until 1974, Kaiser hired as craft workers for that plant only persons who had had prior craft experience. Because blacks had long been excluded from craft unions, few were able to present such credentials. As a consequence, prior to 1974, only 1.83% (5 out of 273) of the skilled craft workers at the Gramercy plant were black, even though the workforce in the Gramercy area was approximately 39% black.
>
> Pursuant to the national agreement, Kaiser altered its craft hiring practice in the Gramercy plant. Rather than hiring already trained outsiders, Kaiser

established a training program to train its production workers to fill craft openings. Selection of craft trainees was made on the basis of seniority, with the proviso that at least 50% of the new trainees were to be black until the percentage of black skilled craft workers in the Gramercy plant approximated the percentage of blacks in the local labor force.

During 1974, the first year of the operation of the Kaiser-USWA affirmative action plan, 13 craft trainees were selected from Gramercy's production workforce. Of these, seven were black and six white. The most senior black selected into the program had less seniority than several white production workers whose bids for admission were rejected. Thereafter, one of those white production workers, respondent Brian Weber (hereafter respondent), instituted this class action in the United States District Court for the Eastern District of Louisiana.

The complaint alleged that the filling of craft trainee positions at the Gramercy plant pursuant to the affirmative action program had resulted in junior black employees' receiving training in preference to senior white employees, thus discriminating against respondent and other similarly situated white employees in violation of §§ 703(a) and (d) of Title VII. The District Court held that the plan violated Title VII, entered a judgment in favor of the plaintiff class, and granted a permanent injunction prohibiting Kaiser and the USWA "from denying plaintiffs, Brian F. Weber and all other members of the class, access to on-the-job training programs on the basis of race." A divided panel of the Court of Appeals for the Fifth Circuit affirmed, holding that all employment preferences based upon race, including those preferences incidental to bona fide affirmative action plans, violated Title VII's prohibition against racial discrimination in employment. ... We reverse.

We emphasize at the outset the narrowness of our inquiry. Since the Kaiser-USWA plan does not involve state action, this case does not present an alleged violation of the Equal Protection Clause of the Fourteenth Amendment. Further, since the Kaiser-USWA plan was adopted voluntarily, we are not concerned with what Title VII requires or with what a court might order to remedy a past proved violation of the Act. The only question before us is the narrow statutory issue of whether Title VII forbids private employers and unions from voluntarily agreeing upon bona fide affirmative action plans that accord racial preferences in the manner and for the purpose provided in the Kaiser-USWA plan. That question was expressly left open in *McDonald v. Santa Fe Trail Transp. Co.*, 427 U.S. 273, 281 n. 8 (1976), which held, in a case not involving affirmative action, that Title VII protects whites as well as blacks from certain forms of racial discrimination.

Respondent argues that Congress intended in Title VII to prohibit all race-conscious affirmative action plans. Respondent's argument rests upon a literal interpretation of §§ 703(a) and (d) of the Act. Those sections make it unlawful to "discriminate … because of … race" in hiring and in the selection of apprentices for training programs. Since, the argument runs, *McDonald v. Santa Fe Trail Transp. Co.* settled that Title VII forbids discrimination against whites as well as blacks, and since the Kaiser-USWA affirmative action plan operates to discriminate against white employees solely because they are white, it follows that the Kaiser-USWA plan violates Title VII.

Respondent's argument is not without force. But it overlooks the significance of the fact that the Kaiser-USWA plan is an affirmative action plan voluntarily adopted by private parties to eliminate traditional patterns of racial segregation. In this context, respondent's reliance upon a literal construction of §§ 703(a) and (d) and upon *McDonald* is misplaced. It is a "familiar rule, that a thing may be within the letter of the statute and yet not within the statute, because not within its spirit, nor within the intention of its makers." *Holy Trinity Church v. United States*, 143 U.S. 457, 459 (1892). The prohibition against racial discrimination in §§ 703(a) and(d) of Title VII must therefore be read against the background of the legislative history of Title VII and the historical context from which the Act arose. Examination of those sources makes clear that an interpretation of the sections that forbade all race-conscious affirmative action would "bring about an end completely at variance with the purpose of the statute," and must be rejected.

Congress' primary concern in enacting the prohibition against racial discrimination in Title VII of the Civil Rights Act of 1964 was with "the plight of the Negro in our economy." 110 Cong.Rec. 6548 (1964) (remarks of Sen. Humphrey). Before 1964, blacks were largely relegated to "unskilled and semi-skilled jobs." Because of automation, the number of such jobs was rapidly decreasing. As a consequence, "the relative position of the Negro worker [was] steadily worsening. In 1947, the nonwhite unemployment rate was only 64 percent higher than the white rate; in 1962, it was 124 percent higher."

Congress considered this a serious social problem. As Senator Clark told the Senate: "The rate of Negro unemployment has gone up consistently as compared with white unemployment for the past 15 years. This is a social malaise and a social situation which we should not tolerate. That is one of the principal reasons why the bill should pass." Congress feared that the goals of the Civil Rights Act—the integration of blacks into the mainstream of American society—could not be achieved unless this trend were reversed. And Congress recognized that that would not be possible unless blacks were able to secure jobs "which have a future." As Senator Humphrey explained to the Senate:

> What good does it do a Negro to be able to eat in a fine restaurant if he cannot afford to pay the bill? What good does it do him to be accepted in a hotel that is too expensive for his modest income? How

can a Negro child be motivated to take full advantage of integrated educational facilities if he has no hope of getting a job where he can use that education?

Without a job, one cannot afford public convenience and accommodations. Income from employment may be necessary to further a man's education, or that of his children. If his children have no hope of getting a good job, what will motivate them to take advantage of educational opportunities?

These remarks echoed President Kennedy's original message to Congress upon the introduction of the Civil Rights Act in 1963. "There is little value in a Negro's obtaining the right to be admitted to hotels and restaurants if he has no cash in his pocket and no job." Accordingly, it was clear to Congress that "[t]he crux of the problem [was] to open employment opportunities for Negroes in occupations which have been traditionally closed to them, and it was to this problem that Title VII's prohibition against racial discrimination in employment was primarily addressed."

It plainly appears from the House Report accompanying the Civil Rights Act that Congress did not intend wholly to prohibit private and voluntary affirmative action efforts as one method of solving this problem. The Report provides:

No bill can or should lay claim to eliminating all of the causes and consequences of racial and other types of discrimination against minorities. There is reason to believe, however, that national leadership provided by the enactment of Federal legislation dealing with the most troublesome problems will create an atmosphere conducive to voluntary or local resolution of other forms of discrimination.

Given this legislative history, we cannot agree with respondent that Congress intended to prohibit the private sector from taking effective steps to accomplish the goal that Congress designed Title VII to achieve. ...

Our conclusion is further reinforced by examination of the language and legislative history of § 703(j) of Title VII. Opponents of Title VII raised two related arguments against the bill. First, they argued that the Act would be interpreted to require employers with racially imbalanced workforces to grant preferential treatment to racial minorities in order to integrate. Second, they argued that employers with racially imbalanced workforces would grant preferential treatment to racial minorities, even if not required to do so by the Act. Had Congress meant to prohibit all race-conscious affirmative action, as respondent urges, it easily could have answered both objections by providing that Title VII would not require or permit racially preferential integration efforts. But Congress did not choose such a course. Rather, Congress added § 70(j), which addresses only the first objection. The section provides that nothing contained in Title VII "shall be interpreted to require any [p. 206] employer ... to grant preferential treatment ... to any group because of the race ... of such ... group on account of a de facto racial imbalance in the employer's workforce." The section does not state that "nothing in Title VII shall be interpreted to permit" voluntary affirmative efforts to correct racial imbalances. The natural inference is that Congress chose not to forbid all voluntary race-conscious affirmative action. ...

We need not today define in detail the line of demarcation between permissible and impermissible affirmative action plans. It suffices to hold that the challenged Kaiser-USWA affirmative action plan falls on the permissible side of the line. The purposes of the plan mirror those of the statute. Both were designed to break down old patterns of racial segregation and hierarchy. Both were structured to "open employment opportunities for Negroes in occupations which have been traditionally closed to them."

At the same time, the plan does not unnecessarily trammel the interests of the white employees. The plan does not require the discharge of white workers and their replacement with new black hirees. Nor does the plan create an absolute bar to the advancement of white employees; half of those trained in the program will be white. Moreover, the plan is a temporary measure; it is not intended to maintain racial balance, but simply to eliminate a manifest racial imbalance. Preferential selection of craft trainees at the Gramercy plant will end as soon as the percentage of black skilled craft workers in the Gramercy plant approximates the percentage of blacks in the local labor force.

We conclude, therefore, that the adoption of the Kaiser-USWA plan for the Gramercy plant falls within the area of discretion left by Title VII to the private sector voluntarily to adopt affirmative action plans designed to eliminate conspicuous racial imbalance in traditionally segregated job categories. Accordingly, the judgment of the Court of Appeals for the Fifth Circuit is reversed.

MR. JUSTICE REHNQUIST, with whom THE CHIEF JUSTICE joins, dissenting.

In a very real sense, the Court's opinion is ahead of its time: it could more appropriately have been handed down five years from now, in 1984, a year coinciding with the title of a book from which the Court's opinion borrows, perhaps subconsciously, at least one idea. Orwell describes in his book a governmental official of Oceania, one of the three great world powers, denouncing the current enemy, Eurasia, to an assembled crowd:

> It was almost impossible to listen to him without being first convinced and then maddened. ... The speech had been proceeding for perhaps twenty minutes when a messenger hurried onto the platform and a

> scrap of paper was slipped into the speaker's hand. He unrolled and read it without pausing in his speech. Nothing altered in his voice or manner, or in the content of what he was saying, but suddenly the names were different. Without words said, a wave of understanding rippled through the crowd. Oceania was at war with Eastasia! ... The banners and posters with which the square was decorated were all wrong! ...
>
> [T]he speaker had switched from one line to the other actually in mid-sentence, not only without a pause, but without even breaking the syntax. [G. Orwell, *Nineteen Eighty-Four* 181–182 (1949).]

Today's decision represents an equally dramatic and equally unremarked switch in this Court's interpretation of Title VII.

The operative sections of Title VII prohibit racial discrimination in employment simpliciter. Taken in its normal meaning, and as understood by all Members of Congress who spoke to the issue during the legislative debates, this language prohibits a covered employer from considering race when making an employment decision, whether the race be black or white. Several years ago, however, a United States District Court held that "the dismissal of white employees charged with misappropriating company property while not dismissing a similarly charged Negro employee does not raise a claim upon which Title VII relief may be granted." *McDonald v. Santa Fe Trail Transp. Co.*, 427 U.S. 273, 278 (1976). This Court unanimously reversed, concluding from the "uncontradicted legislative history" that "Title VII prohibits racial discrimination against the white petitioners in this case upon the same standards as would be applicable were they Negroes. ..."

We have never wavered in our understanding that Title VII "prohibits all racial discrimination in employment, without exception for any group of particular employees." In *Griggs v. Duke Power Co.*, 401 U.S. 424, 431 (1971), our first occasion to interpret Title VII, a unanimous Court observed that "[d]iscriminatory preference, for any group, minority or majority, is precisely and only what Congress has proscribed." And in our most recent discussion of the issue, we uttered words seemingly dispositive of this case: "It is clear beyond cavil that the obligation imposed by Title VII is to provide an equal opportunity for each applicant regardless of race, without regard to whether members of the applicant's race are already proportionately represented in the workforce."

Today, however, the Court behaves much like the Orwellian speaker earlier described, as if it had been handed a note indicating that Title VII would lead to a result unacceptable to the Court if interpreted here as it was in our prior decisions. Accordingly, without even a break in syntax, the Court rejects "a literal construction of § 703(a)" in favor of newly discovered

> "legislative history," which leads it to a conclusion directly contrary to that compelled by the "uncontradicted legislative history" unearthed in *McDonald* and our other prior decisions. Now we are told that the legislative history of Title VII shows that employers are free to discriminate on the basis of race: an employer may, in the Court's words, "trammel the interests of the white employees" in favor of black employees in order to eliminate "racial imbalance." Our earlier interpretations of Title VII, like the banners and posters decorating the square in Oceania, were all wrong.

Justice Rehnquist goes on to review the legislative history of Title VII and reaches a much different conclusion than the majority. He insisted that Congress made clear its intention, which was that "no racial discrimination in employment is permissible under Title VII, not even preferential treatment of minorities to correct racial imbalance." In one particularly incisive passage, Rehnquist quotes two of the Senate leaders of the bill on established seniority rights.

As if directing their comments at Brian Weber, the Senators said:

> Title VII would have no effect on established seniority rights. Its effect is prospective and not retrospective. Thus, for example, if a business has been discriminating the past and as a result has an all-white working force, when the tile comes into effect the employer's obligation would be simply to fill future vacancies on a nondiscriminatory basis. He would not be obliged—or indeed permitted—to fire whites in order to hire Negroes, or to prefer Negroes for future vacancies, or, once Negroes are hired, to give them special seniority rights at the expense of the white workers hired earlier.

Rehnquist sums up by noting that "with virtual clairvoyance the Senate's leading supporters of Title VII anticipated precisely the circumstances of this case and advised their colleagues that the type of minority preference [as here] would violate Title VII's ban on racial discrimination." His argument seems unassailable.

Questions

1. As a matter of logic, Justice Rehnquist seems to have the better argument about reverse discrimination. Does he have the better argument in terms of policy, or is there no difference between them?
2. How might Justice Marshall respond to Justice Rehnquist?

3. Can you develop an argument that the difference between government discrimination in favor of minorities and a private employer doing the same thing is an important one?
4. Assume an employer hired a less-experienced woman to work selling cars because he wanted a "feminine touch" on the sales floor. Should the law permit this?
5. The *Weber* case has been the law since 1978, and Congress substantially modified Title VII in 1991. By refusing to change the *Weber* rule, has Congress approved it? Does that fact prove Rehnquist was wrong?

3. Public Sector Preferences under the 14th Amendment: Two University of Michigan Cases

Because of the state action component, legal claims in the public sector can be brought to vindicate federal constitutional rights. Accordingly, if a student in a public university believes he or she has been the victim of "reverse" discrimination, as in *Bakke*, the individual can use the equal protection clause as a theory of litigation. Two cases involving the University of Michigan came before the Supreme Court in 2003.[16] One of the cases, *Gratz v. Bollinger*, was decided against the College of Liberal Arts' diversity program. The Court ruled that the program was not narrowly tailored to achieve a well-defined goal. Conversely, the program at the School of Law was upheld in *Grutter v. Bollinger*. Portions of that opinion are set forth below.

> [Justice O'Connor delivered the opinion of the Court:]
>
> This case requires us to decide whether the use of race as a factor in student admissions by the University of Michigan Law School (Law School) is unlawful.
>
> The Law School ranks among the Nation's top law schools. It receives more than 3,500 applications each year for a class of around 350 students. Seeking to "admit a group of students who individually and collectively are among the most capable," the Law School looks for individuals with "substantial promise for success in law school" and "a strong likelihood of succeeding in the practice of law and contributing in diverse ways to the well-being of others." More broadly, the Law School seeks "a mix of students with varying backgrounds and experiences who will respect and learn from each other." In 1992, the dean of the Law School charged a faculty committee with crafting a written admissions policy to implement these goals. In particular, the Law School sought to ensure that its efforts to achieve student body diversity complied with this Court's most recent ruling on the use of race in university admissions. Upon the unanimous adoption of the committee's report by the Law School faculty, it became the Law School's official admissions policy.

The hallmark of that policy is its focus on academic ability coupled with a flexible assessment of applicants' talents, experiences, and potential "to contribute to the learning of those around them." The policy requires admissions officials to evaluate each applicant based on all the information available in the file, including a personal statement, letters of recommendation, and an essay describing the ways in which the applicant will contribute to the life and diversity of the Law School. In reviewing an applicant's file, admissions officials must consider the applicant's undergraduate grade point average (GPA) and Law School Admissions Test (LSAT) score because they are important (if imperfect) predictors of academic success in law school.

The policy makes clear, however, that even the highest possible score does not guarantee admission to the Law School. Nor does a low score automatically disqualify an applicant. Rather, the policy requires admissions officials to look beyond grades and test scores to other criteria that are important to the Law School's educational objectives. So-called soft variables, such as "the enthusiasm of recommenders, the quality of the undergraduate institution, the quality of the applicant's essay, and the areas and difficulty of undergraduate course selection" are all brought to bear in assessing an "applicant's likely contributions to the intellectual and social life of the institution."

The policy aspires to "achieve that diversity which has the potential to enrich everyone's education and thus make a law school class stronger than the sum of its parts." The policy does not restrict the types of diversity contributions eligible for "substantial weight" in the admissions process, but instead recognizes "many possible bases for diversity admissions." The policy does, however, reaffirm the Law School's longstanding commitment to "one particular type of diversity," that is, "racial and ethnic diversity with special reference to the inclusion of students from groups which have been historically discriminated against, like African-Americans, Hispanics and Native Americans, who without this commitment might not be represented in our student body in meaningful numbers." By enrolling a "critical mass of [underrepresented] minority students," the Law School seeks to "ensure their ability to make unique contributions to the character of the Law School."

The policy does not define diversity "solely in terms of racial and ethnic status." Nor is the policy "insensitive to the competition among all students for admission to the [L]aw [S]chool." Rather, the policy seeks to guide admissions officers in "producing classes both diverse and academically outstanding, classes made up of students who promise to continue the tradition of outstanding contribution by Michigan Graduates to the legal profession."

Petitioner Barbara Grutter is a white Michigan resident who applied to the Law School in 1996 with a 3.8 grade point average and 161 LSAT score. The Law School initially placed petitioner on a waiting list, but subsequently rejected her application. In December 1997, petitioner filed suit in the United

States District Court for the Eastern District of Michigan against the Law School, the Regents of the University of Michigan, Lee Bollinger (Dean of the Law School from 1987 to 1994, and President of the University of Michigan from 1996 to 2002), Jeffrey Lehman (Dean of the Law School), and Dennis Shields (Director of Admissions at the Law School from 1991 until 1998). Petitioner alleged that respondents discriminated against her on the basis of race in violation of the Fourteenth Amendment. …

The Equal Protection Clause provides that no State shall "deny to any person within its jurisdiction the equal protection of the laws." Because the Fourteenth Amendment "protects persons, not groups," all "governmental action based on race—a group classification long recognized as in most circumstances irrelevant and therefore prohibited—should be subjected to detailed judicial inquiry to ensure that the personal right to equal protection of the laws has not been infringed." *Adarand Constructors, Inc. v. Peña*, 515 U.S. 200, 227 (1995).

We have held that all racial classifications imposed by government "must be analyzed by a reviewing court under strict scrutiny." This means that such classifications are constitutional only if they are narrowly tailored to further compelling governmental interests. "Absent searching judicial inquiry into the justification for such race-based measures," we have no way to determine what "classifications are 'benign' or 'remedial' and what classifications are in fact motivated by illegitimate notions of racial inferiority or simple racial politics." *Richmond v. J. A. Croson Co.*, 488 U.S. 469, 493 (1989). We apply strict scrutiny to all racial classifications to "smoke out illegitimate uses of race by assuring that [government] is pursuing a goal important enough to warrant use of a highly suspect tool."

With these principles in mind, we turn to the question whether the Law School's use of race is justified by a compelling state interest. Before this Court, as they have throughout this litigation, respondents assert only one justification for their use of race in the admissions process: obtaining "the educational benefits that flow from a diverse student body." In other words, the Law School asks us to recognize, in the context of higher education, a compelling state interest in student body diversity. …

The Law School's educational judgment that such diversity is essential to its educational mission is one to which we defer. The Law School's assessment that diversity will, in fact, yield educational benefits is substantiated by respondents and their amici. Our scrutiny of the interest asserted by the Law School is no less strict for taking into account complex educational judgments in an area that lies primarily within the expertise of the university. Our holding today is in keeping with our tradition of giving a degree of deference to a university's academic decisions, within constitutionally prescribed limits.

We have long recognized that, given the important purpose of public education and the expansive freedoms of speech and thought associated with the university environment, universities occupy a special niche in our constitutional tradition. In announcing the principle of student body diversity as a compelling state interest, Justice Powell invoked our cases recognizing a constitutional dimension, grounded in the First Amendment, of educational autonomy: "The freedom of a university to make its own judgments as to education includes the selection of its student body." Our conclusion that the Law School has a compelling interest in a diverse student body is informed by our view that attaining a diverse student body is at the heart of the Law School's proper institutional mission, and that "good faith" on the part of a university is "presumed" absent "a showing to the contrary."

As part of its goal of "assembling a class that is both exceptionally academically qualified and broadly diverse," the Law School seeks to "enroll a 'critical mass' of minority students." The Law School's interest is not simply "to assure within its student body some specified percentage of a particular group merely because of its race or ethnic origin." That would amount to outright racial balancing, which is patently unconstitutional. Rather, the Law School's concept of critical mass is defined by reference to the educational benefits that diversity is designed to produce. …

These benefits are not theoretical but real, as major American businesses have made clear that the skills needed in today's increasingly global marketplace can only be developed through exposure to widely diverse people, cultures, ideas, and viewpoints. What is more, high-ranking retired officers and civilian leaders of the United States military assert that, "[b]ased on [their] decades of experience," a "highly qualified, racially diverse officer corps … is essential to the military's ability to fulfill its principle mission to provide national security." The primary sources for the Nation's officer corps are the service academies and the Reserve Officers Training Corps (ROTC), the latter composed of students already admitted to participating colleges and universities. At present, "the military cannot achieve an officer corps that is both highly qualified and racially diverse unless the service academies and the ROTC used limited race-conscious recruiting and admissions policies." To fulfill its mission, the military "must be selective in admissions for training and education for the officer corps, and it must train and educate a highly qualified, racially diverse officer corps in a racially diverse setting." We agree that "[i]t requires only a small step from this analysis to conclude that our country's other most selective institutions must remain both diverse and selective. …"

Even in the limited circumstance when drawing racial distinctions is permissible to further a compelling state interest, government is still "constrained in how it may pursue that end: [T]he means chosen to accomplish the [government's] asserted purpose must be specifically and narrowly framed to accomplish that purpose." The purpose of the narrow tailoring requirement is to ensure that "the means chosen 'fit' the compelling goal so closely that there is little or no possibility that the motive for the classification was illegitimate racial prejudice or stereotype."

To be narrowly tailored, a race-conscious admissions program cannot use a quota system—it cannot "insulate each category of applicants with certain desired qualifications from competition with all other applicants." Instead, a university may consider race or ethnicity only as a "plus in a particular applicant's file," without "insulating the individual from comparison with all other candidates for the available seats." In other words, an admissions program must be "flexible enough to consider all pertinent elements of diversity in light of the particular qualifications of each applicant, and to place them on the same footing for consideration, although not necessarily according them the same weight."

We find that the Law School's admissions program bears the hallmarks of a narrowly tailored plan. As Justice Powell made clear in *Bakke*, truly individualized consideration demands that race be used in a flexible, nonmechanical way. It follows from this mandate that universities cannot establish quotas for members of certain racial groups or put members of those groups on separate admissions tracks. Nor can universities insulate applicants who belong to certain racial or ethnic groups from the competition for admission. Universities can, however, consider race or ethnicity more flexibly as a "plus" factor in the context of individualized consideration of each and every applicant. ...

In summary, the Equal Protection Clause does not prohibit the Law School's narrowly tailored use of race in admissions decisions to further a compelling interest in obtaining the educational benefits that flow from a diverse student body. The judgment of the Court of Appeals for the Sixth Circuit, accordingly, is affirmed.

[Dissent by Justice Scalia:]

Unlike a clear constitutional holding that racial preferences in state educational institutions are impermissible, or even a clear anti-constitutional holding that racial preferences in state educational institutions are OK, today's Grutter-Gratz split double header seems perversely designed to prolong the controversy and the litigation. Some future lawsuits will presumably focus on whether the discriminatory scheme in question contains enough evaluation of the applicant "as an individual," and sufficiently avoids "separate admissions tracks" to fall under Grutter rather than Gratz. Some will focus on whether a university has gone beyond the bounds of a "good faith effort" and has so zealously pursued its "critical mass" as to make it an unconstitutional de facto quota system, rather than merely "a permissible goal." Other lawsuits may focus on whether, in the particular setting at issue, any educational benefits flow from racial diversity. Still other suits may challenge the bona fides of the institution's expressed commitment to the educational benefits of diversity that immunize the discriminatory scheme in Grutter. (Tempting targets, one would suppose, will be those universities that talk the talk of multiculturalism and racial diversity in the courts but walk the walk of tribalism and racial segregation on their campuses—through minority-only student organizations, separate minority housing opportunities, separate minority student centers, even separate minority-only graduation ceremonies.) And still other suits may claim that the institution's racial preferences have gone below or above the mystical Grutter-approved "critical mass." Finally, litigation can be expected on behalf of minority groups intentionally short changed in the institution's composition of its generic minority "critical mass." I do not look forward to any of these cases. The Constitution proscribes government discrimination on the basis of race, and state-provided education is no exception.

[Dissent by Justice Thomas:]

Beyond the harm the Law School's racial discrimination visits upon its test subjects, no social science has disproved the notion that this discrimination "engenders attitudes of superiority or, alternatively, provokes resentment among those who believe that they have been wronged by the government's use of race. These programs stamp minorities with a badge of inferiority and may cause them to develop dependencies or to adopt an attitude that they are 'entitled' to preferences."

It is uncontested that each year, the Law School admits a handful of blacks who would be admitted in the absence of racial discrimination. Who can differentiate between those who belong and those who do not? The majority of blacks are admitted to the Law School because of discrimination, and because of this policy all are tarred as undeserving. This problem of stigma does not depend on determinacy as to whether those stigmatized are actually the "beneficiaries" of racial discrimination. When blacks take positions in the highest places of government, industry, or academia, it is an open question today whether their skin color played a part in their advancement. The question itself is the stigma—because either racial discrimination did play a role, in which case the person may be deemed "otherwise unqualified," or it did not, in which case asking the question itself unfairly marks those blacks who would succeed without discrimination. Is this what the Court means by "visibly open"?

Finally, the Court's disturbing reference to the importance of the country's law schools as training grounds meant to cultivate "a set of leaders with legitimacy in the eyes of the citizenry," ibid., through the use of racial discrimination deserves discussion. As noted earlier, the Court has soundly rejected the remedying of societal discrimination as a justification for governmental use of race. For those who believe that every racial disproportionality in our society is caused by some kind of racial discrimination, there can be no distinction between remedying societal discrimination and erasing racial disproportionalities in the country's leadership caste. And if the lack of proportional racial representation among our leaders is not caused by societal discrimination, then "fixing" it is even less of a pressing public necessity.

Questions

1. How does Justice O'Connor define the standard for a "compelling state interest?" How does the law school's admission policy meet that standard?
2. Do you think Justice Scalia successfully refutes the idea of a compelling state interest? How can special student groups on campus be acceptable if diversity is important?
3. Why is the law school admission policy "narrowly tailored," but the liberal arts policy was not?
4. If you were a citizen and taxpayer in Michigan, would you vote for or against the *Gratz* decision?
5. What is the main point of Justice Thomas's dissent? Is his perspective more authoritative than that of the white justices? Do you think Justice Thurgood Marshall would have agreed with Justice Thomas?

4. Bona Fide Occupational Qualifications: Johnson Controls and Hooter Girls

Congress recognized in Title VII that there might be instances in which an employer had a legitimate and necessary reason to discriminate in hiring. There are some recognized examples, such as hiring female corrections officers to work in certain jobs in a prison for women. Generally speaking, though, a BFOQ (bona fide occupation qualification) is difficult to establish. This section contains material from the Supreme Court's definitive pronouncement on gender BFOQs and a discussion of Hooters restaurants' hiring policies, which excludes men from server jobs. The Supreme Court case involved the Johnson Controls company, which excluded some women from jobs working in a battery locker.[17]

[Justice Blackmun delivered the opinion of the Court:]

In this case we are concerned with an employer's gender-based fetal-protection policy. May an employer exclude a fertile female employee from certain jobs because of its concern for the health of the fetus the woman might conceive?

Johnson Controls, Inc., manufactures batteries. In the manufacturing process, the element lead is a primary ingredient. Occupational exposure to lead entails health risks, including the risk of harm to any fetus carried by a female employee.

Before the Civil Rights Act of 1964, became law, Johnson Controls did not employ any woman in a battery-manufacturing job. In June 1977, however, it announced its first official policy concerning its employment of women in lead-exposure work:

Protection of the health of the unborn child is the immediate and direct responsibility of the prospective parents. While the medical profession and the company can support them in the exercise of this responsibility, it cannot assume it for them without simultaneously infringing their rights as persons.

Since not all women who can become mothers wish to become mothers (or will become mothers), it would appear to be illegal discrimination to treat all who are capable of pregnancy as though they will become pregnant.

Consistent with that view, Johnson Controls "stopped short of excluding women capable of bearing children from lead exposure," but emphasized that a woman who expected to have a child should not choose a job in which she would have such exposure. The company also required a woman who wished to be considered for employment to sign a statement that she had been advised of the risk of having a child while she was exposed to lead. The statement informed the woman that although there was evidence "that women exposed to lead have a higher rate of abortion," this evidence was "not as clear … as the relationship between cigarette smoking and cancer," but that it was, "medically speaking, just good sense not to run that risk if you want children and do not want to expose the unborn child to risk, however small. …"

Five years later, in 1982, Johnson Controls shifted from a policy of warning to a policy of exclusion. Between 1979 and 1983, eight employees became pregnant while maintaining blood lead levels in excess of 30 micrograms per deciliter. This appeared to be the critical level noted by the Occupational Health and Safety Administration (OSHA) for a worker who was planning to have a family. The company responded by announcing a "policy that women who are pregnant or who are capable of bearing children will not be placed into jobs involving lead exposure or which could expose them to lead through the exercise of job bidding, bumping, transfer or promotion rights. …"

The District Court granted summary judgment for defendant-respondent Johnson Controls. … The Court of Appeals for the Seventh Circuit, sitting en banc, affirmed the summary judgment by a 7-to-4 vote. The majority held that the proper standard for evaluating the fetal-protection policy was the defense of business necessity; that Johnson Controls was entitled to summary judgment under that defense; and that even if the proper standard was a BFOQ, Johnson Controls still was entitled to summary judgment.

The Court of Appeals first reviewed fetal-protection opinions from the Eleventh and Fourth Circuits. Those opinions established the three-step business necessity inquiry: whether there is a substantial health risk to the fetus; whether transmission of the hazard to the fetus occurs only through women; and whether there is a less discriminatory alternative equally capable of preventing the health hazard to the fetus. The Court of Appeals agreed with the Eleventh and Fourth Circuits that "the components of the business necessity defense the courts of appeals and the EEOC have utilized in fetal protection cases balance the interests of the employer, the employee and the unborn child in a manner consistent with Title VII. ..."

Applying this business necessity defense, the Court of Appeals ruled that Johnson Controls should prevail. Specifically, the court concluded that there was no genuine issue of material fact about the substantial health-risk factor because the parties agreed that there was a substantial risk to a fetus from lead exposure. ...

Having concluded that the business necessity defense was the appropriate framework and that Johnson Controls satisfied that standard, the court proceeded to discuss the BFOQ defense and concluded that Johnson Controls met that test, too. The en banc majority ruled that industrial safety is part of the essence of respondent's business, and that the fetal-protection policy is reasonably necessary to further that concern. The majority emphasized that, in view of the goal of protecting the unborn, "more is at stake" than simply an individual woman's decision to weigh and accept the risks of employment. ...

With its ruling, the Seventh Circuit became the first Court of Appeals to hold that a fetal-protection policy directed exclusively at women could qualify as a BFOQ. We granted certiorari, 494 U. S. 1055 (1990), to resolve the obvious conflict between the Fourth, Seventh, and Eleventh Circuits on this issue, and to address the important and difficult question whether an employer, seeking to protect potential fetuses, may discriminate against women just because of their ability to become pregnant. ...

The bias in Johnson Controls' policy is obvious. Fertile men, but not fertile women, are given a choice as to whether they wish to risk their reproductive health for a particular job. Section 703(a) of the Civil Rights Act of 1964 prohibits sex based classifications in terms and conditions of employment, in hiring and discharging decisions, and in other employment decisions that adversely affect an employee's status. Respondent's fetal-protection policy explicitly discriminates against women on the basis of their sex. The policy excludes women with childbearing capacity from lead-exposed jobs and so creates a facial classification based on gender.

Nevertheless, the Court of Appeals assumed, as did the two appellate courts who already had confronted the issue, that sex-specific fetal-protection policies do not involve facial discrimination. These courts analyzed the policies as though they were facially neutral, and had only a discriminatory effect upon the employment opportunities of women. Consequently, the courts looked to see if each employer in question had established that its policy was justified as a business necessity. The business necessity standard is more lenient for the employer than the statutory BFOQ defense. The court assumed that because the asserted reason for the sex-based exclusion (protecting women's unconceived offspring) was ostensibly benign, the policy was not sex-based discrimination. That assumption, however, was incorrect.

First, Johnson Controls' policy classifies on the basis of gender and childbearing capacity, rather than fertility alone. Respondent does not seek to protect the unconceived children of all its employees. Despite evidence in the record about the debilitating effect of lead exposure on the male reproductive system, Johnson Controls is concerned only with the harms that may befall the unborn offspring of its female employees. This Court faced a conceptually similar situation in *Phillips v. Martin Marietta Corp.*, 400 U.S. 542 (1971), and found sex discrimination because the policy established "one hiring policy for women and another for men each having pre-school-age children." Johnson Controls' policy is facially discriminatory because it requires only a female employee to produce proof that she is not capable of reproducing.

Our conclusion is bolstered by the Pregnancy Discrimination Act of 1978 in which Congress explicitly provided that, for purposes of Title VII, discrimination "on the basis of sex" includes discrimination "because of or on the basis of pregnancy, childbirth, or related medical conditions." "The Pregnancy Discrimination Act has now made clear that, for all Title VII purposes, discrimination based on a woman's pregnancy is, on its face, discrimination because of her sex." In its use of the words "capable of bearing children" in the 1982 policy statement as the criterion for exclusion, Johnson Controls explicitly classifies on the basis of potential for pregnancy. Under the PDA, such a classification must be regarded, for Title VII purposes, in the same light as explicit sex discrimination. Respondent has chosen to treat all its female employees as potentially pregnant; that choice evinces discrimination on the basis of sex.

We concluded above that Johnson Controls' policy is not neutral because it does not apply to the reproductive capacity of the company's male employees in the same way as it applies to that of the females. Moreover, the absence of a malevolent motive does not convert a facially discriminatory policy into a neutral policy with a discriminatory effect. Whether an employment practice involves disparate treatment through explicit facial discrimination does not depend on why the employer discriminates but rather on the explicit terms of the discrimination. … The beneficence of an employer's purpose does not undermine the conclusion that an explicit gender-based policy is sex discrimination under 703(a) and thus may be defended only as a BFOQ. …

Under 703(e)(1) of Title VII, an employer may discriminate on the basis of "religion, sex, or national origin in those certain instances where religion, sex, or national origin is a bona fide occupational qualification reasonably necessary to the normal operation of that particular business or enterprise." We therefore turn to the question whether Johnson Controls' fetal-protection policy is one of those "certain instances" that come within the BFOQ exception.

The BFOQ defense is written narrowly, and this Court has read it narrowly. See, e. g., *Dothard v. Rawlinson*, 433 U.S. 321, 332–337 (1977); *Trans World Airlines, Inc. v. Thurston*, 469 U.S. 111, 122–125 (1985). We have read the BFOQ language of 4(f) of the Age Discrimination in Employment Act of 1967 (ADEA) which tracks the BFOQ provision in Title VII, just as narrowly. See *Western Air Lines, Inc. v. Criswell*, 472 U.S. 400 (1985). Our emphasis on the restrictive scope of the BFOQ defense is grounded on both the language and the legislative history of 703.

The wording of the BFOQ defense contains several terms of restriction that indicate that the exception reaches only special situations. The statute thus limits the situations in which discrimination is permissible to "certain instances" where sex discrimination is "reasonably necessary" to the "normal operation" of the "particular" business. Each one of these terms certain, normal, particular prevents the use of general subjective standards and favors an objective, verifiable requirement. But the most telling term is "occupational"; this indicates that these objective, verifiable requirements must concern job-related skills and aptitudes. …

Johnson Controls argues that its fetal-protection policy falls within the so-called safety exception to the BFOQ. Our cases have stressed that discrimination on the basis of sex because of safety concerns is allowed only in narrow circumstances. In *Dothard v. Rawlinson*, this Court indicated that danger to a woman herself does not justify discrimination. We there allowed the employer to hire only male guards in contact areas of maximum-security male penitentiaries only because more was at stake than the "individual woman's decision to weigh and accept the risks of employment." We found sex to be a BFOQ inasmuch as the employment of a female guard would create real risks of safety to others if violence broke out because the guard was a woman. Sex discrimination was tolerated because sex was related to the guard's ability to do the job maintaining prison security. We also required in *Dothard* a high correlation between sex and ability to perform job functions and refused to allow employers to use sex as a proxy for strength although it might be a fairly accurate one. …

Similarly, some courts have approved airlines' layoffs of pregnant flight attendants at different points during the first five months of pregnancy on the ground that the employer's policy was necessary to ensure the safety of passengers. … In two of these cases, the courts pointedly indicated that fetal, as opposed to passenger, safety was best left to the mother.

We considered safety to third parties in *Western Airlines, Inc. v. Criswell* in the context of the ADEA. We focused upon "the nature of the flight engineer's tasks," and the "actual capabilities of persons over age 60" in relation to those tasks. Our safety concerns were not independent of the individual's ability to perform the assigned tasks, but rather involved the possibility that, because of age-connected debility, a flight engineer might not properly assist the pilot, and might thereby cause a safety emergency. Furthermore, although we considered the safety of third parties in *Dothard* and *Criswell*, those third parties were indispensable to the particular business at issue. In *Dothard*, the third parties were the inmates; in Criswell, the third parties were the passengers on the plane. We stressed that in order to qualify as a BFOQ, a job qualification must relate to the "essence," or to the "central mission of the employer's business. …"

Third-party safety considerations properly entered into the BFOQ analysis in *Dothard* and *Criswell* because they went to the core of the employee's job performance. Moreover, that performance involved the central purpose of the enterprise. *Dothard*, 433 U. S., at 335 ("The essence of a correctional counselor's job is to maintain prison security"); *Criswell*, 472 U. S., at 413 (the central mission of the airline's business was the safe transportation of its passengers). The unconceived fetuses of Johnson Controls' female employees, however, are neither customers nor third parties whose safety is essential to the business of battery manufacturing. No one can disregard the possibility of injury to future children; the BFOQ, however, is not so broad that it transforms this deep social concern into an essential aspect of battery-making.

Our case law, therefore, makes clear that the safety exception is limited to instances in which sex or pregnancy actually interferes with the employee's ability to perform the job. This approach is consistent with the language of the BFOQ provision itself, for it suggests that permissible distinctions based on sex must relate to ability to perform the duties of the job. Johnson Controls suggests, however, that we expand the exception to allow fetal-protection policies that mandate particular standards for pregnant or fertile women. We decline to do so. Such an expansion contradicts not only the language of the BFOQ and the narrowness of its exception but the plain language and history of the Pregnancy Discrimination Act. …

We conclude that the language of both the BFOQ provision and the PDA which amended it, as well as the legislative history and the case law, prohibit an employer from discriminating against a woman because of her capacity to become pregnant unless her reproductive potential prevents her from performing the duties of her job. We reiterate our holdings in *Criswell* and *Dothard* that an employer must direct its concerns about a woman's ability to perform her job safely and efficiently to those aspects of the woman's job-related activities that fall within the "essence" of the particular business. …

We have no difficulty concluding that Johnson Controls cannot establish a BFOQ. Fertile women, as far as appears in the record, participate in the manufacture of batteries as efficiently as anyone else. Johnson Controls' professed moral and ethical concerns about the welfare of the next generation do not suffice to establish a BFOQ of female sterility. Decisions about the welfare of future children must be left to the parents who conceive, bear, support, and raise them rather than to the employers who hire those parents. Congress has mandated this choice through Title VII, as amended by the Pregnancy Discrimination Act. Johnson Controls has attempted to exclude women because of their reproductive capacity. Title VII and the PDA simply do not allow a woman's dismissal because of her failure to submit to sterilization. …

A word about tort liability and the increased cost of fertile women in the workplace is perhaps necessary. One of the dissenting judges in this case expressed concern about an employer's tort liability and concluded that liability for a potential injury to a fetus is a social cost that Title VII does not require a company to ignore. It is correct to say that Title VII does not prevent the employer from having a conscience. The statute, however, does prevent sex-specific fetal-protection policies. These two aspects of Title VII do not conflict.

More than 40 States currently recognize a right to recover for a prenatal injury based either on negligence or on wrongful death. According to Johnson Controls, however, the company complies with the lead standard developed by OSHA and warns its female employees about the damaging effects of lead. It is worth noting that OSHA gave the problem of lead lengthy consideration and concluded that "there is no basis whatsoever for the claim that women of childbearing age should be excluded from the workplace in order to protect the fetus or the course of pregnancy." Instead, OSHA established a series of mandatory protections which, taken together, "should effectively minimize any risk to the fetus and newborn child." Without negligence, it would be difficult for a court to find liability on the part of the employer. If, under general tort principles, Title VII bans sex-specific fetal-protection policies, the employer fully informs the woman of the risk, and the employer has not acted negligently, the basis for holding an employer liable seems remote at best. …

We, of course, are not presented with, nor do we decide, a case in which costs would be so prohibitive as to threaten the survival of the employer's business. We merely reiterate our prior holdings that the incremental cost of hiring women cannot justify discriminating against them.

Our holding today that Title VII, as amended, forbids sex-specific fetal-protection policies is neither remarkable nor unprecedented. Concern for a woman's existing or potential offspring historically has been the excuse for denying women equal employment opportunities. Congress in the PDA prohibited discrimination on the basis of a woman's ability to become pregnant. We do no more than hold that the Pregnancy Discrimination Act means what it says.

Questions

1. Why did the company change from a policy of warning female employees about the dangers of lead to a policy of keeping them out of specific jobs?
2. What justification did the company offer to support its rule? Do you agree that women should be prohibited from working around high levels of lead? Or only some women? Which ones?
3. In an early and well-known case, an airline company had a policy of hiring only women to serve as flight attendants. If customers demanded female attendants, would that satisfy a BFOQ standard?
4. Why does the Court talk so much about the Pregnancy Discrimination Act? Do you understand from the opinion why Congress passed that legislation? Do you know of any instances in which a pregnant person was not a female?
5. Do you think science can definitively determine a person's gender? For a study arguing that some persons are neither male or female, see Gerald Callahan, *Between XX and XY: Intersexuality and the Myth of Two Sexes* (Chicago: Chicago Review Press, 2009). How should the law treat these individuals?
6. The Court discusses BFOQs based on age. Are there some jobs old people should not be allowed to do? What jobs and how old? In 2010 a 66-year-old runner completed the Leadville 100, usually regarded as one of the hardest races in the country, within the allocated time. Does that prove anything one way or the other about age?
7. At what age should airline pilots be stopped from flying? How old was Chesley B. "Sully" Sullenberger when he safely landed an Airbus A320-214 passenger jet on the Hudson River during an emergency in 2009? The Federal Aviation Agency regulates the retirement age for pilots, and in 2007, it raised the age to 65. See http://www.faa.gov/news/press_releases/news_story.cfm?newsId=10072. Age BFOQs are usually rejected if a test can prove ability to do a job. An example would be a test for vision, physical response times, and other testable characteristics. Legislation may provide for mandatory retirement age in some occupations, such as safety personnel.

So What About Hooters?

The restaurant chain known as "Hooters" has become something of a cultural phenomenon in our time. Hooters gained substantial notoriety in the 1990s with its resistance to the perceived "political correctness" of the EEOC. Hooters then, and Hooters now, hires young women for servers in its restaurants. It does not hire men for these jobs. In fact, the chain's Web site says that only women should apply for the positions.

Is this a legitimate BFOQ? Hardly. Hooters sells food and drink, and the notion that only women can successfully perform the work is preposterous. Hooters gets away with it because it faced down the EEOC when the government tried to force it to hire men applicants for servers. Hooters appealed to its public and got massive support. According to the Hooters Web site, about 500,000 customers sent letters to Congress in 1996 protesting the waste of government resources and 23 members of the House asked the EEOC to drop the case. Hooters believes the EEOC has done so.

A group of men tried to sue the chain using a class-action theory, and Hooters settled that case on favorable terms. The agreement states that "being female is 'reasonably necessary' to the performance of the Hooters Girl's job duties," and Hooters can legally discriminate against men. The Hooters Web site proclaims that its marketing policy is a perfectly legitimate business strategy (http://www.hooters.com/about.aspx). Here is what the company says:

> Sex appeal is legal and it sells. Newspapers, magazines, daytime talk shows, and local television affiliates consistently emphasize a variety of sexual topics to boost sales. Hooters marketing, emphasizing the Hooters Girl and her sex appeal, along with its commitment to quality operations continues to build and contributes to the chain's success. Hooters' business motto sums it up, "You can sell the sizzle, but you have to deliver the steak."

If you visit the Web site, Hooters features a number of pictures of Hooters employees and describes the career opportunities available to its employees.

Questions

1. Hooters' management argues that its business philosophy is perfectly consistent with our social values. That is, if customers support the restaurants, the government should not try to regulate social mores. Do you agree with that argument? If you do, should airlines be permitted to hire only female flight attendants because it may appeal to male patrons?
2. Do you think Hooters should describe its servers as "girls?" If a woman aged 50 applied for a job, could Hooters tell her she was "too old?" Is there a difference between age discrimination and gender discrimination?

3. If Hooters had a restaurant in a neighborhood that was predominantly white, could it hire only white Hooters girls to work there? Why would race discrimination be different from gender discrimination?

III. Americans with Disabilities Act of 1990 and the 2009 Amendments

The Americans with Disabilities Act (ADA), signed by President George H. Bush on July 26, 1990, provided sweeping protections for persons with disabilities across a wide spectrum of social life in this country. We now have buildings and transportation systems designed to accommodate disabilities, and public thoroughfares are accessible to wheelchairs. Title I of the bill deals with employment; its purpose is to eliminate discrimination against prospective job applicants and employees who have disabilities. As happened with Title VII, the U.S. Supreme Court tried to limit the scope and effectiveness of the act, and Congress responded with legislation undoing the Court's decisions.[18] In its 2009 modification, Congress made the following finding of fact: "physical or mental disabilities in no way diminish a person's right to fully participate in all aspects of society, yet many people with physical or mental disabilities have been precluded from doing so because of discrimination; others who have a record of a disability or are regarded as having a disability also have been subjected to discrimination." As of January 2009, the ADA is an expanded and important domain of employment regulation. Its stated purpose is "to provide a clear and comprehensive national mandate for the elimination of discrimination against individuals with disabilities." The act applies to all employers having 15 or more employees, but not to the federal government, because it is covered by other laws.

Consistent with the statute's mandate, the key to understanding how the ADA functions in the employment setting is the requirement of "reasonable accommodation." In simple terms, the law imposes a duty on employers to provide reasonable assistance so that a person with a disability can perform a job. Congress said that all individuals who are "qualified" must be considered for employment. It then defined "qualified individuals" in the following language:

> The term "qualified individual" means an individual who, with or without reasonable accommodation, can perform the essential functions of the employment position that such individual holds or desires. For the purposes of this subchapter, consideration shall be given to the employer's judgment as to what functions of a job are essential, and if an employer has prepared a written description before advertising or interviewing applicants for the job, this description shall be considered evidence of the essential functions of the job.

Accordingly, employers must consider an applicant's qualifications for a position without reference to any disability. If the applicant meets the qualifications on that basis, but has a disability, then the employer must consider whether a reasonable accommodation can be made.

Congress set forth a detailed analysis of the term "reasonable accommodation," and the related concept of "undue hardship." If an accommodation involves undue hardship, it is not reasonable. Here is how the statute explains the duty to accommodate:

> The term "reasonable accommodation" may include
>
> (A) making existing facilities used by employees readily accessible to and usable by individuals with disabilities; and (B) job restructuring, part-time or modified work schedules, reassignment to a vacant position, acquisition or modification of equipment or devices, appropriate adjustment or modifications of examinations, training materials or policies, the provision of qualified readers or interpreters, and other similar accommodations for individuals with disabilities.

The law then elaborates on the meaning of "undue hardship" in the following sections:

> (A) In general, the term "undue hardship" means an action requiring significant difficulty or expense, when considered in light of the factors set forth in subparagraph (B).
>
> (B) Factors to be considered in determining whether an accommodation would impose an undue hardship on a covered entity, factors to be considered include:
>
> (i) the nature and cost of the accommodation needed under this chapter;
>
> (ii) the overall financial resources of the facility or facilities involved in the provision of the reasonable accommodation; the number of persons employed at such facility; the effect on expenses and resources, or the impact otherwise of such accommodation upon the operation of the facility;
>
> (iii) the overall financial resources of the covered entity; the overall size of the business of a covered entity with respect to the number of its employees; the number, type, and location of its facilities; and
>
> (iv) the type of operation or operations of the covered entity, including the composition, structure, and functions of the workforce of such entity; the geographic separateness, administrative, or fiscal relationship of the facility or facilities in question to the covered entity.

The definition of a "disability" under the ADA is broad. When the Supreme Court decided a case involving a woman with limited arm movement that arose out of her employment, the Court said that was not a disability, because it did not substantially limit a major life activity. In a related decision, the Court found that a person having impaired vision, but whose vision could be corrected, was not a person with a disability.

The 2009 amendments reject the Court's rulings explicitly and thoroughly. The ADA states that the term disability means:

> (A) a physical or mental impairment that substantially limits one or more major life activities of such individual;
> (B) a record of such an impairment; or
> (C) being regarded as having such impairment. …

The statute continues with a description of major life activities, major bodily functions, the meaning of "regarded as having" an impairment, and a list of rules to interpret the act broadly in light of its purposes.[19]

One of the cases which the Supreme Court correctly decided involved the professional golf association.[20] The relevant facts of the case are straightforward. A golfer named Casey Martin had a promising career as a professional golfer. He also had a physical condition that made it difficult for him to walk. Some, but not all golf events, require that players walk the course. Martin asked for a reasonable accommodation that would allow him to use a golf cart. The Court first had to decide whether the PGA fell under the coverage of the ADA, which the majority answered in the affirmative. It then had to determine if Martin's use of a cart could be a reasonable accommodation or if it gave him an unfair advantage over other players. Again, the majority ruled in favor of Martin. The excerpt below gives the majority's reasoning and part of Justice Scalia's dissent.

[Justice Stevens wrote the majority opinion. He begins with an extended discussion of the way golfers can qualify to play in PGA tournaments. Stevens then turns to the rules of golf:]

> Three sets of rules govern competition in tour events. First, the "Rules of Golf," jointly written by the United States Golf Association (USGA) and the Royal and Ancient Golf Club of Scotland, apply to the game as it is played, not only by millions of amateurs on public courses and in private country clubs throughout the United States and worldwide, but also by the professionals in the tournaments conducted by petitioner, the USGA, the Ladies' Professional Golf Association, and the Senior Women's Golf Association. Those rules do not prohibit the use of golf carts at any time.
>
> Second, the "Conditions of Competition and Local Rules," often described as the "hard card," apply specifically to petitioner's professional tours. The hard cards for the PGA TOUR and NIKE TOUR require players to walk the golf course during tournaments, but not during open qualifying rounds. On the SENIOR PGA TOUR, which is limited to golfers age 50 and older, the contestants may use golf carts. Most seniors, however, prefer to walk.

The basic Rules of Golf, the hard cards, and the weekly notices apply equally to all players in tour competitions. As one of petitioner's witnesses explained with reference to "the Masters Tournament, which is golf at its very highest level … the key is to have everyone tee off on the first hole under exactly the same conditions and all of them be tested over that 72-hole event under the conditions that exist during those four days of the event."

[The opinion says Martin is a talented golfer with an impressive list of accomplishments. It then describes his disability:]

Martin is also an individual with a disability as defined in the Americans with Disabilities Act of 1990 (ADA or Act). Since birth he has been afflicted with Klippel-Trenaunay-Weber Syndrome, a degenerative circulatory disorder that obstructs the flow of blood from his right leg back to his heart. The disease is progressive; it causes severe pain and has atrophied his right leg. During the latter part of his college career, because of the progress of the disease, Martin could no longer walk an 18-hole golf course. Walking not only caused him pain, fatigue, and anxiety, but also created a significant risk of hemorrhaging, developing blood clots, and fracturing his tibia so badly that an amputation might be required. For these reasons, Stanford made written requests to the Pacific 10 Conference and the NCAA to waive for Martin their rules requiring players to walk and carry their own clubs. The requests were granted.

When Martin turned pro and entered petitioner's Q-School, the hard card permitted him to use a cart during his successful progress through the first two stages. He made a request, supported by detailed medical records, for permission to use a golf cart during the third stage. [The PGA] refused to review those records or to waive its walking rule for the third stage. Martin therefore filed this action. A preliminary injunction entered by the District Court made it possible for him to use a cart in the final stage of the Q-School and as a competitor in the NIKE TOUR and PGA TOUR. Although not bound by the injunction, and despite its support for petitioner's position in this litigation, the USGA voluntarily granted Martin a similar waiver in events that it sponsors, including the U.S. Open. …

At trial, petitioner did not contest the conclusion that Martin has a disability covered by the ADA, or the fact "that his disability prevents him from walking the course during a round of golf." Rather, petitioner asserted that the condition of walking is a substantive rule of competition, and that waiving it as to any individual for any reason would fundamentally alter the nature of the competition. Petitioner's evidence included the testimony of a number of experts, among them some of the greatest golfers in history. Arnold Palmer, Jack Nicklaus, and Ken Venturi explained that fatigue can be a critical factor in a tournament, particularly on the last day when psychological pressure is at a maximum. Their testimony makes it clear that, in their view, permission to use a cart might well give some players a competitive advantage over other players who must walk. They did not, however, express any opinion on whether a cart would give Martin such an advantage.

Rejecting petitioner's argument that an individualized inquiry into the necessity of the walking rule in Martin's case would be inappropriate, the District Court stated that it had "the independent duty to inquire into the purpose of the rule at issue, and to ascertain whether there can be a reasonable modification made to accommodate plaintiff without frustrating the purpose of the rule" and thereby fundamentally altering the nature of petitioner's tournaments. The judge found that the purpose of the rule was to inject fatigue into the skill of shot-making, but that the fatigue injected "by walking the course cannot be deemed significant under normal circumstances." Furthermore, Martin presented evidence, and the judge found, that even with the use of a cart, Martin must walk over a mile during an 18-hole round, and that the fatigue he suffers from coping with his disability is "undeniably greater" than the fatigue his able-bodied competitors endure from walking the course. ...

As a result, the judge concluded that it would "not fundamentally alter the nature of the PGA Tour's game to accommodate him with a cart." The judge accordingly entered a permanent injunction requiring petitioner to permit Martin to use a cart in tour and qualifying events. ...

[The Court of Appeals for the Ninth Circuit ruled in Martin's favor. It upheld the trial court's finding that Martin's use of a cart would not "fundamentally alter" the game of golf. The Supreme Court concluded that the PGA was subject to the ADA as a public accommodation because it offered golfing opportunities to the public generally. With regard to the use of a golf cart, the Court continued:]

Petitioner [PGA] does not contest that a golf cart is a reasonable modification that is necessary if Martin is to play in its tournaments. Martin's claim thus differs from one that might be asserted by players with less serious afflictions that make walking the course uncomfortable or difficult, but not beyond their capacity. In such cases, an accommodation might be reasonable but not necessary. In this case, however, the narrow dispute is whether allowing Martin to use a golf cart, despite the walking requirement that applies to the PGA TOUR, the NIKE TOUR, and the third stage of the Q-School, is a modification that would "fundamentally alter the nature" of those events.

In theory, a modification of petitioner's golf tournaments might constitute a fundamental alteration in two different ways. It might alter such an essential aspect of the game of golf that it would be unacceptable even if it affected all competitors equally; changing the diameter of the hole from three to six inches might be such a modification. Alternatively, a less significant change that has only a peripheral impact on the game itself might nevertheless give a disabled player, in addition to access to the competition as required by Title

III, an advantage over others and, for that reason, fundamentally alter the character of the competition. We are not persuaded that a waiver of the walking rule for Martin would work a fundamental alteration in either sense.

As an initial matter, we observe that the use of carts is not itself inconsistent with the fundamental character of the game of golf. From early on, the essence of the game has been shot-making—using clubs to cause a ball to progress from the teeing ground to a hole some distance away with as few strokes as possible. That essential aspect of the game is still reflected in the very first of the Rules of Golf, which declares: "The Game of Golf consists in playing a ball from the teeing ground into the hole by a stroke or successive strokes in accordance with the rules." Over the years, there have been many changes in the players' equipment, in golf course design, in the Rules of Golf, and in the method of transporting clubs from hole to hole. Originally, so few clubs were used that each player could carry them without a bag. Then came golf bags, caddies, carts that were pulled by hand, and eventually motorized carts that carried players as well as clubs. "Golf carts started appearing with increasing regularity on American golf courses in the 1950's. Today they are everywhere. And they are encouraged. For one thing, they often speed up play, and for another, they are great revenue producers." There is nothing in the Rules of Golf that either forbids the use of carts, or penalizes a player for using a cart. That set of rules, as we have observed, is widely accepted in both the amateur and professional golf world as the rules of the game. The walking rule that is contained in petitioner's hard cards, based on an optional condition buried in an appendix to the Rules of Golf, is not an essential attribute of the game itself.

Indeed, the walking rule is not an indispensable feature of tournament golf either. As already mentioned, petitioner permits golf carts to be used in the SENIOR PGA TOUR, the open qualifying events for petitioner's tournaments, the first two stages of the Q-School, and, until 1997, the third stage of the Q-School as well. Moreover, petitioner allows the use of carts during certain tournament rounds in both the PGA TOUR and the NIKE TOUR. In addition, although the USGA enforces a walking rule in most of the tournaments that it sponsors, it permits carts in the Senior Amateur and the Senior Women's Amateur championships. ...

[G]olf is a game in which it is impossible to guarantee that all competitors will play under exactly the same conditions or that an individual's ability will be the sole determinant of the outcome. For example, changes in the weather may produce harder greens and more head winds for the tournament leader than for his closest pursuers. A lucky bounce may save a shot or two. Whether such happenstance events are more or less probable than the likelihood that a golfer afflicted with Klippel-Trenaunay-Weber Syndrome would one day qualify for the NIKE TOUR and PGA TOUR, they at least demonstrate that pure chance may have a greater impact on the outcome of elite golf tournaments than the fatigue resulting from the enforcement of the walking rule.

Further, the factual basis of petitioner's argument is undermined by the District Court's finding that the fatigue from walking during one of petitioner's 4-day tournaments cannot be deemed significant. The District Court credited the testimony of a professor in physiology and expert on fatigue, who calculated the calories expended in walking a golf course (about five miles) to be approximately 500 calories—"nutritionally ... less than a Big Mac." What is more, that energy is expended over a 5-hour period, during which golfers have numerous intervals for rest and refreshment. In fact, the expert concluded, because golf is a low intensity activity, fatigue from the game is primarily a psychological phenomenon in which stress and motivation are the key ingredients. And even under conditions of severe heat and humidity, the critical factor in fatigue is fluid loss rather than exercise from walking. ...

Even if we accept the factual predicate for [the PGA's] argument—that the walking rule is "outcome affecting" because fatigue may adversely affect performance—its legal position is fatally flawed. Petitioner's refusal to consider Martin's personal circumstances in deciding whether to accommodate his disability runs counter to the clear language and purpose of the ADA. As previously stated, the ADA was enacted to eliminate discrimination against "individuals" with disabilities, and to that end Title III of the Act requires without exception that any "policies, practices, or procedures" of a public accommodation be reasonably modified for disabled "individuals" as necessary to afford access unless doing so would fundamentally alter what is offered. To comply with this command, an individualized inquiry must be made to determine whether a specific modification for a particular person's disability would be reasonable under the circumstances as well as necessary for that person, and yet at the same time not work a fundamental alteration. ...

Under the ADA's basic requirement that the need of a disabled person be evaluated on an individual basis, we have no doubt that allowing Martin to use a golf cart would not fundamentally alter the nature of petitioner's tournaments. As we have discussed, the purpose of the walking rule is to subject players to fatigue, which in turn may influence the outcome of tournaments. Even if the rule does serve that purpose, it is an uncontested finding of the District Court that Martin "easily endures greater fatigue even with a cart than his able-bodied competitors do by walking." The purpose of the walking rule is therefore not compromised in the slightest by allowing Martin to use a cart. A modification that provides an exception to a peripheral tournament rule without impairing its purpose cannot be said to "fundamentally alter" the tournament. What it can be said to do, on the other hand, is to allow Martin the chance to qualify for and compete in the athletic events petitioner offers to those members of the public who have the skill and desire to enter. That is exactly what the ADA requires. As a result, Martin's request for a waiver of the walking rule should have been granted.

[Justice Scalia's dissenting comments on the point that the rules of golf describe the "essential" game:]

Nowhere is it writ that PGA TOUR golf must be classic "essential" golf. Why cannot the PGA TOUR, if it wishes, promote a new game, with distinctive rules (much as the American League promotes a game of baseball in which the pitcher's turn at the plate can be taken by a "designated hitter")? If members of the public do not like the new rules—if they feel that these rules do not truly test the individual's skill at "real golf" (or the team's skill at "real baseball") they can withdraw their patronage. But the rules are the rules. They are (as in all games) entirely arbitrary, and there is no basis on which anyone—not even the Supreme Court of the United States—can pronounce one or another of them to be "nonessential" if the rule maker (here the PGA TOUR) deems it to be essential.

If one assumes, however, that the PGA TOUR has some legal obligation to play classic, Platonic golf—and if one assumes the correctness of all the other wrong turns the Court has made to get to this point—then we Justices must confront what is indeed an awesome responsibility. It has been rendered the solemn duty of the Supreme Court of the United States, laid upon it by Congress in pursuance of the Federal Government's power "[t]o regulate Commerce with foreign Nations, and among the several States," to decide What Is Golf. I am sure that the Framers of the Constitution, aware of the 1457 edict of King James II of Scotland prohibiting golf because it interfered with the practice of archery, fully expected that sooner or later the paths of golf and government, the law and the links, would once again cross, and that the judges of this august Court would someday have to wrestle with that age-old jurisprudential question, for which their years of study in the law have so well prepared them: Is someone riding around a golf course from shot to shot *really* a golfer? The answer, we learn, is yes. The Court ultimately concludes, and it will henceforth be the Law of the Land, that walking is not a "fundamental" aspect of golf.

Either out of humility or out of self-respect (one or the other) the Court should decline to answer this incredibly difficult and incredibly silly question. To say that something is "essential" is ordinarily to say that it is necessary to the achievement of a certain object. But since it is the very nature of a game to have no object except amusement (that is what distinguishes games from productive activity), it is quite impossible to say that any of a game's arbitrary rules is "essential." Eighteen-hole golf courses, 10-foot-high basketball hoops, 90-foot baselines, 100-yard football fields—all are arbitrary and none is essential. The only support for any of them is tradition and (in more modern times) insistence by what has come to be regarded as the ruling body of the sport—both of which factors support the PGA TOUR's position in the present case. (Many, indeed, consider walking to be *the central feature* of the game of golf—hence Mark Twain's classic criticism of the sport: "a good walk spoiled.") I suppose there is some point at which the rules of a well-known game are changed to such a degree that no reasonable person would call it the same game. If the PGA TOUR competitors were required to dribble a large, inflated ball and put it through a round hoop, the game could no longer reasonably be called golf. But this criterion—destroying recognizability as the same generic game—is surely not the test of "essentialness" or "fundamentalness" that the Court applies, since it apparently thinks that merely changing the diameter of the *cup* might "fundamentally alter" the game of golf. ....

The statute, of course, provides no basis for this individualized analysis that is the Court's last step on a long and misguided journey. The statute seeks to assure that a disabled person's disability will not deny him *equal access* to (among other things) competitive sporting events—not that his disability will not deny him an *equal chance to win* competitive sporting events. The latter is quite impossible, since the very *nature* of competitive sport is the measurement, by uniform rules, of unevenly distributed excellence. This unequal distribution is precisely what determines the winners and losers—and artificially to "even out" that distribution, by giving one or another player exemption from a rule that emphasizes his particular weakness, is to destroy the game. That is why the "handicaps" that are customary in social games of golf—which, by adding strokes to the scores of the good players and subtracting them from scores of the bad ones, "even out" the varying abilities—are *not* used in professional golf. In the Court's world, there is one set of rules that is "fair with respect to the able-bodied" but "individualized" rules, mandated by the ADA, for "talented but disabled athletes." The ADA mandates no such ridiculous thing. Agility, strength, speed, balance, quickness of mind, steadiness of nerves, intensity of concentration—these talents are not evenly distributed. No wild-eyed dreamer has ever suggested that the managing bodies of the competitive sports that test precisely these qualities should try to take account of the uneven distribution of God-given gifts when writing and enforcing the rules of competition. And I have no doubt Congress did not authorize misty-eyed judicial supervision of such a revolution.

Questions

1. The Court spends considerable time talking about the rules of golf. What if a company developed a golf ball that flew much straighter than conventional balls, and the rules of golf declared that the design was illegal for tournament play? Would it be ethical for other players to use the ball, or should the PGA seek to ban the design altogether? For a report on the new ball, see the article in the *New York Times* confirming that the design does work: http://www.nytimes.com/2011/05/10/sports/golf/10ball.html?nl=todaysheadlines&emc=tha27.
2. Casey Martin was Tiger Woods's teammate at Stanford. Would you look at this case differently if Tiger said Casey could have been the world's best golfer if he hadn't had to ride in a golf cart?
3. What if an individual wanted to play PGA golf using a prosthetic device that gave him greater power in his arm than that of an ordinary human? Would the Supreme Court uphold this accommodation?
4. Should different standards apply if Casey Martin wanted a job as a golf pro and the owner of the golf shop said he needed somebody who could stand for long periods while instructing golfers? Should Martin be accommodated then?
5. Justice Scalia calls this case "silly" because all games have arbitrary rules. Is Scalia just being "silly" by characterizing Martin's claim as one not deserving legal scrutiny? Or is that what Scalia means?

Suggested Exercises

1. Create a presentation that collects facts on employment, income, health care coverage, education, and life expectancy for white men, white women, minority men, and minority women. Offer an explanation for the differences in each category.
2. Write an essay summarizing Justice Marshall's concurring opinion in the *Bakke* case. Discuss whether the case of *Plessy v. Ferguson* should be considered a worse opinion than the Court's opinion in the *Dred Scott* case.
3. In designated teams, conduct a debate on the issue of affirmative action. The proposition for debate is, "The only way to stop race discrimination is to stop discriminating on the basis of race."
4. Write a paper describing the development of the law against sexual harassment. Begin with the use of the term "sex" in the 1964 Civil Rights Act, and conclude with the Supreme Court's opinion in the case of *Oncale v. Sundowner Offshore Services, Inc., 523 US 75*(1999).
5. Review the changes made in the Americans with Disabilities Act in 2009. Write an argumentative paper either supporting or opposing those changes.

6. Research the Hooters case, and make a presentation arguing that what the company does is unethical and exploitative of women. Or that it's not.

Notes

1. Various sites reported the story. See, e.g., http://www.theroot.com/buzz/gop-party-member-sends-email-obama-parents-apes.
2. Dr. Boyce Watkins, "Republican Birther Puts Obama's Face on a Chimp . . ." http://thyblackman.com/2011/04/18/dr-boyce-watkins-republican-birther-puts-obamas-face-on-a-chimp/.
3. Winthrop Jordan, *White over Black: American Attitudes Toward the Negro, 1550–1812* (Chapel Hill: University of North Carolina Press, 1968), p. 233.
4. See, e.g., http://www.nydailynews.com/news/national/2011/04/19/2011-04-19_goper_says_sorry_again_for_racist_obama_email_claims_to_have_received_threats.html?r=news.
5. *Ricci v. DeStefano*, 129 S. Ct. 2658 (2009).
6. *Regents of the University of California v. Bakke*, 438 U.S. 265 (1978). Justice Marshall cites several well-known studies of black history in his opinion. His footnotes are deleted from the opinion, but the basic works are the following: John Hope Franklin, *From Slavery to Freedom: A History of African Americans* (New York: Alfred A. Knopf, 4th ed. 1974 [8th ed. 2000]); Richard Kluger, *Simple Justice: The History of Brown v. Board of Education and Black America's Struggle for Equality* (New York: Alfred A. Knopf, 1976); C. Vann Woodward, *The Strange Career of Jim Crow* (New York: Oxford University Press, 3rd rev. ed., 1974).
7. For an informative and in-depth look at income inequality in the United States, see Timothy Noah, "The Great Divergence," *Slate*, at http://www.slate.com/id/2266025/entry/2266026/.
8. See http://www.eeoc.gov/employees/lawsuit.cfm for further information.
9. http://www.eeoc.gov/eeoc/statistics/enforcement/charges.cfm
10. *Stalter v. Wal-Mart Stores*, 195 F.3d 285 (7th Cir. 1999).
11. *Griggs v. Duke Power Co.*, 401 U.S. 424 (1971).
12. *Wards Cove Packing Co. v. Antonio*, 490 U.S. 642 (1989).
13. http://www.eeoc.gov/policy/docs/factemployment_procedures.html
14. http://frwebgate.access.gpo.gov/cgi-bin/get-cfr.cgi?TITLE=29&PART=1607&SECTION=5&YEAR=2000&TYPE=TEXT
15. http://www.dol.gov/opa/media/press/ofccp/OFCCP20110146.htm
16. *Gratz v. Bollinger*, 539 U.S. 244 (2003); *Grutter v. Bollinger*, 539 U.S. 306 (2003).
17. *United Automobile, Aerospace & Agricultural Implement Workers of America (UAW) v. Johnson Controls, Inc.*, 499 US.187 (1991).
18. 42 U.S.C., Ch. 126, Sec. 12101 et seq. (2009). For an in-depth treatment of the statutory language, see http://www.ada.gov/pubs/ada.htm.
19. Section 12102 contains the language added in 2009.
20. *PGA Tour v. Martin*, 532 U.S. 661 (2001).

5. Human Resource Management

I. The Human Resource Management Function: An Overview

Human resource management, or HRM, emerged from historical relations between workers and the owners and managers of firms. As Karl Marx pointed out in his analysis of capitalism, employers do not purchase labor from workers. Rather, they purchase the potential for labor, and then deal with the problem of exchanging wages for actual labor. In one of the most famous passages of *Capital*, Marx described the world of wage labor as a "hidden abode," where employers exploit labor by taking the "surplus" value of work in the form of profit.[1] According to this analysis, owners always pay less in wages than the value of the commodity produced by labor, and this process drives the engine of capitalism by creating accumulated wealth. The wage-labor bargain is not a contract for the outright purchase of a quantity of labor, because the terms of the arrangement are incomplete. Workers are hired to report for work at a given time and date, and the employer subsequently assigns work to be accomplished. Managing workers thus requires monitoring, rewarding, and disciplining them on a routine basis.

The analysis changes when an "independent" contracting arrangement exists, because there is a bargain for both a price (not a wage) and a known quantity of labor. For that reason, managing *employees*—as opposed to a contractor—has always been a crucial dimension of capitalist organization. The law recognizes a crucial distinction between contractors and employees, a subject covered in Chapter One. HR managers may choose to purchase contract labor rather than to enter into an employment relationship for various reasons, including the regulatory environment that imposes costs on employment. Likewise, the government has an interest in making sure that employees are designated as employees and not as independent contractors so that workers are protected under appropriate laws.

Historically, the term "industrial relations" (IR) described the field of study covering all aspects of employment relations. In an impressive book on the subject, Bruce Kaufman traces the origins of IR to developments in the United States during the beginning of the 20th century, specifically crediting John Commons and John D. Rockefeller, Jr. as the founders of the discipline.[2] Scholars such as Commons and his students at the University of Wisconsin studied labor problems, and developed policies to improve the more destructive consequences of class conflict that were described by Marx.[3] Rockefeller, at one time the richest man on the planet, implemented and popularized a process of organizational justice that is still followed today. The "Colorado Industrial Plan," as it was known, featured a system of employee representation that gave workers a voice in the operation of the firm; disputes were settled by third-party arbitration.

In the aftermath of the Great Depression and the New Deal, organized labor played the dominant role in dealings between labor and management, and "personnel management" performed the function of administering the different components of an employment relationship. Large firms generally managed workers by reference to the terms of the labor agreement, which set out such matters as wages, benefits, working conditions, and disciplinary procedures. Leading firms that were not organized, such as Coca-Cola and IBM, typically followed unionized trends in compensation and benefits. Union influence began to decline in the late 1970s, and personnel management evolved into the field of HRM. During the 1980s, human resource policies focused on "union avoidance" as a means of controlling labor costs; that strategy was so successful that the avidly nonunion Wal-Mart became the model for low-wage employment. By the end of the first decade of the 21st century, unions had only a marginal effect on employment relations. HRM played an increasingly important role in protecting the firm from employment-related lawsuits.

Scholars have differing views on the precise contours of HRM as distinct from its predecessors. A well-known book by Karen Legge suggests that HRM contrasts with personnel management, in that HRM is more strategically integrated within the firm and adds value in its contribution to the firm's overall mission and competencies.[4] Toward this end, HRM emphasizes culture, teamwork, employee motivation, and empowerment as opposed to a reliance on rules, job classification, detailed task assignments, and adherence to systematized work environments. HR managers are therefore concerned with understanding the organization's overall goals, strengths, capabilities, and vision and participating in their development. Regardless of the exact dimensions of HRM, there is general agreement in its major functions, which is the content of this chapter. The table below provides an overview of HR activities.

HRM Category	Description
Hiring	Managing the recruitment process, interviewing, and selecting employees
Compensating	Developing pay and benefit policies, administering the system
Performance Management	Training, promoting, motivating, and stabilizing the workforce
Conflict Resolution	Dealing with disciplinary procedures, providing organizational justice systems, avoiding litigation

II. Recruiting and Selecting

A. Job Descriptions

The first step in hiring a workforce is to describe the jobs necessary to accomplish the firm's objectives. Assume, for example, that a group decides to form a company that furnishes medical and personal care for the elderly ("Older Is Okay" or "OO"). The demographics of retirement indicate that there will be more retirees over the next few decades, that they will live longer, and that improved medical care will mean a better quality of life. Among various other jobs, the OO Company wants several occupational therapists on its staff. How would the HR director go about hiring qualified individuals? One starting point is to look at the Occupational Handbook prepared by the Bureau of Labor Statistics. Here is what that document says about occupational therapists.[5]

> *Significant Points*
> - Employment is expected to grow much faster than average, and job opportunities should be good, especially for therapists treating the elderly.
> - Occupational therapists are regulated in all 50 States; requirements vary by State.
> - Occupational therapists are increasingly taking on supervisory roles, allowing assistants and aides to work more closely with clients under the guidance of a therapist.
>
> *Nature of the Work*
> Occupational therapists help patients improve their ability to perform tasks in living and working environments. They work with individuals who suffer from a mentally, physically, developmentally, or emotionally disabling

condition. Occupational therapists use treatments to develop, recover, or maintain the daily living and work skills of their patients. The therapist helps clients not only to improve their basic motor functions and reasoning abilities, but also to compensate for permanent loss of function. The goal is to help clients have independent, productive, and satisfying lives.

Occupational therapists help clients to perform all types of activities, from using a computer to caring for daily needs such as dressing, cooking, and eating. Physical exercises may be used to increase strength and dexterity, while other activities may be chosen to improve visual acuity or the ability to discern patterns. For example, a client with short-term memory loss might be encouraged to make lists to aid recall, and a person with coordination problems might be assigned exercises to improve hand-eye coordination. Occupational therapists also use computer programs to help clients improve decision-making, abstract-reasoning, problem-solving, and perceptual skills, as well as memory, sequencing, and coordination—all of which are important for independent living.

Patients with permanent disabilities, such as spinal cord injuries, cerebral palsy, or muscular dystrophy, often need special instruction to master certain daily tasks. For these individuals, therapists demonstrate the use of adaptive equipment, including wheelchairs, orthoses, eating aids, and dressing aids. They also design or build special equipment needed at home or at work, including computer-aided adaptive equipment. They teach clients how to use the equipment to improve communication and control various situations in their environment.

Some occupational therapists treat individuals whose ability to function in a work environment has been impaired. These practitioners might arrange employment, evaluate the work space, plan work activities, and assess the client's progress. Therapists also may collaborate with the client and the employer to modify the work environment so that the client can succeed at work.

Assessing and recording a client's activities and progress is an important part of an occupational therapist's job. Accurate records are essential for evaluating clients, for billing, and for reporting to physicians and other healthcare providers.

Occupational therapists may work exclusively with individuals in a particular age group or with a particular disability. In schools, for example, they evaluate children's capabilities, recommend and provide therapy, modify classroom equipment, and help children participate in school activities. A therapist may work with children individually, lead small groups in the classroom, consult with a teacher, or serve on an administrative committee. Some therapists provide early intervention therapy to infants and toddlers who have, or are at risk of having, developmental delays. Therapies may include facilitating the use of the hands and promoting skills for listening, following directions, social play, dressing, or grooming.

Other occupational therapists work with elderly patients. These therapists help the elderly lead more productive, active, and independent lives through a variety of methods. Therapists with specialized training in driver rehabilitation assess an individual's ability to drive using both clinical and on-the-road tests. The evaluations allow the therapist to make recommendations for adaptive equipment, training to prolong driving independence, and alternative transportation options. Occupational therapists also work with clients to assess their homes for hazards and to identify environmental factors that contribute to falls.

Occupational therapists in mental health settings treat individuals who are mentally ill, developmentally challenged, or emotionally disturbed. To treat these problems, therapists choose activities that help people learn to engage in and cope with daily life. Activities might include time management skills, budgeting, shopping, homemaking, and the use of public transportation. Occupational therapists also work with individuals who are dealing with alcoholism, drug abuse, depression, eating disorders, or stress-related disorders.

Work environment. In large rehabilitation centers, therapists may work in spacious rooms equipped with machines, tools, and other devices generating noise. The work can be tiring because therapists are on their feet much of the time. Therapists also face hazards such as back strain from lifting and moving clients and equipment.

Occupational therapists working for one employer full-time usually work a 40-hour week. Around 31 percent of occupational therapists worked part-time. It is not uncommon for occupational therapists to work for more than one employer at multiple facilities, which may involve significant travel time. Those in schools may participate in meetings and other activities during and after the school day.

Occupational therapists help patients learn to perform all types of activities, from using a computer to caring for daily needs such as dressing, cooking, and eating.

Training, Other Qualifications, and Advancement

Occupational therapists are regulated in all 50 States. Individuals pursuing a career as an occupational therapist usually need to earn a post-baccalaureate degree from an accredited college or university or education deemed equivalent.

Education and training. A master's degree or higher in occupational therapy is the typical minimum requirement for entry into the field. In addition, occupational therapists must attend an academic program accredited by the Accreditation Council for Occupational Therapy Education (ACOTE) in order to sit for the national certifying exam. In 2009, 150 master's degree programs or combined bachelor's and master's degree programs were accredited, and 4 doctoral degree programs were accredited. Most schools have full-time programs, although a growing number are offering weekend or part-time programs as well. Coursework in occupational therapy programs include the physical, biological, and behavioral sciences as well as the application of occupational therapy theory and skills. All accredited programs require at least 24 weeks of supervised fieldwork as part of the academic curriculum.

People considering this profession should take high school courses in biology, chemistry, physics, health, art, and the social sciences. College admissions offices also look favorably on paid or volunteer experience in the healthcare field. Relevant undergraduate majors include biology, psychology, sociology, anthropology, liberal arts, and anatomy.

Licensure. All States regulate the practice of occupational therapy. To obtain a license, applicants must graduate from an accredited educational program and pass a national certification examination. Those who pass the exam are awarded the title "Occupational Therapist Registered (OTR)." Specific eligibility requirements for licensure vary by State; contact your State's licensing board for details.

Some States have additional requirements for therapists who work in schools or early intervention programs. These requirements may include education-related classes, an education practice certificate, or early intervention certification.

Certification and other qualifications. Certification is voluntary. The National Board for Certifying Occupational Therapy certifies occupational therapists through a national certifying exam. Those who pass the test are awarded the title Occupational Therapist Registered (OTR). In some States, the national certifying exam meets requirements for regulation while other States have their own licensing exam.

Occupational therapists are expected to continue their professional development by participating in continuing education courses and workshops. In fact, a number of States require continuing education as a condition of maintaining licensure.

Occupational therapists need patience and strong interpersonal skills to inspire trust and respect in their clients. Patience is necessary because many clients may not show immediate improvement. Ingenuity and imagination in adapting activities to individual needs are assets. Those working in home healthcare services also must be able to adapt to a variety of settings.

Advancement. Therapists are increasingly taking on supervisory roles in addition to their supervision of occupational therapy assistants and aides.

Occupational therapists may advance their careers by taking on administrative duties at hospitals or rehabilitation centers.

Occupational therapists also can advance by specializing in a clinical area and gaining expertise in treating a certain type of patient or ailment. Therapists may specialize in gerontology, mental health, pediatrics, and physical rehabilitation. In addition, some occupational therapists choose to teach classes in accredited occupational therapy educational programs.

Employment

Occupational therapists held about 104,500 jobs in 2008. The largest number of occupational therapist jobs was in ambulatory healthcare services, which employed about 29 percent of occupational therapists. Other major employers were hospitals, offices of other health practitioners (including offices of occupational therapists), public and private educational services, and nursing care facilities. Some occupational therapists were employed by home healthcare services, outpatient care centers, offices of physicians, individual and family services, community care facilities for the elderly, and government agencies.

A small number of occupational therapists were self-employed in private practice. These practitioners treated clients referred by other health professionals. They also provided contract or consulting services to nursing care facilities, schools, adult day care programs, and home healthcare agencies.

Job Outlook

Employment is expected to grow much faster than average. Job opportunities should be good, especially for occupational therapists treating the elderly.

Employment change. Employment of occupational therapists is expected to increase by 26 percent between 2008 and 2018, much faster than the average for all occupations. The increasing elderly population will drive growth in the demand for occupational therapy services. The demand for occupational therapists should continue to rise as a result of the increasing number of individuals with disabilities or limited function who require therapy services. Older persons have an increased incidence of heart attack and stroke, which will spur demand for therapeutic services. Growth in the population 75 years and older—an age group that suffers from high incidences of disabling conditions—also will increase demand for therapeutic services. In addition, medical advances now enable more patients with critical problems to survive—patients who ultimately may need extensive therapy. However, growth may be dampened by the impact of Federal legislation imposing limits on reimbursement for therapy services.

Hospitals will continue to employ a large number of occupational therapists to provide therapy services to acutely ill inpatients. Hospitals also will need occupational therapists to staff their outpatient rehabilitation programs.

Employment growth in schools will result from the expansion of the school-age population and the federally funded extension of services for disabled students. Therapists will be needed to help children with disabilities prepare to enter special education programs.

Job prospects. Job opportunities should be good for licensed occupational therapists in all settings, particularly in acute hospital, rehabilitation, and orthopedic settings because the elderly receive most of their treatment in these settings. Occupational therapists with specialized knowledge in a treatment area also will have increased job prospects. Driver rehabilitation, training for the elderly, and ergonomic consulting are emerging practice areas for occupational therapy.

Earnings

Median annual wages of occupational therapists were $66,780 in May 2008. The middle 50 percent earned between $55,090 and $81,290. The lowest 10 percent earned less than $42,820, and the highest 10 percent earned more than $98,310. Median annual wages in the industries employing the largest numbers of occupational therapists in May 2008 were

Home health care services	*$74,510*
Nursing care facilities	*72,790*
Offices of other health care practitioners	*69,360*
General medical and surgical hospitals	*68,100*
Elementary and secondary schools	*60,020*

Based on this information, positions at OO may be difficult and costly to fill. The HR department would need to consider whether less qualified therapists might be able to perform some functions offered by the company. Is there a job description in the handbook for therapists who do not have the education and training of a certified therapist?

As a practical matter, an efficient method to screen and recruit candidates in the case above would be to use a consultant who specializes in health care staffing. An example is "Club Staffing," which provides services to employers and employees seeking work in the field. Their advertisement promises, "Thanks to our vast recruiting network and leading-edge staffing services, we can fill your therapist jobs, medical imaging jobs or laboratory jobs and other allied positions across the country with the most qualified professionals." The site invites employees to submit personal information as a preliminary step in the application process.[6]

B. Finding and Selecting Candidates

Once a job description has been developed, a recruiter might advertise in local media outlets such as newspapers, television, and radio. Relying on the reach of internet technology, some companies such as Monster offer a range of online services to employers and employees (http://www.monster.com/). The Web site provides a range of features, including searchable job databases using keywords, locations, and industries. Monster also has tips for preparing résumés, negotiating salaries, following up on interviews, and other items of interest to job seekers. Prospective employees also can post résumés and complete applications online. For employers, the site offers posting opportunities based on specified fees for different types of jobs.

Many companies maintain their own Web sites for attracting potential employees. In early 2011 *CBS Sunday Morning* featured a story on the Container Store, a company that sells storage devices.[7] Although the company's product is certainly not "trendy," the company itself was characterized as one of the best places to work in the country. If you visit the Web site, prospective employees can find information about careers with the company and testimonials from current employees. The Web site proclaims, "We're a company known for impeccable customer service and expert salespeople. We're a company that insists on having fun. Simply put, **we approach retail differently**. In fact, for these reasons and more, we've been at the top of FORTUNE magazine's list of '100 Best Companies to Work for in America' 11 years in a row."[8]

In addition to soliciting applications, employers are using online programs to perform preliminary screening of applicants. Because there are large numbers of people seeking employment of any kind, firms may be pressed to sort out legitimate and qualified applicants from the pool. According to a recent report, "Employment assessments can range from online exams for a specific computer skill to personality tests intended to predict customer service prowess to extensive evaluations of potential executives. A study published last year by consulting firm Rocket-Hire found that about two-thirds of companies use some form of pre-employment assessment tools." The assessment strategies may extend to performance evaluation and promotion. While there are issues associated with online assessment, such as cheating on a test, software providers continue to improve the product. Most likely, those technological strategies for selection will become widespread.[9]

Based on the materials in Chapter 3, you know that some job qualifications and questions are not legal. An applicant could not be asked, for example, whether they were in excellent health, how old they are, the nature of their religious affiliations, or other information that might violate the protections of the civil rights laws. To avoid those pitfalls, employers typically ask open-ended questions that allow the applicant to shape an answer. Some of the most common are the following:

- What are your long-term career goals?
- Why are you interested in this job (or company)?
- What kind of people would you prefer to work with in a team setting?

- What salary would you require to work here?
- What's the most difficult problem you faced in a work setting and what did you do?
- What personality type would you find most difficult to work with?

The questions are fairly generic, but they allow applicants to express something important about themselves while avoiding legal impediments.

The development of "social media" sites allows employers to acquire more information about prospective employees, but it may also present some risks of legal consequence. Some legal experts characterize an Internet search as being similar to an interview, except the search may reveal the applicant's age, family status, or other kinds of information. One way to avoid the problem is to rely only on information the applicant furnishes. Alternatively, the employer might ask for consent to undertake a search. The extent to which the employer can control an employee's use of social media is discussed later in the chapter.

C. Verifying Employee Information

There are different means by which the prospective employee's application can be verified. This is important to avoid liability for negligent hiring, as well as to ensure the credentials are what they appear to be. The potential legal liability arises out of well-established doctrines of negligence. In a recent California case, a plaintiff attempted to get damages from a plumbing company after a former employee shot and killed the plaintiff's mother. The plaintiff claimed that the plumbing company hired an individual whom they should have known was a threat to the company's clients. The court cited the standard rule as follows: "Liability for negligent hiring is based upon the reasoning that if an enterprise hires individuals with characteristics which might pose a danger to customers or other employees, the enterprise should bear the loss caused by the wrongdoing of its incompetent or unfit employees." A legal duty exists when the employer "knew or should have known that hiring the employee created a particular risk or hazard and that particular harm materializes."[10] The plaintiff lost this case, because the company had fired the individual two years before the shooting. Consider the case of a female English teacher, fired after she was caught naked in a public park with a 15-year-old student. She was sentenced to probation and registration as a sex offender.[11] If a school in another state hired her and the same thing happened, should the school be liable to the victim for failing to investigate the teacher's background? What damages could the victim recover?

Conducting a background investigation can be costly and time consuming, but there are firms that will perform a search of public records for the employer. If an employer uses that method of screening, the activity is covered by the federal Fair Trade Commission's (FTC) authority to regulate consumer reports under the Fair Credit

Reporting Act. The FTC provides an informative explanation about the regulations on its Web site.[12]

Using Consumer Reports: What Employers Need to Know

Your advertisement for cashiers nets 100 applications. You want credit reports on each applicant. You plan to eliminate those with poor credit histories. What are your obligations?

You are considering a number of your long-term employees for major promotions. Can you check their credit reports to ensure that only financially responsible individuals are considered?

A job candidate has authorized you to obtain a credit report. The applicant has a poor credit history. Although the credit history is considered a negative factor, it's the applicant's lack of relevant experience that's more important to you. You turn down the application. What procedures must you follow?

As an employer, you may use consumer reports when you hire new employees and when you evaluate employees for promotion, reassignment, and retention—as long as you comply with the Fair Credit Reporting Act (FCRA). Sections 604, 606, and 615 of the FCRA spell out your responsibilities when using consumer reports for employment purposes.

The FCRA is designed primarily to protect the privacy of consumer report information and to guarantee that the information supplied by consumer reporting agencies is as accurate as possible. Amendments to the FCRA—which went into effect September 30, 1997—significantly increase the legal obligations of employers who use consumer reports. Congress expanded employer responsibilities because of concern that inaccurate or incomplete consumer reports could cause applicants to be denied jobs or cause employees to be denied promotions unjustly. The amendments ensure (1) that individuals are aware that consumer reports may be used for employment purposes and agree to such use, and (2) that individuals are notified promptly if information in a consumer report may result in a negative employment decision.

What Is a Consumer Report?

A consumer report contains information about your personal and credit characteristics, character, general reputation, and lifestyle. To be covered by the FCRA, a report must be prepared by a consumer reporting agency (CRA)—a business that assembles such reports for other businesses.

Employers often do background checks on applicants and get consumer reports during their employment. Some employers only want an applicant's or employee's credit payment records; others want driving records and criminal histories. For sensitive positions, it's not unusual for employers to order investigative consumer reports—reports that include interviews with an applicant's or employee's friends, neighbors, and associates. All of these types of reports are consumer reports if they are obtained from a CRA.

Applicants are often asked to give references. Whether verifying such references is covered by the FCRA depends on who does the verification. A reference verified by the employer is not covered by the Act; a reference verified by an employment or reference checking agency (or other CRA) is covered. Section 603(o) provides special procedures for reference checking; otherwise, checking references may constitute an investigative consumer report subject to additional FCRA requirements.

Key Provisions of the FCRA Amendments

Written Notice and Authorization

Before you can get a consumer report for employment purposes, you must notify the individual in writing—in a document consisting solely of this notice—that a report may be used. You also must get the person's written authorization before you ask a CRA for the report. (Special procedures apply to the trucking industry.)

Adverse Action Procedures

If you rely on a consumer report for an "adverse action"—denying a job application, reassigning or terminating an employee, or denying a promotion—be aware that:

> Step 1: Before you take the adverse action, you must give the individual a pre-adverse action disclosure that includes a copy of the individual's consumer report and a copy of "A Summary of Your Rights Under the Fair Credit Reporting Act"—a document prescribed by the Federal Trade Commission. The CRA that furnishes the individual's report will give you the summary of consumer rights.
>
> Step 2: After you've taken an adverse action, you must give the individual notice—orally, in writing, or electronically—that the action has been taken in an adverse action notice. It must include:
>
> - The name, address, and phone number of the CRA that supplied the report;
> - A statement that the CRA that supplied the report did not make the decision to take the adverse action and cannot give specific reasons for it; and
> - A notice of the individual's right to dispute the accuracy or completeness of any information the agency furnished, and his or her right to an additional free consumer report from the agency upon request within 60 days.

Certifications to Consumer Reporting Agencies
Before giving you an individual's consumer report, the CRA will require you to certify that you are in compliance with the FCRA and that you will not misuse any information in the report in violation of federal or state equal employment opportunity laws or regulations.

In 1998, Congress amended the FCRA to provide special procedures for mail, telephone, or electronic employment applications in the trucking industry. Employers do not need to make written disclosures and obtain written permission in the case of applicants who will be subject to state or federal regulation as truckers. Finally, no pre-adverse action disclosure or Section 615(a) disclosure is required. Instead, the employer must, within three days of the decision, provide an oral, written, or electronic adverse action disclosure consisting of: (1) a statement that an adverse action has been taken based on a consumer report; (2) the name, address, and telephone number of the CRA; (3) a statement that the CRA did not make the decision; and (4) a statement that the consumer may obtain a copy of the actual report from the employer if he or she provides identification.

In Practice ...
You advertise vacancies for cashiers and receive 100 applications. You want just credit reports on each applicant because you plan to eliminate those with poor credit histories. What are your obligations?

You can get credit reports—one type of consumer report—if you notify each applicant in writing that a credit report may be requested and if you receive the applicant's written consent. Before you reject an applicant based on credit report information, you must make a pre-adverse action disclosure that includes a copy of the credit report and the summary of consumer rights under the FCRA. Once you've rejected an applicant, you must provide an adverse action notice if credit report information affected your decision.

You are considering a number of your long-term employees for a major promotion. You want to check their consumer reports to ensure that only responsible individuals are considered for the position. What are your obligations?

You cannot get consumer reports unless the employees have been notified that reports may be obtained and have given their written permission. If the employees gave you written permission in the past, you need only make sure that the employees receive or have received a "separate document" notice that reports may be obtained during the course of their employment—no more notice or permission is required. If your employees have not received notice and given you permission, you must notify the employees and get their written permission before you get their reports.

In each case where information in the report influences your decision to deny promotion, you must provide the employee with a pre-adverse action disclosure. The employee also must receive an adverse action notice once you have selected another individual for the job.

A job applicant gives you the okay to get a consumer report. Although the credit history is poor and that's a negative factor, the applicant's lack of relevant experience carries more weight in your decision not to hire. What's your responsibility?

In any case where information in a consumer report is a factor in your decision—even if the report information is not a major consideration—you must follow the procedures mandated by the FCRA. In this case, you would be required to provide the applicant a pre-adverse action disclosure before you reject his or her application. When you formally reject the applicant, you would be required to provide an adverse action notice.

The applicants for a sensitive financial position have authorized you to obtain credit reports. You reject one applicant, whose credit report shows a debt load that may be too high for the proposed salary, even though the report shows a good repayment history. You turn down another, whose credit report shows only one credit account, because you want someone who has shown more financial responsibility. Are you obliged to provide any notices to these applicants?

Both applicants are entitled to a pre-adverse action disclosure and an adverse action notice. If any information in the credit report influences an adverse decision, the applicant is entitled to the notices—even when the information isn't negative.

Noncompliance

There are legal consequences for employers who fail to get an applicant's permission before requesting a consumer report or who fail to provide pre-adverse action disclosures and adverse action notices to unsuccessful job applicants. The FCRA allows individuals to sue employers for damages in federal court. A person who successfully sues is entitled to recover court costs and reasonable legal fees. The law also allows individuals to seek punitive damages for deliberate violations. In addition, the Federal Trade Commission, other federal agencies, and the states may sue employers for noncompliance and obtain civil penalties.

After reading the government's description of the requirements, do you think it gives employees too much protection? Is it too burdensome for employers? Returning to the case of the English teacher, how else could a school district protect itself against a negligent hiring lawsuit?

III. Compensation and Benefits

According to an article in the *New York Times* on May 19, 2011, job prospects for new college graduates remained bleak.[13] The report stated, "The median starting salary for students graduating from four-year colleges in 2009 and 2010 was $27,000, down from $30,000 for those who entered the work force in 2006 to 2008. … That is a decline of 10 percent, even before taking inflation into account." Declining salaries are only part of the problem. Many of the jobs taken by college graduates did not require a degree, depending largely on the graduate's disciplinary field. The *Times* found, "Young graduates who majored in education and teaching or engineering were most likely to find a job requiring a college degree, while area studies majors—those who majored in Latin American studies, for example—and humanities majors were least likely to do so." More problematically for the American workforce, college graduates who took lower-level jobs forced individuals without degrees into even worse jobs. The downward ratcheting effect resulted in higher unemployment rates for high school graduates or dropouts. The trend in employment levels and pay exacerbates the three-decade wage stagnation in place before the 2007 recession and affects compensation policies generally, which is the topic of this section.

A leading textbook on compensation uses a framework designed around policies, procedures, and objectives.[14] The first policy involves creating a compensation structure that has internal coherence, and is based on a rational system which can be explained and understood. The second policy is to address the problem of market competitiveness, which ensures that individuals are attracted to the organization and are satisfied with their pay. Following from the first two policies, the third factor is individual rewards that are fair and equitable. Last, the program must be administratively feasible and satisfy legal requirements. A compensation system incorporating the four policies will satisfy the objectives of efficiency, fairness, and compliance. Keeping these points in mind, we can explore the basic structure of pay and related benefits.

A straightforward and understandable way of compensating workers is to describe jobs and attach pay rates to the specific job. Union contracts usually contain such information in an appendix to the agreement. Some common factors associated with rates of pay are skill, physical and mental effort, responsibility and working conditions. So, for example, a union contract in a grocery store may have a job classification called "head meat cutter," a position requiring considerable expertise and responsibility, with a pay rate of about $18.00 per hour, plus benefits. A generic classification of "meat cutter" is hired at a rate of $11.30 per hour and is given raises based on length of service earned in increments of 1,040 hours worked, with a top rate of $17.65. A similar process applies to other classifications, such as seafood clerks, meat wrappers, and delicatessen clerks. This approach satisfies the policies of transparency, competitiveness, fairness, and legal compliance.

What can American workers generally expect in terms of average wages and benefits? The Bureau of Labor Statistics compiles detailed information about pay and benefits for American workers and publishes that information on a regular basis. Below are excerpts from the December 2010 report, published in March 2011.[15] Note how much of total compensation is paid in wages, specific benefits, and differences between private and public sector employment. Some labor costs are mandatory, such as Social Security, workers' compensation, and unemployment insurance, but other benefits are discretionary with employers.

EMPLOYER COSTS FOR EMPLOYEE COMPENSATION—DECEMBER 2010

Private industry employers spent an average of $27.75 per hour worked for total employee compensation in December 2010, the U.S. Bureau of Labor Statistics reported today. Wages and salaries averaged $19.64 per hour worked and accounted for 70.8 percent of these costs, while benefits averaged $8.11 and accounted for the remaining 29.2 percent. Total compensation costs for state and local government workers averaged $40.28 per hour worked in December 2010. Total employer compensation costs for civilian workers, which include private industry and state and local government workers, averaged $29.72 per hour worked in December 2010.

Employer Costs for Employee Compensation (ECEC), a product of the National Compensation Survey, measures employer costs for wages, salaries, and employee benefits for nonfarm private and state and local government workers.

Paid leave costs in private industry

Private industry employer costs for paid leave benefits averaged $1.89 per hour worked.

Private industry paid leave benefit costs were highest for management, professional, and related occupations, $4.17 per hour, or 8.4 percent of total compensation, in December 2010. Costs were lowest among service occupations, 59 cents, or 4.3 percent of total compensation. Included in this amount were employer costs for vacations, holidays, sick leave, and personal leave. Paid leave benefit costs are often directly linked to wages; therefore, higher paid occupations or industries will typically show higher estimates for this compensation component.

Employer costs for paid leave benefits averaged $2.77 per hour worked for union workers, significantly higher than the $1.79 per hour average for nonunion workers. Paid leave costs in goods-producing industries were $2.11, greater than the average for service-providing industries, $1.84, in December 2010. The average cost per hour worked for paid leave in service-providing industries ranged from $3.87 in information to 40 cents in leisure and hospitality.

Paid leave costs varied widely by establishment size in private industry. Paid leave costs for establishments with fewer than 100 workers were $1.28 per hour worked versus $1.95 for establishments with 100 to 499 employees and $3.44 with 500 employees or more.

Legally required benefits costs in private industry

The average cost for legally required benefits was $2.28 per hour worked in private industry (8.2 percent of total compensation) in December 2010. Social Security comprises the largest legally required benefit cost component at $1.32 per hour or 4.8 percent of total compensation. Legally required benefits such as Social Security and Medicare are often directly linked to wages; therefore, higher paid occupations or industries will typically show higher cost estimates for this compensation component.

Costs for other legally required benefits include Workers' compensation, which averaged 42 cents per hour worked (1.5 percent of total compensation); State unemployment insurance, which averaged 18 cents per hour worked (0.7 percent); and Federal unemployment insurance, which averaged just 3 cents per hour worked (0.1 percent).

Employer costs for legally required benefits varied by occupation, industry, bargaining status, and establishment size. The average cost per hour worked for legally required benefits ranged from $3.43 for management, professional, and related occupations to $1.42 per hour for service occupations. The proportion of total compensation represented by legally required benefits ranged from 10.2 percent for service and natural resources, construction, and maintenance workers to 6.9 percent for management, professional, and related workers. Worker's compensation employer costs for construction industry workers were especially notable, averaging $1.32 per hour worked in December 2010.

Other benefit categories in private industry

Private industry employer costs averaged $2.22 per hour worked for insurance benefits (life, health, and disability insurance), or 8.0 percent of total compensation. In addition to insurance, the other benefit categories were: supplemental pay (overtime and premium, shift differentials, and nonproduction bonuses), which averaged 75 cents per hour worked (2.7 percent); and retirement and savings, which averaged 97 cents per hour (3.5 percent).

Table A. Relative importance of employer costs for employee compensation, December 2010

Compensation component	Civilian workers (federal)	Private industry	State and local government
Wages and salaries	69.7%	70.8%	65.6%
Benefits	30.3	29.2	34.4
Paid leave	7.0	6.8	7.5
Supplemental pay	2.3	2.7	0.8
Insurance	8.8	8.0	11.9
Health benefits	8.4	7.5	11.6
Retirement and savings	4.5	3.5	8.1
Defined benefit	2.7	1.5	7.3
Defined contribution	1.8	2.0	0.8
Legally required	7.8	8.2	6.0

The information above provides an overview of compensation in the United States. Firms obviously have broad latitude concerning pay rates and methods. Among other techniques, employers can adopt pay for performance plans, which reward employees with bonuses based on meeting certain goals or production quotas. Such programs are particularly useful to compensate managerial employees, such as chief executive officers.

In theory, executives are compensated for their contributions to the enterprise's bottom line, but many studies show that they are rewarded even when the firm's stock declines and the company loses money. The problem came into public focus during the 2008 bailouts of several large financial firms. Tax money was used to prop up the companies, but public opinion forced government officials to cut executive pay. The ongoing debate over that situation centers on the importance of pay to executives and their benefit to the enterprise. Bloggers have devoted considerable energy to the subject.[16] In 2011 the Securities and Exchange Commission proposed rules to give shareholders a greater say on executive compensation and "golden parachutes."[17] Despite the adverse publicity, CEOs are hardly living on the sidewalks.

Consider, for example, the case of Vikram Pandit, the head of the Citigroup banking empire. The company got $45 billion in taxpayer bailouts in 2008, and Pandit generously offered to work for $1 a year at that time. The *New York Times* reported in May 2011 that Pandit would receive "as much as $16.5 million in stock and options as well as a cash payment valued at more than $6.65 million as part of a special profit-sharing program for top executives." Pandit's sacrifice appears to have been magnanimously recompensed. And how did the rest of the pack fare in relation to their efforts toward the well-being of the American economy? The *Times* summed up as follows: "Bank of America's chief executive, Brian T. Moynihan, received about $10.2 million in total compensation for 2010, according to Equilar, a compensation research and consulting firm. Jamie Dimon, JPMorgan's chairman and chief executive, was awarded a $23.6 million pay package last year, making him the highest paid of any Wall Street chief. The heads of Goldman Sachs, Morgan Stanley and Wells Fargo were paid somewhere in between."[18]

With regard to regular workers, pay for performance systems can be complicated to develop and administer, and they require the support of employees. One of the most successful—and enduring—examples of such compensation schemes was implemented at the Lincoln Electric Company during the depths of the Great Depression in 1934.[19] Lincoln was one of the leading firms to adopt a program of "welfare capitalism" during the 1910s, and the company developed a program of employee representation to ensure worker involvement in the enterprise. Frank Koller, a Canadian journalist, published a book-length study of Lincoln in 2010, tracing the company from its origins to its current standing as the largest manufacturer of electric arc welding equipment in the world. In 2008, Koller reports, Lincoln gave each employee an envelope with a check that "represented roughly 61 percent of each employee's base earnings: The average bonus being handed out was $28,873. Furthermore, no permanent Lincoln Electric employees in the United States were laid off for economic reasons in 2008."[20]

Lincoln continues its progressive employment policies today. On its Web site, the company affirms its commitment to guaranteed job security and human resource policies. Lincoln makes the following statement about its compensation strategies: "The Company is famous for its productive and highly-skilled work force, as well as its unique compensation system, Incentive Management. Incentive Management is widely studied in business schools and industrial management circles. The system compensates and encourages individual and team initiative and responsibility at all levels of employment within the U.S. subsidiary." The statement continues that the firm "has never experienced a work stoppage in its 100-plus year history." For interested applicants, Lincoln provides information about the kinds of jobs and working conditions. An "assembler," to illustrate, is described as follows: "Assembly positions may include either individual or assembly line work. Individual assembly positions involve off-line assembly of finished products or parts that are used in finished products. Pay for individual assembly positions is based on the number of units produced by the individual worker. Assembly line work typically involves working with a group of other employees on the assembly of a finished product."[21] Koller concludes that few companies can match Lincoln's success because "pay for performance" is difficult to sustain over a long period.

IV. Performance Management

Once employees are hired and their compensation is determined, the next important HR function is to train, evaluate, and develop, and if necessary, to discipline the worker. The process is a continuous one, and makes up one of the major tasks of the HRM portfolio. This section takes up the several elements, and discusses the important dimensions of each one.

A. Training

As a general rule, every employee is given at least some training. A new employee must be introduced to the company's rules, policies, values, and expectations. An orientation session usually will cover the provisions of the employer's handbook pertaining to an employee's benefits, performance, and behavior on the job. A large food manufacturer furnishes employees with an extensive description of the company's expectations for employees, and what employees can expect from the employer. The handbook begins with a statement of the company's philosophy, which is to recognize and respect the interests of consumers, customers, employees, stockholders, and the community. The company's core values focus on growth, empowered employees, and the creation of responsibility and trust. The handbook continues to set out an employee's benefits, attendance requirements, rules of personal conduct, and the company's disciplinary system. An orientation session gives employees the opportunity to learn about the company and their rights, duties, and privileges as an employee.

Another common method of training takes place on the job. To illustrate the point, recall that an earlier part of this chapter dealt with the job classification of head meat cutter at a grocery store. Reflect a moment on how a head of beef goes from the pasture to your plate in the form of a steak. After cattle are sold to a packing operation, they are processed from a live animal to a consumable commodity sold through a retail grocery outlet. At one time, most grocers had butchers who took whole beef carcasses and cut them into various kinds of meat. Those workers were sufficiently distinct that they had their own craft unions, such as the Amalgamated Butcher Workmen, and performance standards could be negotiated in a labor agreement. Packinghouses began to offer more customized products, and skilled butchers were less in demand. Large grocery chains still needed some meat cutting expertise, which meant that qualified individuals could find work fairly easily. Workers who had the necessary skills might be assigned training duties to develop new meat cutters. Such on-the-job learning is a common feature of many kinds of work.

Moving to another level of training, consider a common skill that pervades today's workplace: communicating with others through e-mail. Secondary education prepares individuals for certain activities in society, and writing was historically regarded as an essential skill. New forms of communication tended to discount formal writing capabilities, such as correct spelling and grammar, and the result was that employers could no longer rely on a high school diploma, or even some higher education, as a guarantee of literacy. The point had particular relevance to electronic communication, which largely displaced formal written documents. But who wants to be regarded as an illiterate simply because words appear on a screen instead of on paper?

To remedy this particular problem, individual training consultants have stepped in to fill the vacuum. Several good books have been published on the subject, and they provide a background for training courses.[22] The actual instruction may be undertaken by an in-house trainer if a qualified person is available within the company. Alternatively, the employer can hire an outside consultant who specializes in the particular subject. The consultant provides training oriented toward the particular employer, and instructs employees on basic principles such as correct grammar, punctuation, tone, diction, and other elements of writing. The benefit of this method is that employees have expert, but individualized, training carried out by a professional with experience in the activity and knowledge of the topic. The disadvantage is the cost associated with hiring a contractor.

Another option is to send employees for instruction away from the workplaces. A number of management consulting firms offer training courses, sometimes awarding certificates and other indicia of accomplishment. An example of a successful venture along these lines is the Mountain States Employers Council in Denver, Colorado. The organization was founded in the late 1940s to assist employers with their unionized workforces. Member companies paid a set amount of dues, and in return received help with grievances, arbitration, unionizing campaigns, negotiations, and other aspects of labor relations. As unions declined, MSEC began dealing with other management issues, such as training, legal compliance, and employee relations in general. The firm now has an elaborate course offering covering all aspects of employment (including how to write effective letters, reports, and e-mails) and awards its own certificates of accomplishment. Here is how MSEC advertises its seminar on the legal environment of employment:

> Did you know that employment law claims comprise approximately 15% of all lawsuits filed? In addition, employment law claims are also more likely to go to trial that any other type of claim. Yet human resources, managers and supervisors understandably find that the number of legal issues they need to be aware of can be overwhelming. Courts have weighed in and stated that the failure to train managers and supervisors on basic employment law issues is an "extraordinary mistake."

Their one-day training course covers basic information about employment law. It essentially summarizes the content of the first four chapters of this book. Obviously, some awareness of legal issues is essential for managers.

The final point about training is how training needs can be determined. By looking at the job descriptions used in hiring and compensating, managers can compile information about the specific abilities associated with each job. Returning to the occupational therapist position described earlier, it becomes clear that the job requires continuous training to remain current in the field. Licensing requirements, in fact, may dictate a certain level of training be completed within specified periods. Attorneys have a duty to attend a certain number of training sessions, known as "bar refreshers," to keep their licenses current. Those who fall below the designated amount of training are threatened with removal from the bar. Other training needs may be determined by looking at an employee's job performance, which is the next topic.

B. Evaluating Performance

The standard method of evaluating employees is the "performance appraisal" conducted at various points in the employment continuum. Appraisals are used to reward good performance and correct bad performance. They may be tied into the company's compensation program so that a positive appraisal leads to a higher raise or a promotion. A negative appraisal, conversely, could lead to disciplinary action to deal with a particular problem, such as poor attendance.

Taking factors from the job description helps to ground the appraisal process. Returning to the example of a meat cutter in a grocery store, the job description may incorporate such tasks as dealing with customers, maintaining an attractive display of meat products, ensuring that products have not exceeded their sale dates, cooperating with related departments such as seafood and deli, and helping to oversee the work of junior employees. Using these general areas, the appraisal could consist of a rating scale of "exceeds expectations" (5 points) to "does not meet expectations" (1 point). By breaking the job duties into various elements, the appraisal form creates a detailed view of performance. For example, the "dealing with customers" factor might include specific behaviors, such as promptly greeting customers, responding to questions fully, maintaining a neat and clean appearance, and so forth. The ratings on each item can be summed up to obtain a numerical score for a general area. If the employee performed poorly on an item, such as putting outdated meat products into a sales case or failing to stock depleted inventory, further managerial action would be warranted.

Some HR specialists have suggested that performance appraisals may not be the best method for dealing with employee performance. One expert points out that regular performance appraisals can create anxiety for both managers and employees and have a number of weaknesses associated with their use, such as subjective evaluations, a tendency to focus on recent events, and a "grouping" effect that lumps employees together.[23] Citing results of a new survey, she says, "More than half (51 percent) of 631 respondents believe reviews don't provide accurate appraisals of their work, and nearly one-fourth dread them" as a part of the job. Instead of appraisals given at a regular interval, employees should have feedback on an ongoing basis emphasizing prompt engagement. The process is facilitated by online technologies that allow immediate, one-to-one interaction between team members and managers.[24]

As the material suggests, evaluating employees is a complicated task. It may depend on such factors as the organizational structure of the company, the demographics of the workforce, and the type of work involved. Evaluation is also closely related to compensation, and a good compensation plan such as the one at Lincoln Electric may make evaluations unnecessary, because pay is closely tied to performance. In any case, poor performance must be corrected by some system of sanctions. Most employers have safeguards in place to ensure that discipline is fair and consistent. Those safeguards help to reduce the risk of lawsuits challenging disciplinary action. The case below illustrates the possible problems an employer encounters in today's legal environment.

C. Disciplinary Action: Is "Sexting" on the Job Protected?

When employers impose discipline on an employee, it may prompt litigation based on the employee's legal protections. Civil rights laws, for example, impose liability on employers for such activities as sexual harassment of a fellow employee in the workplace. Another situation calling for prompt disciplinary action is workplace violence, which has become an important issue for employers. A company could decide to implement a "zero tolerance" approach to threats, physical assaults, and intimidation. Any application of discipline necessarily must consider the specific facts of the case and take into consideration any conflicting evidence raised by the alleged perpetrator. Discharge is the most severe penalty available to employers, and is used to deal with the most egregious offenses.

Handbooks typically spell out the kinds of infractions that will lead to discipline and the procedure for administering it. To illustrate, employees who fail to comply with timekeeping rules such as clocking in and out for breaks and shifts, may be given an initial written reminder. If the problem persists, the employer proceeds through a formal written warning, a short suspension, and finally, termination. Discipline is intended to rehabilitate an employee rather than punish him or her, and it is therefore progressive in nature. By allowing the employee to improve her performance, or to comply with existing rules, the employer avoids the appearance of arbitrary decision making.

Given the expanding scope of employment litigation, policies can be a crucial element in defending against the claims of discharged employees. One of the emerging areas of HRM has to do with electronic media, such as e-mail, text messaging, and Internet usage. Employees may try to assert a right of privacy when using those communication channels. The Supreme Court recently decided a case involving a California police officer who used equipment provided by the employer to send erotic text messages to his wife, and also to his mistress at the time.[25] Recall that when the government is the employer, the "state action" concept is satisfied and an employee can raise constitutional issues about any discipline.

The officer worked for the City of Ontario, California. The city decided that it would provide pagers to the police force. It had in place a policy stating that the city "reserves the right to monitor and log all network activity including e-mail and Internet use, with or without notice. Users should have no expectation of privacy or confidentiality when using these resources." The plaintiff, Quon, signed a statement that he had read and understood the policy. The city intended to treat text messages as a type of e-mail under the policy, and Quon was instructed on this point.

When Quon exceeded his quota of messages, many of which were not related to work, the city asked the service provider to furnish transcripts of the texts. The city reviewed the record of Quon's transmissions, and Quon was disciplined for violating the policy. He then sued, claiming a violation of his right of privacy. The Ninth Circuit Court of Appeals ruled in favor of Quon, finding that he had a reasonable expectation of privacy and that the search of his messages was unconstitutional. The U.S. Supreme Court reversed. While conceding that Quon may have had a right of privacy regarding the texts, the city's search of those records was not unreasonable, and therefore did not violate Quon's Fourth Amendment protections.

The Court begins its analysis with a discussion of an employee's expectation of privacy. The opinion conceded that Quon might have an expectation of privacy is his texts, but the Court avoided an explicit ruling on this point. The reason, as the Court explained, is that technology is still developing in this area, and it is unclear what employees might understand to be their rights of access. The opinion states, "The Court must proceed with care when considering the whole concept of privacy expectations in communications made on electronic equipment owned by a government employer. The judiciary risks error by elaborating too fully on the Fourth Amendment implications of emerging technology before its role in society has become clear." Quon might have understood that his texts would not be reviewed if he paid the overage charges, and under those circumstances, he reasonably could have anticipated they would remain private.

The Court ruled against Quon because it found the search was a reasonable one, even if Quon had a privacy right. The reasonableness of the search turned on the employer's justification for looking at the texts, and the fact that the search was not "unreasonably intrusive." That is, the police department had a legitimate, work-related cause to examine Quon's texts, and it confined the search to only those records. The appellate court was incorrect in holding the search to violate Quon's constitutional rights. The Court added a cautionary observation about the evolving nature of electronic communication and employee rights in the workplace:

> Rapid changes in the dynamics of communication and information transmission are evident not just in the technology itself but in what society accepts as proper behavior. As one amicus ["friend of the court"] brief notes, many employers expect or at least tolerate personal use of such equipment by employees because it often increases worker efficiency. Another amicus points out that the law is beginning to respond to these developments, as some States have recently passed statutes requiring employers to notify employees when monitoring their electronic communications. At present, it is uncertain how workplace norms, and the law's treatment of them, will evolve.

The same logic applied to any claimed violation of the Stored Communication Act. The Court dismissed that argument by stating that the plaintiffs "point to no authority for the proposition that the existence of statutory protection renders a search per se unreasonable under the Fourth Amendment." Accordingly, the discipline was appropriate.

In private sector employment, constitutional safeguards do not apply to employees. Employers have more latitude to develop policies and to inform employees that they do not have an expectation of privacy in electronic communications. Still, an overly harsh policy may not suit employees who routinely use social media for personal purposes. According to some commentary, more than half of the office employees in this country spend at least 15 minutes during the workday accessing their social media pages. To discourage all use of the Internet at work could be counterproductive.

Moreover, an overly restrictive policy could negatively affect employee morale, and possibly result in successful litigation. In the case of *Pietrylo v. Hillstone Restaurant Group*,[26] the plaintiffs were awarded damages when a jury found that the employer violated the Stored Communications Act by intentionally and wrongly accessing content on an employee's chat book. The court ruled, "Evidence was presented that Houston's managers accessed the Spec-Tator on several different occasions, even though it was clear on the Web site that the Spec-Tator was intended to be private and only accessible to invited members." That fact indicated the managers acted with knowledge of their wrongdoing. The jury also found that the employer had not violated the employees' common law right of privacy when it terminated the plaintiffs. The court also upheld that finding.

The above materials suggest that a suitable policy should try to accommodate some employee interests in privacy while protecting the employer's interests in ensuring that employees are complying with the company's needs for efficient work practices, and are not disseminating false and malicious information about the employer or other employees. The policy might state, for example, that all electronic communications using company equipment are considered to be the property of the employer, including e-mails, texts, or other media sources, and employees have no expectation of privacy in such communications. At the same time, the employer will not routinely screen or monitor an employee's electronic activity unless there is a job-related justification for doing so.

V. Managing Conflict

Conflict is endemic in any organization. Effective organizations manage conflict so as to avoid any undesirable consequences, such as violence, harassment, intimidation, or inadequate work performance. Toward that end, companies need explicit policies to provide methods for resolving conflict and providing "organizational justice." A large body of research shows that employees who feel the company provides fair procedures for resolving conflict, such as instances of sexual harassment, are less likely to engage in negative behaviors to retaliate against the employer. Conflict resolution involves a number of techniques, ranging from simple complaint procedures up to outside third-party dispute resolution. This section of the materials briefly surveys two theories of conflict management, and then examines various options, beginning with the least formal and proceeding up to the quasi-judicial forum of arbitration.

A. Theories of Conflict Management

What principles should guide an organization when it develops a program of conflict management? One of the most influential perspectives for understanding organizational conflict is to view it as a compromise between the interests of management and the interests of the employee. As the Supreme Court indicated in the Quon case, along with many others, managers in public employment can balance the need for managerial efficiency against the constitutional rights of employees. Even if an employee has a right to engage in free speech, for example, that speech cannot disrupt the workplace and interfere with the activities of other employees. The "managerial grid" developed by two scholars, Robert Blake and Jane Mouton, proposes a similar analysis to resolve conflict. Under this theory, managers take into consideration the needs of the organization in achieving its goals, and balance them with the needs of employees in resolving their conflicts.

A recent paper suggests a different way of looking at conflict.[27] This approach argues that conflict should focus on the needs of employees only. Management needs clear and objective rules to provide justice for all employees. To illustrate, employees may be forbidden from threatening or harassing other employees, or stealing or selling drugs at work, or drinking on the job, or any number of other rules of conduct. As the famous sociologist Max Weber observed, such rules are based on "formal rationality." But Weber went on to say that rules must also be applied with discretion, based on particular circumstances. He called this "substantive rationality," meaning it was justice as administered in a particular case, as opposed to justice in the abstract. Using a model of conflict management based on a balance of objective rules and individual circumstances allows managers to administer discipline clearly and equitably.

An example will show how the process works. A high school student, Jason Tate, became famous for a week in May 2011. He used paper letters pasted on a school wall to invite a girl to go to the prom with him. The school headmistress punished him by suspending him and banning him from the prom. The case attracted national media attention. Jason was interviewed on the *Today* show, had a Facebook page with thousands of followers, and generated a barrage of hostile e-mail to the school. The headmistress finally gave in and rescinded the punishment after a week of abuse.[28]

Using Weber's framework, the case is simple. The formal rule is that defacement of school property will be severely punished. Punishment could include expulsion, suspension, or exclusion from a school event. But administrators would also take mitigating factors into consideration. If the incident did not attack or demean any student or school employee, or involve permanent marking, or bring the school into disrepute, the penalty could be reduced. Since Tate's prom invitation was in the latter category, his punishment should be lighter. If the headmistress had insisted on the correctness of the policy, but explained why Tate's case fell within the scope of mitigation, she could have avoided the ultimate indignity of backing down in front of national television cameras after days of resistance.

Whatever theory applies to conflict management, there are well-defined procedures used to deal with conflict. They range from processes which are completely controlled by management, to processes in which the ultimate decision making is under the control of someone outside the organization. It may seem intuitively wrong that managers would surrender their discretion to deal with employees, but many large companies now use external systems of conflict resolution. The reason, in a word, is litigation. What follows is a description of different techniques to deal with conflict.

B. Open-Door Policies

As its name implies, the open-door concept invites employees to present an informal complaint through conversation with a manager. The advantage of this technique is that it may result in prompt action without a great deal of effort on the employee's part. If an employee presented a case to a manager that she was underpaid relative to her effort, and she documented her argument, the manager could adjust the matter by raising her salary. This strategy avoids complaints to a federal agency, a lengthy and disruptive process of gathering evidence, and other activities that consume time and emotional energy. The disadvantage of this process, obviously, is that the manager might dismiss the complaint as unfounded, and the employee would be left without further recourse.

C. Ombudsperson or Mediator

Another common method of conflict management is to designate an impartial third person to negotiate an adjustment to a dispute. The third party seeks information from both the complaining party and the managers directly responsible. Using that information, the mediator attempts to negotiate a voluntary settlement of the conflict. Mediation generally is more formal than an "open-door" policy, and the mediator may have some degree of authority to require the parties to attend meetings, provide information, and actively participate in the process.

Mediation is an important tool in labor relations, and the federal government provides services to employers and labor unions in an effort to avoid strikes and reach a negotiated settlement. In the labor arena, mediators offer valuable help in arranging meetings, preparing agendas, communicating information, and evaluating positions. A skilled mediator can help the parties to work through personal issues, retreat from untenable positions, and clarify the underlying intent of a proposal. Similarly, a mediator can assist employees and managers in uncovering the roots of a workplace conflict and propose ways of addressing the problem. An employee who has a personal dislike of her supervisor might be transferred to another department or given different duties, for example. In any event, mediation is often useful in focusing the nature of the dispute.

D. Impartial Arbitration

Arbitration has a long history in the American workplace. John D. Rockefeller Jr. introduced the system into the mines owned by Colorado Fuel & Iron to address the adverse publicity from the Ludlow Massacre in 1914. Speaking to miners in Pueblo, Rockefeller promised them competitive wages, the right of individuals to join a union, and a system of arbitration to deal with disputes. The *Denver Post* on October 3, 1915, devoted a front page story to Rockefeller's speech. The *Post* said, "The plan was presented by Mr. Rockefeller in person to representatives of the miners from every C.FI. & I. camp in the state. The representatives were elected by the workmen themselves at secret meetings, from which all company representatives were barred." The report predicted that the Rockefeller plan would set a standard for industrial relations and observed, "It goes further in its guarantees than many labor unions ever attempted to go." The Rockefeller or Colorado Industrial Plan, as it came to be known, had an important influence on labor relations from World War I up to the Wagner Act in 1935, when "company unions" became illegal.[29]

As unions gained members and economic power, they displaced the dispute procedures implemented by Rockefeller and other employers. Unions negotiated for grievance and arbitration procedures that adopted many of the techniques already in place. Generally, the process requires employees to present a grievance to the union, which then moves it through various levels of management in an effort to resolve the issue. If that fails, the union will demand arbitration.

Typically, the arbiter is a labor relations expert who has sufficient experience to be listed with an agency such as the Federal Mediation and Conciliation Service. When the parties contact the FMCS, they receive a panel containing five or seven names, and they then alternate striking a name from the list until only one person remains. The arbiter arranges a hearing date, and conducts a hearing similar to a trial, but without the same degree of formality. The parties present evidence and make arguments about the case. The arbiter duly renders an award, which settles the dispute. The costs of arbitration are usually shared by the company and the union.

Many large firms, such as the Anheuser-Busch Company, now use third-party arbitration to resolve workplace issues for nonunion employees. In a detailed study of the plan, two legal scholars noted: "The Dispute Resolution Program (the 'program' or 'DRP') combines binding arbitration with a comprehensive dispute resolution process, focusing on early resolution, fairness, and open communication. During its ten years of existence, the program has been very successful at both early resolutions of problems as well as reducing the company's outside legal fees."[30] They emphasize that "Procedurally, the company ensures that the program is meticulously fair to employees. Its financial contribution to the process, its contractual promise of no retaliation, its commitment to early resolution, and its provision of mediation are all examples of the company going beyond the legal requirements of a compulsory arbitration system." As a result, the DRP is "not simply a litigation avoidance strategy, but a comprehensive dispute resolution strategy."

Despite its advantages for both employees and employers, arbitration may have some negative consequences. The most notorious case in this area involves KBR Construction and an employee named Jamie Leigh Jones. The company hired her to perform work in Iraq. Shortly after she arrived on the site, Jones was sexually assaulted by another KBR employee. She attempted to sue KBR for failing to provide sufficient protection against this type of incident, but KBR responded that Jones was bound by an arbitration clause in the agreement. The case worked its way through the judicial system, and is set for presentation to the U.S. Supreme Court in mid-2011. Jones has testified at congressional hearings regarding the abuse of arbitration, and Congress has taken up bills to limit the use of commercial and employment arbitration.[31] The Supreme Court, however, has made several rulings that indicate employees will be bound by an employer's arbitration requirement.[32] As a result, employers may increasingly use this technique to resolve disputes.

Notes

1. Karl Marx, *Capital*, vol. I. For an influential contemporary treatment of capitalism, see David Harvey, *The Enigma of Capital and the Crises of Capitalism* (Oxford: Oxford University Press, 2010). Harvey explains the financial crash of 2008 in terms of an accumulation crisis.
2. Bruce E. Kaufman, *The Global Evolution of Industrial Relations: Events, Ideas, and the IIRA* (Geneva: International Labour Office, 2004), pp. 81–160.
3. See, for example, Charles Dickens, *Hard Times* (London, 1854).
4. Karen Legge, *Human Resource Management: Rhetorics and Realities, Anniversary Edition* (London: Palgrave MacMillan, 2005), pp. 133–74.
5. Occupational Handbook, http://www.bls.gov/oco/; Job elements for occupational therapist: http://www.bls.gov/oco/ocos078.htm.
6. http://clubstaffing.com/
7. http://www.cbsnews.com/video/watch/?id=7358608n
8. http://www.containerstore.com/careers/index.html
9. Ed Frauenheim, "More Companies Go with Online Tests to Fill in the Blanks," *Workforce Management*, online at http://www.workforce.com/archive/feature/training-development/more-companies-go-online-tests-fill-blanks/index.php. May 31, 2011.
10. *Phillips v. TLC Plumbing, Inc.*, 172 Cal.App.4th 1133 (2009).
11. Robert Allen, "Ridgeview Parents Divided on Arrest Secrecy," *Fort Collins Coloradoan*, May 19, 2011, p. A1.
12. http://business.ftc.gov/documents/bus08-using-consumer-reports-what-employers-need-know

13. Catherine Rampell, "Many with New College Degree Find the Job Market Humbling," *New York Times*, May 19, 2011, p. A1.
14. George T. Milkovich and Jerry M. Newman, *Compensation* (New York: McGraw-Hill, 7th ed. 2002), p. 13.
15. http://www.bls.gov/news.release/ecec.nr0.htm (released March 10, 2011).
16. For an interesting set of comments on the subject, see http://blogs.reuters.com/great-debate/tag/executive-compensation/.
17. For a good overview on trends, see the following Web site: http://blogs.law.harvard.edu/corpgov/2011/01/16/focus-in-2011-will-remain-on-executive-compensation/.
18. Eric Dash, "As Citi Revives, Pandit Wins Big Pay Package," *New York Times*, May 18, 2011. The article is posted at http://dealbook.nytimes.com/2011/05/18/pandits-take-of-citigroups-profits/?nl=todaysheadlines&emc=tha25. The reader comments are worth consideration. While some explain the justification for such compensation, others suggest that Citibank executives should be in jail.
19. Frank Koller, *Spark: How Old-Fashioned Values Drive a Twenty-First Century Corporation: Lessons from Lincoln Electric's Unique Guaranteed Employment Program* (New York: Public Affairs, 2010).
20. Koller, p. xii.
21. https://lincolnelectric.selectrakonline.com/Recruitment/Recruit.aspx
22. David Shipley and Will Schwalbe, *Send: The Essential Guide to Email for Office and Home.* New York: Knopf, 2007).
23. Rita Pyrillis, "Is Your Performance Review Underperforming?" Workforce Management. Online: http://www.workforce.com/archive/feature/hr-management/is-your-performance-review-underperforming/index.php.
24. One such software provider is Rypple, which believes that performance management has outlived its usefulness in the modern workplace. According to its Web site, "Rypple embeds the best management practices into social software. It focuses on people, not process. It connects goals, recognition, feedback and coaching to everyday work. It keeps us engaged and on track." You can visit their company at http://rypple.com/tour.
25. *Quon v. City of Ontario*, 560 U.S. ___ (2010).
26. Civil Case No. 06-5754 (FSH), United States District Court, D. New Jersey (2009).
27. Michael Gross, Raymond Hogler, and Christine Henle, "Process, People, and Conflict Management in Organizations: A Viewpoint Based on Weber's Formal and Substantive Rationality," *International Journal of Conflict Management* (in press).
28. CBS News, "CT Teen Who Posted Sign on School Allowed to Attend Prom," Online at: http://newyork.cbslocal.com/2011/05/14/ct-teen-who-posted-sign-on-school-allowed-to-attend-prom/.
29. For a general survey of the subject, see Raymond L. Hogler and Guillermo J. Grenier, *Employee Participation and Labor Law in the American Workplace* (New York: Quorum Books, 1992).
30. Richard A. Bales and Jason N. W. Plowman, "Compulsory Arbitration as Part of a Broader Employment Dispute Resolution Process: The Anheuser-Busch Example," *Hofstra Labor and Employment Law Journal*, vol. 26 (2008), pp. 1–32.

31. Jones's testimony can be viewed at http://www.youtube.com/watch?v=jn6yG-_KqnI&feature=related. Senator Al Franken, one of the leading advocates of restricting arbitration, questioned an employment lawyer about the process. This material is available at http://www.youtube.com/watch?v=g-OCEzoTy1A. A discussion of the proposal is at http://www.civilrights.org/archives/2011/05/1185-arbitration-fairness.html.
32. For example, in *14 Penn Plaza v. Pyett*, 129 S.Ct. 1456 (2009), the Court said that a union contract required the grievant to submit his age discrimination claim to the arbiter. Another case, *Rent-A-Center, West, Inc., v. Jackson*, 130 S.Ct. 2772 (2010), the Court held that the plaintiff's claim that the arbitration agreement was unenforceable should be made to the arbiter. The Court's rulings indicate that Jones will be forced to submit her case to arbitration, although an arbiter might rule that some parts of the claim were not sufficiently connected to her employment to be subject to arbitration.

CPSIA information can be obtained at www.ICGtesting.com
Printed in the USA
LVOW051059070112

262840LV00009BA/3/P

9 781609 270063